Benjamin Chapman Burt

A History of modern Philosophy

From the Renaissance to the Present - Vol. II

Benjamin Chapman Burt

A History of modern Philosophy
From the Renaissance to the Present - Vol. II

ISBN/EAN: 9783337073510

Printed in Europe, USA, Canada, Australia, Japan

Cover: Foto ©ninafisch / pixelio.de

More available books at **www.hansebooks.com**

A HISTORY

OF

MODERN PHILOSOPHY

(From the Renaissance to the Present)

BY

B. C. BURT, A.M.

AUTHOR OF A "BRIEF HISTORY OF GREEK PHILOSOPHY," OF TRANSLATIONS OF
ERDMANN'S "GRUNDRISS DER GESCHICHTE DER PHILOSOPHIE DES NEUN-
ZEHNTEN JAHRHUNDERTS," AND HEGEL'S "RECHTS-, PFLICHTEN-,
UND RELIGIONSLEHRE;" SOMETIME DOCENT (LECTURER)
IN THE HISTORY OF PHILOSOPHY AT
CLARK UNIVERSITY

In Two Volumes
Vol. II.

CHICAGO
A. C. McCLURG AND COMPANY
1892

MAY 1908

COPYRIGHT
BY A. C. McCLURG AND CO.
A. D. 1892

TABLE OF CONTENTS.

THIRD PERIOD OF MODERN PHILOSOPHY.
(Continued.)

	PAGE
§ 115. *Johann Christoph Friedrich von Schiller* (Works; Philosophy)	9–11
§ 116. *The "Faith Philosophers"*	11
§ 117. *Johann Georg Hamann* (Works; Philosophy)	11–13
§ 118. *Johann Gottfried Herder* (Works; Philosophy)	13–15
§ 119. *Friedrich Heinrich Jacobi* (Works; Philosophy; Result)	15–18
§ 120. *Jacob Friedrich Fries* (Works; Philosophy; Result)	18–22
§ 121. *Karl Leonhard Reinhold* (Works; Philosophy; Result)	22–25
§ 122. *Gottlob Ernst Schulze* (Works; Philosophy)	25–26
§ 123. *Salomon Maimon* (Works; Philosophy)	26–28
§ 124. *Jacob Sigismund Beck* (Works; Philosophy)	28, 29
§ 125. *Johann Gottlieb Fichte* (Works; Philosophy: Introduction; Theoretical Science of Knowledge; Practical Philosophy: Theory of Right and Theory of Morals; Later Philosophy of Fichte; Result)	30–40
§ 126. *Fichtians*	40, 41
§ 127. *Von Schlegel* (Works; Philosophy: Earlier Standpoint; Later Standpoint)	41–43
§ 128. *Schleiermacher* (Works; Philosophy; Doctrine of the Absolute and of Religion; Psychology and Dialectic; Ethics; Result)	43–49
§ 129. *Von Schelling* (Works; Philosophy; First Period: Philosophy of Nature, and Transcendental Idealism; Philosophy of the Absolute: "System of Identity;" The Philosophy of Freedom, — Positive Philosophy; Result; Schellingians)	50–68
§ 130. *Lorenz Oken* (Works; Philosophy: God; Nature and Man)	68–71
§ 131. *Henrik Steffens* (Works; Philosophy)	71, 72
§ 132. *Johann Erich von Berger* (Works; Philosophy)	72–74

CONTENTS.

	PAGE
§ 133. *Carl Wilhelm* **Ferdinand** *Solger* (Works; Philosophy)	74, 75
§ 134. *Franz Baader* (Works; Philosophy: Logic, Theory of Knowledge, or Transcendental Philosophy; Philosophy of Nature; Ethics; Result)	76–80
§ 135. *Karl Christian Friedrich* **Krause** (Works; Philosophy: Ground-Science, Analytic and Synthetic Courses; The Sciences of Nature, Reason, and Composite Essence; Morals, Rights, Politics, Philosophy of History; Result)	81–87
§ 136. *Georg Wilhelm F. Hegel* (Works; Philosophy: Deduction of the Principle; Logic: Doctrine of Being, Doctrine of Essence, Doctrine of the Notion; Philosophy of Nature; Philosophy of Spirit: Introduction; Doctrine of Subjective Spirit; Doctrine of Objective Spirit; Doctrine of the Absolute Spirit [Art, Religion, Philosophy]; Result)	88–118
§ 137. *Hegelians*	118
§ 138. *Christian* **Hermann Weisse** (Works; Philosophy)	119, 120
§ 139. *Ludwig* **Andreas Feuerbach** (Works; Philosophy)	120–122
§ 140. *Schopenhauer* (Works; Philosophy: Theory of Idea; Theory of Will; Theory of Art; Theory of Ethics; Result)	122–127
§ 141. *Herbart* (Works; Philosophy: Introduction; Metaphysics; Methodology; Ontology; Synechology; Idology; Psychology; Æsthetics; Result)	128–137
§ 142. *Beneke* (Works; Philosophy: Introduction; Psychology; Metaphysics; Practical Philosophy; Result)	137–142
§ 143. *Gustav Theodor* **Fechner** (Works; Philosophy; Result)	142–145
§ 144. *Materialists*	145
§ 145. *Friedrich Adolf Trendelenburg* (Works; Philosophy: The Conception of Philosophy; Mathematical Philosophy; Physical Philosophy; Organic Philosophy; Ethical Philosophy; Philosophy of the Unconditioned: The Philosophical Standpoint; Result)	145–151
§ 146. *Hermann* **Ulrici** (Works; Philosophy; Result)	151–155
§ 147. *Von Hartmann* (Works; Scope and Method of the Philosophy of the Unconscious; I. Phenomenology of the Unconscious; Unconscious in the Bodily Life; The Unconscious in the Human Mind; II. The Metaphysics of the Unconscious: Brain and Ganglia as Conditions of Animal Consciousness; Matter as Will and Idea; Individuality; The Unconscious as Individual; The Unconscious as the Supra-Con-	

scious; Generation; Individuation; The Supreme Wisdom of the Unconscious and the Perfection of the World; The Misery and the Irrationality of Existence; The Goal of Evolution and the Significance of Consciousness; Ultimate Principles: the Unconscious as Will; The Idea; The Identical Substance of both Attributes; The Possibility of Metaphysical Knowledge; Result) . 155-173

§ 148. *Rudolph Hermann Lotze* (Works; Philosophy: Problem, Method, and Divisions; Metaphysics; Ontology; Cosmology; Phenomenology; Philosophy of Nature; Psychology: Empirical Psychology; Speculative Psychology; Practical Philosophy; Ethics: Introduction; Maxims of Conduct; Determinism; The Forms and Relations of the Realization of the External Good [The Individual, The Family, Intercourse, Society, The State]; Æsthetics: Beauty and Fancy; The Actualization of the Beautiful and its Kinds; The Philosophy of Religion; Result) 173-199

§ 149. *Italian Systems* 199
§ 150. *Melchiore Gioja* 199
§ 151. *Romagnosi* 199, 200
§ 152. *Pasquale Galluppi* (Works; Philosophy; Result) 200, 201
§ 153. *Antonio Rosmini-Serbati* (Works; Philosophy: Introduction; The Sciences of Intuition; Ideology; Logic; Sciences of Perception: Psychology; Cosmology; The Science of Reasoning; Ontological Sciences [Ontology proper, Natural Theology]; Deontology [General and Special]; Result) . 201-217
§ 154. *Vincenzo Gioberti* (Works; Philosophy) . . . 217, 218
§ 155. *Terenzio Mamiani* (Works; Philosophy) . . . 218, 219
§ 156. *Scholasticism* 219
§ 157. *Italian Positivism (Ferrari and Franchi)* 220
§ 158. *English Systems* 220
§ 159. *Hartley* (Philosophy; Result) 220-222
§ 160. *James Mill* (Works; Philosophy; Psychology; Education; Ethics; Æsthetics; Result) 222-225
§ 161. *Jeremy Bentham* (Works; Philosophy) . . . 225-227
§ 162. *John Stuart Mill* (Works; Philosophy: Metaphysics; Theory of Nature; Ethics: Freedom; Criterion of Right and Wrong; The Ultimate Sanction of the Principle of Utility; The Proofs of the Principle of Utility; The Connection between Justice and Utility; Natural Theology and Religion; Result) 227-240

§ 163. *Herbert Spencer* (Works; Philosophy: First Principles; Unknowable; The Knowable: Conception of Philosophy; Data of Philosophy; Evolution (and Dissolution); **The** Interpretation of Evolution; Conclusion; **Principles** of **Biology**: The Data of Biology; Inductions of **Biology**; **The** Evolution of **Life**; Morphological Development; Physiological Development; The **Laws** of Multiplication; The **Principles of Psychology**: The Data of Psychology; **Inductions of Psychology**; **General Synthesis**; Special **Synthesis**; **Physical Synthesis**; **Special Analysis**; General **Analysis**; Congruities; **Corollaries**; The **Principles of** Sociology: **Data of Sociology**; The **Inductions of** Sociology; **Domestic Institutions**; **Ceremonial Institutions**; **Political Institutions**; **Ecclesiastical Institutions**; **The Principles** of Ethics: **Data of** Ethics; **Result**) . . 240–289

§ 164. *George Henry Lewes* (Works; Philosophy: Problem, Scope, and Method of Metaphysics; Methodological and Psychological Principles; Theory of Knowledge: I. Limitations of Knowledge; II. Principles of Certitude; III. From the Known to the Unknown; Matter and Force; Force and Cause; The Absolute in the Correlations of Feeling and Motion; Result) 289–302

§ 165. *William Whewell* (Works; Philosophy) . . . 302–306

§ 166. *Thomas Hill Green* (Works; Philosophy: Introduction; Metaphysics of Knowledge; The Relation of Man as Intelligence to the Spiritual Principle in Nature; The Freedom of Man as Intelligence; The Will; Desire, Intellect, and Will; The Moral Ideal and Moral Progress: I. The Good and Moral Good; II. Characteristics of the Moral Ideal; III. Origin and Development of the Moral Ideal; The Application of Moral Philosophy to the Guidance of Conduct: Practical Value of the Moral Ideal; Practical Value of a Theory of the Moral Ideal; Practical Value of Hedonistic Philosophy; Practical Value of Utilitarianism compared with that of the Theory of the Good as Human Perfection; The Principles of Political Obligation: Religion; Result) 306–319

§ 167. *American Philosophy* 319–321

A HISTORY OF MODERN PHILOSOPHY.

17391

DIVISION III. THIRD PERIOD OF MODERN PHILOSOPHY (*Continued*).

§ 115.

Johann Christoph Friedrich von Schiller[1] (1759–1805). — Schiller, the poet, attended a Latin school and a military academy, and took a degree in medicine. He practised medicine for a time in the army, but abandoned it for literary pursuits, — of his success in which it is not necessary to speak here. In 1789, through Goethe's influence, he was appointed professor of history in the University of Jena (in consequence of the writing of the "History of the Thirty Years' War"). During about ten years spent at Jena he "frequently met Fichte, Schelling, the two Schlegels, Wilhelm von Humboldt, and many other writers eminent in science, philosophy, and literature." He gave up history for philosophy, his studies in which included the reading of the English moralists, Lessing, Garve, Rousseau, and especially Kant. Schiller is a fine example of the union in a single individual of both poetic and philosophic genius.

Works. — Schiller's philosophical works include the following: "Briefe über die aesthetische Erziehung des Menschengeschlechts" ("Letters on the Æsthetic Education of the Human Race"), (1795); a number of special esthetical essays, perhaps the best among which are: "Ueber

---

[1] Schiller's Esthetical and Philosophical Essays, Noack; Erdmann.

den Grund unser Vergnügen an tragischen Gegenständen" ("On the Ground of our Pleasure in Tragical Subjects"), (1792); "Ueber Anmuth und Würde" ("On Grace and Dignity"), (1793); "Ueber Naïve und Sentimentalische Dichtung" ("On Naïve and Sentimental Poetry"), (1796); "Philosophische Briefe" (1786-1789); "Ueber den Zusammenhang der thierischen Natur des Menschen mit seiner geistigen" ("On the Connection between the Animal Nature of Man and his Spiritual Nature"), (1780).

Philosophy. — Truth, according to Schiller, is the harmony of sense and reason. Esthetically this harmony consists in grace rather than dignity, which latter is due to the over-preponderance of the rational or spiritual in its union with the sensible. Grace in the human countenance, for example, is a golden mean between that complete characterlessness of expression which betokens the absence of influence of the spiritual over the physical in man, and that rigidity of feature which is the result of an overpowering will or spiritual nature in man. Likewise, inward grace, or grace of soul, is a certain blending of the sensuous feelings and the moral sentiments. This grace of soul is the true nobility of soul, true character, true culture; for the very fact that the spiritual and sensible are found together in man is a postulate of their necessary relation and inner harmony. If this be so, then ideal human nature cannot be merely that "intelligible nature" of which Kant speaks, and before which he would have the sensible nature completely humiliated; morality is spiritual *beauty*, not merely spiritual dignity or sublimity. Kant, led by a practical necessity, the necessity laid upon a moral reformer in an immoral age, "proposed the idea of duty with harshness enough to ruffle the Graces, and one which could easily tempt a feeble mind to seek for moral perfection in the sombre paths of an ascetic and monastic life;" but the *principles* of the Kantian philosophy, however expressed ordinarily by him and by others, are unshakable: moral perfection is man's ideal destiny. It is simply necessary to understand that the "moral perfection of man" cannot be realized except through the association of sensible inclination with moral conduct. That "strongly impure inclinations" often usurp the name of virtue, is not a reason for putting a stigma upon disinterested inclinations, for making of the law "which is the most sublime witness of our grandeur, the most crushing argument for our fragility." True morality is spontaneous; it is reason obeyed from inclination and with a "sentiment of joy." "A noble soul has no other merit than to be a noble soul," is its own ideal. In the esthetic ideal of humanity is contained deliverance from that physical necessity to which the drudging laborer is subject, and from that moral constraint of which the ascetic is a victim, — in a word, true freedom for all.

§ 116.

The "Faith-Philosophers." — The three next-following thinkers — Hamann, Herder, Jacobi — may be grouped together as "Faith-Philosophers," because of their common doctrine that the ultimately real is an object, not of discursive understanding, but of purely intuitive reason, or faith. They are most properly classed, perhaps, as "Realists," since they make reality independent of our activity, and something merely passively apprehended by us.

§ 117.

Johann Georg Hamann[1] (1730-1788). — Hamann (born at Königsberg) was a moody, "mystical" intellect, developed by desultory studies in theology, law, philosophy, criticism, and the reading of romances. After two failures as private tutor, and a third as traveller for a commercial house at Riga, he took up his abode at Königsberg to care for an aged father. He had inner mental conflicts, which seem to have been set at rest by Bible study. For many years he was engaged as employee in the excise service

---

[1] See Noack.

at Königsberg, and became superintendent of a warehouse. He retired, with a small pension, at the age of fifty-five. A large leisure during his business engagements permitted extensive reading and much correspondence and intercourse with friends. The eccentric subjectivity of his character and reflections has become proverbial; he is commonly known as the "Magus of the North."

Works. — Among the philosophical works of Hamann, which are chiefly fugitive productions ("fliegende Blätter," as he styled them), are "Sokratische Denkwürdigkeiten" ("Socratic Memorabilia"), (1759); "Briefe" ("Letters"), collected by his friend Jacobi.

Philosophy. — Hamann had no system. His philosophy is contained in an antipathy to abstraction, and the enunciation and illustration, rather than demonstration, of Bruno's "Principium Coincidentiæ Oppositorum" (see vol. i. p. 46). Sense and understanding, revelation and reason, human and divine knowledge, nature and history, are not opposed, but agree and are one. (A fundamental error, says Hamann, of the Kantian philosophy, was the treating of them as opposites.) Philosophy is at once idealism and realism; there is nothing in understanding that was not already in sense. The essential unity of the two appears in speech, which is a product, not of (abstract) reason merely, but of faith rather, or the innate faculty for belief upon which tradition and history, in which language has sprung into existence, primarily rest. Abstractly regarded, the conceptions sense and understanding, revelation and reason, etc., represent no real things, but are merely auxiliary notions: abstract philosophy is mere "grammar" of knowledge. The whole secret of religion is contained in the idea of the man-becoming of God. This is the only religious truth of importance for dwellers upon this earth. The formal dogmas and laws of the church are merely pedagogical and governmental instrumentalities. The distinction between rights and morals, civil and religious life, state and church, is artificial and false. There is no proof of any philosophical truth; philosophical truth is an object of faith, inner experience.

§ 118.

Johann Gottfried Herder[1] (1744–1803). — Herder was born at Mohrungen, in East Prussia. A congenital peculiar sensitiveness of feeling in him was increased by harsh influences at school, by solitary communings with nature, and by adverse practical experiences. An attempt to study medicine, at Königsberg University, was frustrated by a fainting-fit in the dissecting-room, and Herder turned to theology. He attended lectures of Kant on logic, metaphysics, moral philosophy, and physical geography. He was greatly stimulated by Kant, whom he always, — even after he had been inwardly repelled by his doctrines and been piqued at Kant's criticism of one of his works — looked upon (according to a confession of his) as a "pattern of an acute, methodical, independent thinker," and regarded with the "highest reverence and gratitude." An intercourse (which extended over many years) with Hamann, also a deeply sensitive nature, left a marked and lasting impression on him. He was characterized by versatility of tastes and ability which led him through a very wide range of reading and study (in which poetry occupied a conspicuous place), and on the other hand, by a strong individuality, which caused opposition on his part to imitative classicism in German literature, and the earnest advocacy of individual and national independence of effort. His chief interest was in humanity, and particularly in its natural aspects and conditions, — a fact in keeping with the character of his philosophy. He held the positions of court-preacher and member of the Consistory at Bückeburg and at Weimar, and enjoyed, at the latter place, the friendship of Goethe, Wieland, and Jean Paul Richter.

Works. — Herder's principal philosophical works are: "Vom Erkennen und Empfinden der menschlichen Seele"

---

[1] Noack.

("The Knowledge and Feeling of the Human Soul"), (1778); "Gott: einige Gespräche über Spinoza's System" ("God: Dialogues on Spinoza's System"), (1787); "Briefe zur Beförderung der Humanität" ("Letters on the Advancement of Mankind"), (1793-1797); "Ideen zur Philosophie der Geschichte der Menschheit" ("Ideas for the Philosophy of the History of Mankind"), (1784-1791), — the most important of Herder's philosophical works. We may mention also two others: "Verstand und Erfahrung, Vernunft und Sprache, eine Metakritik zur Kritik der reinen Vernunft" (1799), — a criticism of Kant's "Critique of Pure Reason," — and "Kalligone" (1800), — a criticism of Kant's "Critique of Judgment."

Philosophy. — Knowledge is of the truly existent, not of phenomena merely. It is in no sense *a priori*, but a product of experience. Sense merely receives; understanding merely takes cognizance of what sense receives and of the "given." Sense and understanding are, indeed, not two faculties, but one, whose function is just to apprehend existence as such. The unity of the two is contained in the faculty of speech, with which reason is born. Experience results in faith, or belief in the future according to the norm of the present. Obedience to faith is reason, the function of which is the applying the idea of the unconditioned to the conditioned. The idea of the unconditioned is necessarily contained in reason, and the mind capable of it applies it to all things, — sees God in everything. God is the eternal, primal, impersonal force within, not outside, nature; working everywhere with perfect wisdom and goodness; revealing itself in finite creations which are but living copies of it. Its omnipresence is evinced in an eternal process of "giving and taking," attraction and repulsion, self-involution and self-sacrifice, — the unity and alternation of opposites. This law is most clearly exemplified in man, who is, indeed, the microcosm. Man is not, as Spinoza (of whose doctrine of God, Herder's is but a modification) taught, swallowed up in God or nature, but possesses a true individuality: every creature, in fact, has its own world, and remains always self-identical. Man possesses from the beginning the individual germ of that which he is through experience to become; he possesses in the highest degree the energy for the exhibition of the nature of the whole to which he feels himself as belonging. His special excellence lies in the power of speech and the possession of a physiological organization ministering to that. The problem of human life is the attainment by the individual and the race as nearly as possible to the ideal of humanity; no one does actually attain to this, but the race is, in spite of retrogressions, progressing towards it. The present earthly life is only preparatory to a higher condition of the individual and of the race. The destiny of both is but the natural consequence of their acts and thoughts. Earthly humanity blossoms in religion, which is also the germ of all culture and science. It is a part of human nature; the Christian religion, or rather the religion of Christ (compare Lessing, vol. i. p. 265), was, and was intended, as the expression of the most genuine humanity.

§ 119.

Friedrich Heinrich Jacobi[1] (1743–1819). — Jacobi was the son of a Düsseldorf merchant, and was educated for a commercial career, which for a time he followed. Abandoning this, he entered political service as a privy councillor for the duchies of Juliers and Berg. His leisure at this time and afterwards was devoted to philosophical and literary tasks, and to correspondence or personal intercourse with a wide circle of intellectual friends, among whom were Mendelssohn, Herder, Baader, Schelling, Goethe, and Wieland. He was at one time (1807–1813) president of the Bavarian Academy of Sciences, and member of the Privy Council at Munich. His training as a philosophical thinker was a result not so much of Scholastic methods, as

[1] Zeller; Jacobi's "Vorrede, zugleich Einleitung, etc.;" Noack; Erdmann.

of reading, correspondence, conversation, — conditioned, however, as it appears, by strong natural tastes and inclinations. He first became acquainted — in his philosophical studies — with the materialistic and sensualistic doctrines of the Swiss atomist Le Sage, of Bonnet, and of French thinkers. By these he was repelled. He studied Hume and the Scotch school, Spinoza, Kant, Hamann, Schelling, and, indeed, kept, as it is said, a watchful eye upon speculative effort generally in his day. He professed to write under the impulsion of a higher irresistible power within him.

Works. — Of Jacobi's works we mention, "Woldemar" (1779), — a philosophical romance; "Briefe über die Lehre Spinoza's" ("Letter [to Mendelssohn] on the Doctrine of Spinoza"), (1785); "David Hume über den Glauben [Faith], oder Idealismus und Realismus" (1787); "Sendschreiben an Fichte" ("Open Letter to Fichte"), (1799); "Ueber das Unternehmen des Kriticismus die Vernunft zu Verstand zu bringen" ("On the Attempt of Criticism to reduce Reason to Understanding"), (1802), — said to be the best introduction to Jacobi's doctrine; and "Von göttlichen Dingen und ihrer Offenbarung [Revelation]" (1811).

Philosophy. — The understanding, as the spontaneous or non-receptive faculty in cognition, is a faculty merely for analyzing and combining already given matter of cognition; it alone, therefore, does not conduct us to reality. As a faculty of knowledge as such, it fails to satisfy a certain demand or need of the soul, — a need which is at once a need of reason and of the heart, which requires a postulation of an extra-mundane being. The most that demonstrative understanding can possibly do in this direction is to suppose a connected totality of phenomena. That it can demonstrate the existence of God is a proposition absurd even in its very terms, since a demonstrated God were no God. God cannot be conceived as in any sense a result, the end of a conditioning process, but must, rather, be the *beginning* of every process, even of that of cognition. Every demonstrative system, further, is fatalistic, and as such contradicts the free utterance of the heart *against* mere blind necessity and *for* the soul's freedom. While, therefore, it is true to say, with Kant, that *scientifically* we can know only phenomena, it cannot be true that we have absolutely no theoretical knowledge of the noumenal or real. Such knowledge we do have in an immediate intuition, — an act which, inasmuch as its object is beyond the present, we may call an act of faith, but which is an act of theoretical faith, — a faith that concerns the real, and not merely the ideal, as does the Kantian moral faith, based on the fact of freedom. By faith (*sense, sensation, feeling, inner experience, presentiment, inspiration, reason,* — all these terms are, with Jacobi, interchangeable) we immediately apprehend the truths of God, freedom, immortality, as real; by faith, further, is it that we perceive the existence of other beings than ourselves in this world. In an act of faith we come into relation with reality; and we do so in so far as we are receptive in our faculty of cognition. The primary, the fundamental, distinction in knowledge is, then, that between knowledge as immediate and knowledge as mediate; the former alone being knowledge of the real, the latter of the phenomenal. Our knowledge of God does not enable us to assert anything positively of him except that he is; if he were not, we were not. A God that could be known (in terms of the understanding) would be no God. God is for us merely an object of feeling. As such, we may and must conceive of him as personal. A knowledge of God through any outward revelation is impossible: the revelation which we have of him is inner. It is universal among men. The belief in God growing out of *this* revelation is the kernel of truth in Christianity. If by reason in its theoretical capacity man immediately apprehends the truth, by reason in its practical capacity he is free and virtuous; the reason which reveals God to him also makes him like God. Freedom and virtue are the free gifts of the Creator. Freedom is not the capacity to choose the evil as well as the good, but is independence of appetite. Of our freedom we have evidence immediately in feeling and in the fact of moral consciousness. Freedom is the root of virtue; we are good, not certainly through impulse to pleasure and happiness, not even through respect to moral law as such, but through love; and natural inclination towards the good is just this love in its efficacy. The idea of duty *presupposes* this love, this spontaneous idea of and regard for absolute worth, instead of being (as according to Kant) presupposed by it. The Kantian ethics is, in the light of this truth, formal and cold. "The law was made for man, and not man for the law; and there are many cases in which the pure letter of the law must and may be forsaken; and the right to pardon for such transgression is the peculiar prerogative of man, the seal of his dignity, his divine nature."[1] The prime virtues are wisdom, goodness, and power of will. They take on various forms, according as the forms and conditions of society vary. From them all other virtues spring. Happiness is related to virtue, not as cause or motive, but as consequence.

Result. — Jacobi, together with the other Faith-Philosophers, so-called, is related to the Scotch intuitional school, and is perhaps the best German representative of pure intuitionism. — Jacobi exerted considerable influence as a thinker. Among his followers were Johann Neeb (1767–1843), professor at Mainz; Friedrich Köppen (1775–1858), professor in Landshut and Erlangen; Cajitan von Weiller (1762–1826), at one time General Secretary of the Academy of Sciences at Munich; Jacob Salat (1766–1851), professor (of theology) at Landshut and Munich; Leopold Reinhold (1787–1844); and others.

§ 120.

Jacob Friedrich Fries[2] (1773–1843). — Fries, son of a leading Moravian in the town of Barby, in Magdeburg

---

[1] See Professor Zeller's exceedingly readable account of Jacobi.
[2] Noack; Fries, "Grundriss der Metaphysik."

(where he was born), was carefully educated in the Moravian schools for a theologian of the Moravian persuasion. After attending the University of Leipsic (1795) — where he studied mathematics and the natural sciences as well as philosophy — and the University of Jena (1796) — where Kant especially engaged his attention — he found himself an "Enlightened" Pietist, a Deist tinctured with the theology of Lessing. Three years were spent by him as domestic tutor in Switzerland, and considerable time (1803, 1804) in travelling. In the year 1801 he habilitated as privat-docent at the University of Jena, received an appointment in 1805 as professor of philosophy and elementary mathematics at Heidelberg, and in 1816 as professor of theoretical philosophy at Jena. The last-named appointment he continued to hold until his death.

Works. — Of his numerous writings may be named here the following: "Reinhold, Fichte und Schelling" (1803); "System der Philosophie als evidenter Wissenschaft" (1804); "Wissen, Glaube und Ahnung" ("Knowledge, Faith, and Presentiment"), (1805); "Neue Kritik der Vernunft" ("New Critique of Reason"), (1807), — his chief work; "System der Logik" (1811); "Handbuch der praktischen Philosophie" (1818-1832); "System der Metaphysik" (1824); "Handbuch der psychischen Anthropologie" (1820); "Mathematische Naturphilosophie" (1822); "Geschichte der Philosophie" (1837-1840).

Philosophy. — Fries's general position is indicated by the fact that in his criticism of Fichte, Reinhold, and Schelling, he asserts the necessity of returning from the "*a priori* road," which these thinkers were keenly pursuing, to the "critical highway" opened by Kant, — begins the cry of "Return to Kant." But in order to carry on properly the work begun by Kant, and to approach and solve rightly the main problem of philosophy, — namely, the just realization of the ideas of reason, — it is, according to Fries, necessary at the beginning to avoid two fundamental errors of Kant, which were, treating the problem of the *a priori* conditions of knowledge as one to be solved by an *a priori* method, and ignoring the fact of immediate knowledge in us, — brought to light, it is true, only by a process of reflection. The immediate subject of philosophy is inner experience. The relation of this to absolute objectivity is not a matter of knowledge; we know nothing of things-in-themselves, and hence cannot compare experience with them to determine the relation in question. The task of philosophy is identical with that of empirical psychology. The *a priori* element in knowledge — the presupposition of our knowing — must be discovered by self-observation and an analysis which separates it from the merely empirical element. The investigation here is a purely anthropological one; philosophy is primarily psychical anthropology. Now, the leading fact of inner experience is that of self-consciousness. By this, man is distinguished from all other beings on the earth; by it he distinguishes himself, as phenomenally one and identical, from the changing objects of outer sense. The faculty of being conscious of self has underlying it the feeling, "I am," which becomes an intuition only by individual intuitions of inner activity. Experience arises when inner intuition becomes inner perception (as Kant taught). The manifold of sensations of inner and outer sense is reduced to unity by the understanding, which, according as its activity, is involuntary or voluntary, is memorial or logical. In its memorial activity is contained the productive imagination, which introduces into experience, upon the occurrence of sensation, the mathematical ideas of quantity, distance, form in space, duration in time, motion in space and time. By the logical activity of the understanding — *i. e.*, by reflection — the ideas of the understanding, the categories, are brought to consciousness. Nothing new — no knowledge of object — is given by this process as such. Knowledge of object as such is through sensible intuition alone; for an *intellectual* intuition does not belong to our nature. But even in sensible intuition, we know only the *fact* of objectivity, not any objective content. An objective content, or what is for us necessarily such, is given only in judgment, which is an immediate postulation in feeling of something not given in experience as such, and is manifested in desire, inclination, impulse. We *know*, then, only phenomena; of noumena we only *judge*. The ideal of knowledge is mathematical; science, whether of the outer or of the inner sense, is the more science the more mathematics it contains or admits of (compare Kant, vol. i. p. 356); nature as phenomenon must not be viewed teleologically, but only mechanically. (Kant decided otherwise.) The same holds true of mind regarded as phenomena; empirical psychology is a natural science. — The norm of judgment, as the capacity to feel interest in, and put a value on, things, is the idea of the fit. With judgment, we enter the realm of ends as distinguished from that of phenomenal objectivity. The highest object of judgment is the end-in-itself, or that which possesses absolute worth. The end viewed in application to ourselves, and as object of faith or belief merely, is a moral end. In the world of moral ends, every individual is either a person having absolute worth (or worth in and for itself), or a thing related to personality and possessing value accordingly; and this world is a realm of reciprocity, of free intelligences. The extension of the idea of the end to all things taken together, occurs by a mental act which unites cognition and faith; *i.e.*, an act of presentiment. By this extension we arrive at the object of religion and the æsthetic sense. By this act we find a certain object for the ideas of reason (which, psychologically speaking, we get by negating the categories as merely finite, — quality negated becoming the absolute, quantity perfection or totality, relation freedom, modality necessary being): God is the highest unity and end of all things; the world is subject to the law of the fit, or beauty; the soul has a real existence as a free being. Corresponding to the ideas of religious, or æsthetic, judgment, are the feelings of devotion, resignation, exaltation, which in the merely æsthetic sphere become the sentiments underlying lyric, dramatic, and epic poetry respectively. — As to philosophy considered as system, knowledge, faith, and presentiment — and hence "nature, the ethical world, and the universe as totality in immediate judgment" — do not admit of being deduced from one another or from anything higher than themselves, — though, on the other hand, we cannot deny their unity in a single world-ground. On the basis of the distinction between the phenomenal and ideal, philosophy may be divided into theoretical and practical philosophy, the latter embracing in its scope both the moral and the æsthetico-religious spheres. As we have seen, the method of theoretical philosophy is observation, analysis, and mathematical deduction; in practical philosophy, these failing us, we are governed by immediate conviction of faith and presentiment, belief, and the sentiment of beauty.

Result. — Fries is perhaps best described as an intuitionist with pronounced empiricistic traits, like the Scotch metaphysicians, to whom directly and indirectly (through Jacobi) he was much indebted. — Fries had a considerable number of followers (forming a sort of school), among whom may be mentioned, as the most important, Friedrich Calker (1790-1870), a professor in Bonn; Wilhelm M. L. De Wette (1780-1849), professor of theology at Berlin and Basel; E. S. Mirbt (1799-1847), professor extraordinary at Jena; E. F. Apelt (1815-1859), professor at Jena; Matthias Jakob Schleiden (1804-1881), at one time professor (of botany) at Jena.

§ 121.

Karl Leonhard Reinhold[1] (1758-1828). — Reinhold was born in Vienna, and educated there as a Catholic theologian; but a rupture occurring between his calling and his convictions, he left his order and Vienna to study

---

[1] Zeller, Noack, Erdmann.

philosophy in Leipsic (under Platner) He first became known in the philosophical world by certain "Letters on the Kantian Philosophy," which received the approval of Kant. Soon after the publication of the "Letters" (in a journal edited by Reinhold in conjunction with his father-in-law, the poet Wieland), and, because of their success, Reinhold received the appointment of professor of philosophy in the University of Jena, where for several years he lectured with extraordinary success. He held afterwards a similar position at the University of Kiel.

Works. — Besides the "Briefe uber die Kantische Philosophie" (1787), we give of Reinhold's works the following, as the most important: "Versuch einer neuen Theorie des menschlichen Vorstellungsvermögens" ("Attempt at a New Theory of the Human Faculty of Thought)," (1789), which did *not* (as did the "Letters") receive the approval of Kant; "Beiträge zur Berechtigung bisheriger Missverständnisse der Philosophie" ("Contributions towards the Correction of Misconceptions of Philosophy hitherto prevailing"), (1790-1794); "Ueber das Fundament des philosophischen Wissens" ("On the Foundation of Philosophical Knowledge)," (1791); "Auswahl vermischter Schriften" (1796).

Philosophy. — Reinhold's philosophical views several times underwent radical change. At first a Kantian, he afterwards leaned towards Fichte's doctrines; then was a follower of the Fichtian-Schellingian Christian Gottfried Bardili; but shifted again, owing, perhaps, to the influence upon him of Hegel's Logic.[1] It is as a Kantian, or as a supplementer of Kantism, that he has any special importance. According to Reinhold, there are in Kant's "criticism" of pure reason two fundamental defects that have to be remedied: (1) the dualism in the faculty of theoretical cognition, — *i.e.*, the separation of sense and understanding; and (2) the absence of a real proof of the unknowability for us of things-in-themselves. To

---

[1] See Erdmann, § 307, 1.

remedy these defects, we must, ignoring for the time being the problem of how the knowledge of objects is possible, consider the process of knowing in and for itself, and we must begin with what is indisputable, — namely, the mere fact of knowing on its subjective side, — the fact of consciousness in general, in which sense and understanding are contained together as parts. The first principle of the investigation is, then, the "principle of consciousness." In all consciousness may clearly be distinguished three things, — an idea, a somewhat ideated, or thought, *i. e.*, object, and a thinker, *i.e.*, subject. The idea is related to both subject and object, — the unity of both. That by which it is related to object is its matter; that by which it is referred to subject is its form. Since all that the subject as such contributes towards the idea is the form of it, the matter must be regarded as "given." In consciousness, then, there are two sides, — one (the subjective), of spontaneity, the other (the objective), of receptivity. Thus we have, deduced from a first principle, a distinction not *deduced*, but taken for granted, by Kant at the beginning of his "criticism" of the faculty of knowledge, and with the result of making that faculty "two-stemmed," instead of "one-stemmed." At the same time it distinctly appears that there must be an unknowable somewhat, which when given form by the subject is represented by the matter of the idea. What is known, or in consciousness, is the idea with its two sides; the thing-in-itself remains outside consciousness. It is a contradiction in terms to speak of an idea as outside consciousness; an idea may be present in consciousness in an obscure manner, but never outside consciousness. — Except as to these two points, the doctrine of Reinhold agrees with that of Kant in the "Critique of Pure Reason." The other "Critiques" were not by him subjected to like criticism. As Reinhold regarded his philosophy as dealing with the very first principles of speculative thought, and as introductory to that of Kant, he styled it "Elementarphilosophie,"—a name by which it is commonly known.

Result.— "It was," says Zeller, "of incalculable advantage to German philosophy when Reinhold made it his task to explain and perfect the Kantian philosophy. He accelerated the general comprehension of Kant's philosophy by several years, and was for adherents and opponents alike the source of information regarding it."—The doctrines of Reinhold underwent criticism and emendation at the hands of a number of thinkers, among them Gottlob Ernst Schulze, Salomon Maimon, and Jacob Sigismund Beck.

§ 122.

Gottlob Ernst Schulze (1761–1833).— Schulze (a native of Thuringia) was a member of the philosophical faculty at Wittenberg, and afterwards professor at Helmstädt and Göttingen.

Works.— Schulze's chief work is "Aenesidemus; oder, uber die Fundamente der von Professor Reinhold gelieferten Elementarphilosophie, nebst einer Vertheidigung des Scepticismus gegen die Anmassungen der Vernunft-Kritik;" "Aenesidemus; or, on the Principles of the Elementary Philosophy put forth by Professor Reinhold, together with a Defence of Scepticism against the Criticism of Reason" (1792). Other works are "Einige Bemerkungen über Kant's philosophische Religionslehre" ("Some Observations upon Kant's Philosophical Theory of Religion" (1795); and "Kritik der theoretischen Philosophie" (1801).

Philosophy.— According to Schulze, Reinhold's "Principle of consciousness" is not a first principle, not universally valid, not even definite beyond misconception. There are states of consciousness in which there is no distinction of subject and object, and the thing-in-itself has no certain existence even for thought. The supposition of it is illogical, inasmuch as it gives objective validity to a category which is *ex hypothesi*, as are all the so-called categories, **only subjective in its** application; namely, that of causality. The supposition is gratuitous, since there is no proof **that the matter as** well as the form of our ideas **may not** have its **source in** the **subject;** or, on the other hand, **the element of** necessity **in** experience which is attributed **to the** subject **might, on** Reinhold-Kantian principles, be attributed to the possible thing-in-itself, inasmuch as, if we have a consciousness of **necessity in** every sense-perception, and **if we do not know things-in-themselves, we** cannot know that they cannot and **do not produce this consciousness.** Scepticism makes no positive **assertions on these points.** Reinhold and Kant make the mistake of **confounding the necessity of being** with **that of being** thought; **they settle** nothing as regards the thing-in-itself or the **limits of** knowledge. — Schulze, later, gave up his sceptical standpoint for one nearly allied to that of Jacobi.

§ 123.

Salomon Maimon[1] (1753-1800). — Maimon was a Polish **Jew (born at Neschwitz, in Lithuania), who** after becoming learned in **Talmudistic and Cabalistic lore,** took up the study of medicine, **philosophy, and** mathematics in **German.** **In Berlin, whither he had gone to** study medicine, **he formed the acquaintance of** Mendelssohn, who befriended him and directed his philosophical studies. **He also made the** acquaintance **of Garve, the well-known critic of Kant, at Breslau, and corresponded with** Reinhold. **His life was one of extreme improvidence, poverty, hardship, and aimless wandering, — that of a mere vagabond, — until he was befriended by a certain Count of Kalkreuth,** who gave **him a home on** one of his estates.

Works. — **A special study by him of Kant's first masterpiece, in which he** **made written** explanations and **objections** to the doctrine of **Kant, was published in** 1790 as " Versuch

[1] Zeller and Noack.

über die Transcendentalphilosophie, nebst einem Anhang über die symbolische Erkenntniss" ("Essay on the Transcendental Philosophy," etc.). Other works, besides essays published in various philosophical journals, are "Streifereien im Gebiete der Philosophie" ("Rambles in the Field of Philosophy"), (1793); "Ueber die Progresse der Philosophie" (1793); "Die Kategorien des Aristoteles" (1794); "Versuch einer neuen Logik, oder Theorie des Denkens" ("Essay at a New Logic, or Theory of Thought") (1794), — Maimon's chief philosophical work; "Kritische Untersuchungen über den menschlichen Geist, oder das höhere Erkenntniss- und Willensvermögen" ("Critical Investigations into the Human Mind and the Higher Faculty of Knowledge and Volition"), (1797). — The philosophical intelligence displayed in Maimon's works won the respect of Kant and the confessed "reverence" of Fichte, who was not a little indebted to him.

Philosophy. — Maimon adopts Reinhold's emendation of Kant as regards the "two-stemmedness" of the faculty of knowledge, and Schulze's criticism of the Reinhold-Kantian doctrine of the thing-in-itself, the idea of which he treats as what mathematicians call an imaginary quantity; *i. e.*, as a limitational conception. His analysis of the primal consciousness is substantially as follows. Prior to experience, as conditions of it, are space and time: in experience as the manifold are sensations, which, though they may be said to be "given," are but the unconscious products of our own thought. Sensations are not the only "given": time and space, as belonging to sense, are also "given," — "given," however, *a priori*, whereas sensations are given *a posteriori*. The "given" cannot by any possibility come from without; a real thing-in-itself is an absolutely impossible conception. From this it is evident that sense is but undeveloped understanding; all that is required to make sense understanding is a consciousness of the process whereby it (unconsciously) arrives at the connected "given." This process is but the exemplification of the law that only those combinations of the manifold can yield a real object in which one element of a combination determines another that is determinable by it, though not capable of determining it. This may be called the Law of Determinability. The determined is in every case the subject, the determinable the predicate of a judgment or primary function of the understanding. If the former is given and the latter to be discovered, the judgment is analytic; otherwise synthetic. From this Law of Determinability the categories are deducible, — they are, in fact, but various statements of it. The Law of Determinability, which is merely the law of thought-necessity, appears as the law of causality or universal necessary sequence only in mathematics, and that because only in mathematics is the "given" an *a priori* "given." We know nothing of universal empirical succession. (Accordingly, Maimon styles himself a sceptical empiricist, or empirical sceptic; but also, since time and space are "given," a dogmatic rationalist, or rational dogmatist. Kant and Reinhold he calls empirical dogmatists and rational sceptics.) The so-called "Dialectic of Reason," Maimon disposes of by referring the ideas of reason to the imagination as the faculty of ideals, thus making the antinomy between the ideas of the unconditioned an antinomy, not in reason as such, but between imagination and reason, and thereby preserving the integrity of the theoretical reason. The ideas of God, Freedom, Immortality, as practical, are, according to Maimon, merely subjective; the autonomy of will is not demonstrable; the categorical imperative is purely imaginary. The motive of moral action is in the "agreeable feeling of one's own worth, whose most essential component is knowledge."

§ 124.

Jacob Sigismund Beck[1] (1761-1842). — Beck was a pupil of Kant at Königsberg, taught in a gymnasium and

---

[1] Noack.

in the university, at Halle, and after 1799 was professor of philosophy in the University of Rostock.

Works. — At Kant's suggestion Beck published (1793-1796) "Erläuternder Auszug aus den kritischen Schriften des Herrn Professors Kant" ("Illustrative Abridgment of the Critical Writings of Professor Kant"). Other works are "Grundriss [Outline] der kritischen Philosophie" (1796); "Commentar über Kant's Metaphysik der Sitten" (1798).

Philosophy. — Beck was a professed interpreter of Kant in the spirit of the more purely transcendental tendency of his doctrines, denying that Kant really taught the doctrine that things-in-themselves are causes of sensations. Accepting the positive results of the teaching of Reinhold, of Schulze, and of Maimon, Beck, partly in consequence, as it would seem, of a Fichtian influence, attempts to complete what those three critics of Kant had begun. Phenomena are at once product and object of consciousness, are explicable solely from the laws of ideation or thought, in general. In ideation there is a primary act by which is (unconsciously) produced a unity of the manifold, an "original synthetic objective unity" through the forms of space and the categories, and a secondary act, in which time and the schemata are conditioning forms by which this unity is counterposed as object, — the "original act of recognition." The secondary act is a direct consequence and reflection of the first; hence our knowledge of object. The forms of ideation are not prior to the act of cognition, but in it and determined by the energy of which it is an exertion: in this act they coincide, as it were, and separate only in an analytical derivative thought. An act which is in no manner conditioned or explicable through the forms of ideation is an act of moral will. Such an act corresponds only to a pure non-temporal, non-physical conception, — a mere ideal, — and has as its object and product humanity in its essence. The ideas of God and immortality aid in the realization of this act, but otherwise have no validity. — Beck finally abandoned the "critical philosophy."

§ 125.

Johann Gottlieb Fichte[1] (1762-1814). — Johann Gottlieb Fichte, son of a ribbon-maker in limited circumstances, was born at Rammenau, in Upper Lusatia. Through the influence of the town-preacher, who, as his instructor, discovered in him very remarkable intellectual endowments, and by the generosity of the Freiherr von Miltitz, he attended the schools of Meissen and Pforta, for a period of six years, to prepare for a theological course in the university. He entered the University of Jena in 1780; studied theology and the philosophical systems of Spinoza and Wolff. Owing to straitened circumstances, while in the university and for several years afterwards, he engaged in private teaching, in tutoring in families (as did Kant before him, and Schelling and Hegel and Herbart after him), and in literary "hack-work." At about the age of twenty-eight he began especially to turn his attention, until then occupied much more with theological than with philosophical subjects, to philosophy, and wrote a work, entitled a "Critique of all Revelation," which was an application of the Kantian philosophy to a theological point. In the summer of 1791 he visited the home of Kant, taking with him the manuscript of this work, in the hope of winning by the work the favor of the Königsberg sage. The work received the approval of Kant, and through his influence gained a publisher (1792). The ascription of the authorship of it to Kant immediately, gave the author of it, when he became known as such, a high reputation. The next year Fichte received the appointment of *professor extraordinarius* at the University of Jena. Though his success as a lecturer was great, he gave offence to the powers that were, and by a want of complaisance lost his place. He had incurred a charge of atheism

---

[1] Zeller, Erdmann, Noack; Fichte's "Introduction to the Science of Knowledge" ("Journal of Spec. Phil.," vol. i.); "Facts of Consciousness" (ibid., vol. v., etc.); "Popular Works" (ed. by Smith); Everett's "Fichte" (Griggs's "Philosophical Classics"); "Encyc. Brit."

by publishing, in a philosophical journal edited by him, an essay of Carl Forberg on the "Determination of the Conception of Religion," in which popular views were antagonized; and by substituting in a partial apology for Forberg's performance such an unorthodox conception as that of the moral order of the world for that of God. A threat on his part to resign his chair in case of a reprimand from the academical senate of the university was followed by his receiving permission to withdraw from the faculty, which he did, in 1799. Settling in Berlin, he was occupied until 1809 with literary work, modifying and lecturing upon his system (he lectured one semester at the University of Erlangen), and earnestly championing the cause of German education and German nationality. In 1809, on the foundation of the University of Berlin, he accepted a professorship in the institution. He became dean of the philosophical faculty, and afterwards rector of the university. His efforts to bring about moral reform among the students of the university — to do away with duelling and student-societies — caused friction in his official management, and he resigned the rectorship. He died by a contagious fever taken while attending his wife, who had been a nurse in the military hospitals of Berlin. He was, and still is, regarded as a moral as well as an intellectual personality of very great nobility and power.

Works. — Fichte's most important works are perhaps the following: "Ueber den Begriff der Wissenschaftslehre, oder sogenannte Philosophie" ("On the Conception of the Science of Knowledge, or so-called Philosophy"), (1794); "Grundlage der gesammten Wissenschaftslehre" ("Foundation of the Entire Science of Knowledge"), (1794); "Ueber die Bestimmung des Gelehrten" ("Nature of the Scholar"), (1794); "Grundriss des Eigenthümlichen der Wissenschaftslehre" ("Outline of what is peculiar to the Science of Knowledge"), (1795); "Grundlage des Naturrechts nach Principien der Wissenschaftslehre" ("Foundation of Natural Right according to the

Principles of the Science of Knowledge" (1796); "System der Sittenlehre" ("System of the Science of Morals"), (1798); "Die Bestimmung des Menschen" ("The Destination of Man"), (1800); "Der geschlossene Handelstaat" ("The Exclusive Commercial State"), (1800); "Ueber die Grundzüge des gegenwärtigen Zeitalters" ("Characteristics of the Present Age"), (1805); "Anweisung zum seligen Leben, oder die Religionslehre" ("Way to the Blessed Life, or Theory of Religion"), (1806); "Ueber das Wesen des Gelehrten und seiner Erscheinungen im Gebiete der Freiheit" ("On the Nature of the Scholar and his Appearance in the Realm of Freedom"), (1806); "Reden an die deutsche Nation" ("Addresses to the German Nation"), (1808).

Philosophy: Introduction. — The problem of philosophy is (according to Fichte) to discover the ground of experience, or those ideas which we have that are accompanied by the feeling of necessity. As the ground of experience is outside experience, the philosopher has first of all to abstract from experience. He thus obtains, on the one hand, an intelligence-in-itself (in so far as he abstracts from concrete intelligence, or subject), and, on the other, a thing-in-itself (in so far as he abstracts from real things, or objects). One of these two must be the ground of experience (and of the other); philosophy, or, better, the science of knowledge, must be either Idealism or Dogmatism. At first blush it appears impossible to decide between the two. The dogmatist can — from his point of view — explain freedom and self-consciousness as mere appearance; the idealist, the thing-in-itself as a mere invention or chimera. A ground of decision lies in a certain peculiar fact, — that though the thing-in-itself can be entirely abstracted from, intelligence cannot, but remains in the last possible abstraction as a necessary presupposition of the abstraction, and therefore as object to itself. The perception of this fact depends upon the creation of it in ourselves by a free act of pure self-consciousness.

The fact is — and this is its peculiarity — both objective and subjective, a fact-act. Further, in the unity of intelligence with itself in self-consciousness, — for the universal notion, the very conception, of intelligence itself, is that it *knows* (all things), and hence has intelligence of itself, — we have a unity which is not at all explicable by dogmatism, since the category of dogmatism, that of (mechanical) cause and effect, contemplates subject and object as two distinct and disparate things, whereas in self-consciousness they are one. On the other hand, it is not possible to deduce the determined world from pure undetermined intelligence; there must be presupposed a certain nature — certain laws — of intelligence; and the feeling of necessity accompanying determined representations may be explained as the feeling by intelligence of the limits of its own essence. The laws of the action of intelligence, as surely as they are grounded in the one nature of the intelligence, constitute in themselves a system. If we gather these laws at random from experience, we do not *prove* them to be laws; we leave it possible for the unstilled dogmatist to assert that they are merely qualities of independently existing classes of things. But such is the method of Critical Transcendental Idealism (of Kant), which therefore puts forth laws of external experience only. Complete Transcendental Idealism must begin from a single fundamental law of reason, which is shown as contained immediately in consciousness. This first law involves as condition a second, and that a third, and so on; and the last, as containing all the conditions of the first act, by which the laws are discovered, must contain the system of all necessary representations, or the total of experience. Idealism does not have this experience in view as a foreknown object and result which it should arrive at; it proceeds from its starting-point according to certain rules, careless as to what the results of its investigation may prove to be. In so far as those final results are found in experience, they are *a posteriori*; in so far as they are necessary consequences of our reasoning, they are *a priori*. Since philosophy is the explanation of experience, a " philosophy that does not agree with experience is wrong in its presupposition or deduction." The *presupposition* of Idealism is one contained in reason itself, and no rational person will admit that human reason contains any problem the solution of which is altogether impossible. The *deduction* is a necessary one; what is postulated is supplemented by its necessary condition, and this by its, and so on until the sum of conditions is shown to be exhausted. These conditions form an organic whole, and this whole is a product or realization of *free* thinking. Hence philosophy is Transcendental Idealism. Now, the first law of thought is that the ego, or pure transcendental self, posits originally absolutely its own being; or the essence of the ego consists in positing itself as being. (By way of explanation, it may here be said that *in the beginning* the ego *is*, and is all that there is, — is only as positing something, and hence posits itself.) This law expressed in terms of bare logic, which abstracts from all subject-matter, is merely the familiar Law of Identity; but the former, rather than the latter (which is by abstraction derivable from it), is the beginning and foundation of real thought. A second equally original fact of consciousness is that the ego *op*posits to itself — or posits over against itself — a non-ego. This act is, equally with the first, an act of the ego, and in so far in contradiction or antithesis to it. (Hence the Logical Law of Contradiction.) The voiding of the contradiction — reconciliation or synthesis of the acts or laws — is possible only in so far as ego and non-ego are conceived as reciprocally limited and limiting. The third law of thought (which, unlike the first two, is not a mere statement of fact, but a deduction) is, Ego *op*posits to the limited or divisible ego (*i. e.*, the merely posited ego, not the ego which embraces, since it posits, both sides of the opposition) a limited, or divisible, ego. In these three principles we have, *deduced*, Kant's categories of affirmation, negation, and limitation. These principles are the first principles of all knowledge. In the method by which they have developed themselves — *i. e.*, position, opposition, reconciliation, or thesis, antithesis, synthesis — we have the method of philosophical knowledge. The third principle — further — contains the foundations of the two main divisions of philosophy; *viz.*, theoretical and practical philosophy, or science of knowledge. The principle underlying the former is, Ego posits itself as determined by the non-ego; the principle underlying the latter is, Ego posits itself as determining the non-ego.

Theoretical Science of Knowledge. — From the principle, just now given, of the theoretical science of knowledge it appears that ego is passive in relation to the non-ego (thesis). But as ego originally posits the non-ego, it is, in being determined by it, active (antithesis). One and the same ego is, then, in one and the same relation both passive and active (passive because and in so far as it is active, and *vice versa*), that is, in it a relation of reciprocity obtains (synthesis). In so far as ego is merely passive, and negation of its opposite, non-ego is *cause and reality*. In so far, further, as it determines itself, it is *substance*. In so far as it determines itself in some limited manner, it is *accident*. There remains an unresolved contradiction in the fact that ego is both determined and self-determining, effect and substance. The resolution of the contradiction can lie only in the supposition of an infinite activity in the non-ego that can be overcome only by an infinite series of acts of the ego, since ego, in a certain sense, posits non-ego as often as it posits itself. The twofold activity of positing and transcending is what may be termed *productive imagination*. The first product of the activity is the realization by the ego of the fact of limitation (the action of the non-ego) in itself,— sensation. The apprehension of the object of this limitation is intuition. The discovery of the cause in its origin in the ego gives the image. The distinguishing of the two, by an act of comparison, *as* image and its cause, is understanding. The discovery by the ego of itself as ultimately both cause and image is judgment, in which the ego emerges as free from non-ego, and wholly practical.

Practical Philosophy: Theory of (1) *Right, and* (2) *Morals.*—The ever-recurrent activity which, in the theoretical sphere, appears as a relation between subject and object, ego and non-ego, continues in the practical sphere, but rather as a relation of the ego to itself, or as self-determination. The non-ego here appears as but a part of the effort of the infinite ego to realize itself,—a fact not apparent in the sphere of the theoretical. From the foregoing it at once follows that the infinite ego contains within itself an infinite number of other egos,—since all non-egos are egos,—standing in a relation or reciprocal limitation. The finite rational being can exist as such only as it finds itself reflected in other beings like itself (since it must have an *other* and must also—since it is *self*-conscious—see itself in its other) : as it in turn reflects for others like itself themselves. (1) Here is the origin and basis of the right (in which, therefore, the non-ego has its *raison d'être*). The law of right is that the freedom of each must be limited by the idea of that of all others: every free being must be treated as an end, and not merely as a means. Natural or original rights (as far as such exist) are such as are founded on the mere conception of personality, and are the right of personal freedom and the right of property (which is acquired through labor). Relations between individuals in the sphere of right are further determined by *contract*, the possibility of a violation of which implies the existence, in an acknowledged independent sphere, of the right of coercion. This right can belong only to a totality of individuals constituting a State, the first duty of which is, precisely, the securing of rights to individuals as such. The source of power in the State is the people as a whole. Popular sovereignty, exercised in the form of pure Democracy, gives, however, not the best, but the worst form of government. The best is government by the Best,— an "Aristocracy." Practically, the State can never *be* perfect, but fulfils its office if it continually approximate the ideal of the best State. The office of protecting the right involves the right to punish — which has for its end the improvement of the criminal and the prevention of crime — and the maintenance of a police. Besides the protection of rights, the State has also the offices of promoting material welfare (by organization of labor) and of educating the people, which is its principal duty. It is a duty of the State to tolerate absolutely free inquiry and free speech. (2) The goal of the infinite activity of the ego can never be anything merely real, but the ideal. The subjective consciousness as such spontaneously realizes itself in the fundamental conception — which is also an impulse or instinct — of rational self-determination, the moral law, the so-called "categorical imperative." With this purely rational impulse is joined another, — the natural, — which it has to bring into harmony with itself. In the natural impulse in its various forms — the bodily desires — are found the materials to which the moral impulse in its purity gives form and law. The harmonization of the natural with the spiritual impulse is a process of progression through three stages, in the first of which natural impulse unrestrainedly rules, the maxim of the subject being individual happiness; in the second, the moral impulse rules but blindly; in the third, the true conception of the moral as such. This progression is never fully completed. The feeling, obtained in the last stage, of harmony with the ideal, of satisfaction, is the response of "conscience" to the fact of the (relative) attainment to the ideal. A condition of the realization of the notion of freedom is the ethical association of men a "church," to be a member of which is the duty of every person. But this does not mean that religion is anything more than a practical belief in a moral order of the world. God cannot be conceived as a personality; for if conceived as a particular substance, he must be conceived as having a body. The essence of religion is morality, and positive religion can be nothing but a body of conventional modes and means of securing the cultivation of the moral sense.

(*So-called*) *Later Philosophy of Fichte.* — Philosophy has thus far been for Fichte the explanation of the ground of experience, but of that ground (as we can now see) in its logical, or better, phenomenological, rather, than in its ontological character. The Absolute, or God, has thus far been treated as a mere ideal, and the pure ego, it has been understood, is not as such given in consciousness, but is outside consciousness or experience as its ground. All that has been stated or implied of it, is that it must be absolute as the presupposition of the absolute positing of itself. When, now, Fichte concentrates thought upon this, it becomes for him the Absolute, lying above and constituting the limitation and non-being of knowledge or consciousness. It is being *and* not-being, it is primordial, is God. Absolute knowledge — the Science of Knowledge — is not this being, but an image or manifestation of it, and indeed its knowledge of itself. But there is only one absolute — namely, being, God. But being, or the absolute, is not mere substance, not the God of Spinoza, of which knowledge is a mere accident. "The real life of knowledge is in its root the inner being and essence of the absolute itself; and there is between the absolute, or God, and knowledge in the deepest root of its life, no difference, but the two become lost in one another."[1] It is the infinite moral will of the universe. In accordance with this view the practical or ethical problem consists in recognizing God as alone real, and all else as not-being, and making

---

[1] See Professor Everett's chapters on the ontology of Fichte in his "Critical Exposition of Fichte's Science of Knowledge" (Griggs's "Philosophical Classics"); also Professor Adamson's article on Fichte in the "Encyclopædia Britannica."

ourselves and others, — humanity, in short, — a revelation of the divine nature. Man's highest felicity is the returning through knowledge — the Science of Knowledge — out of the manifoldness of phenomena to the unity of being. The knowledge of the identity of humanity with God may be given in immediate consciousness, — may be "revealed," as it was to the founder of Christianity ; but the will of God may also be an object of philosophical knowledge. The Bible is merely a pedagogical instrumentality, not to be literally taken. In the development of human nature, the end of which is the becoming rational through freedom, there are five epochs : (1) One of the undisturbed rule of reason in instinct, — the epoch of innocence ; (2) One in which there is a rule of arbitrary external authority, and dogmatism in teaching prevails ; (3) An epoch in which indifference to truth and latitude as to conditions of sinfulness prevail ; (4) An epoch of rational science and incipient righteousness ; (5) An epoch of free self-culture and spiritual salvation. — Fichte, it should be said, did not himself conceive that his philosophical standpoint had ever radically altered. The historians, however, have *generally*[1] thought otherwise.

---

[1] Not always. Professor Adamson says (*loc. cit.*) : " It can neither be admitted that Fichte's views underwent radical change, nor that the Wissenschaftslehre was ever regarded as in itself complete, nor that Fichte was unconscious of the apparent difference between his earlier and later utterances [*Cf.* Professor Zeller]. It is demonstrable by various passages in the works and letters that he never looked upon the Wissenschaftslehre as containing the whole system. It is clear from the chronology of his writings that the modification supposed to be due to other thinkers (Schelling and Schleiermacher), were from the first implicit in his theory, and if one fairly traces the course of thought in the early writings, one can see how he was inevitably led on to the statement of the latter, and at first sight divergent, views. On only one point, the position assigned in the Wissenschaftslehre to the absolute ego, is there any obscurity. From the early work, ' Neue Darstellung der Wissenschaftslehre,' unquestionably to be included in the Jena period, one can see that from the outset the doctrine of the absolute ego was held in a form differing only in statement from the later theory." Professor Everett says : " When we have

Result. — The system of Fichte is a rationalistic attempt at the union of the subjective and objective elements of experience by the deduction of the latter from the former. The attempt is scarcely successful, since the object as such, or thing-in-itself, survives as an object of moral need or intuition, without thereby receiving an explanation of itself as it is in itself. There is in this system no place for a theory of nature as such. Almost with equal truth may it be said also that there is in it no place for a theory of art, since this presupposes both subject and object. The system may be described as subjective practical idealism or rationalism. The advance by it upon that of Kant is one not so much in the adjusting of subject and object as in the harmonizing the subject within itself, as in the deduction of understanding from the pure ego (or of the categories from pure self-consciousness), and of the practical and theoretical faculties from a common root.

§ 126.

Fichtians.[1] — The (earlier) system of Fichte was adopted wholly, or in considerable part, by Schelling (in his first philosophizings); Friedrich Carl Forberg (1770–1848), docent and adjunct at Jena; Friedrich Immanuel Niethammer (1766–1848), professor-extraordinary in the theological faculty at Jena, and co-editor (with Fichte) of a philosophical journal; Johann Baptista Schad (1758–1834), professor at Kharkov (Russia); Friedrich Schlegel

reached the ontology, we have found a point of view from which the system becomes a unit. . . . The so-called earlier and later systems of Fichte are the complemental elements of a single system. The great difference between them is to be found in the fact that, in his earlier works, Fichte started from psychological analysis, and moved towards ontology; in his later, he started from the ontology, and based his psychology directly upon this. The ontology, it must be noticed, does not form the substance of the later statements of the Science of Knowledge. It simply forms the introduction to what is really, in its aim as in its title, a Science of Knowledge."

[1] See Erdmann, § 314, 2; Noack.

(in his earlier period); Friedrich Daniel Ernst Schleiermacher (particularly in his earlier thinking).

§ 127.

Karl Wilhelm Friedrich von Schlegel[1] (1772–1829). — Schlegel, after preparing for a mercantile career, studied philology in Göttingen and Leipsic, taught as *privat-docent* in the University of Jena, and lectured at Dresden, Paris, and Vienna. By the composition of diplomatic papers, he acquired the favor of the government at Vienna, by which, in consequence, he was invested with a title of nobility and several court offices. He, together with his brother, August Wilhelm, was a leader in the Romantic movement in literature, and, on the whole, belongs to the history of literature rather than to that of philosophy.

Works. — Schlegel's principal philosophical works are: (1) "Lucinde" (1799), — an (unfinished) romance; essays in the "Athenæum" (a journal edited by his brother and himself); "Charakteristiken und Kritiken" (1811); (2) "Philosophischen Vorlesungen [Lectures] aus den Jahren 1803–1806;" "Vorlesungen über die Philosophie des Lebens [Life]," (1828); "Vorlesungen über die Philosophie der Geschichte [History]," (1829); "Vorlesungen über die Philosophie der Sprache und des Wortes" (1830). These (as indicated) fall into two groups, expounding two quite different standpoints.

Philosophy: (1) *Earlier Standpoint.* — Schlegel's earlier standpoint, styled by himself the Standpoint of Irony, is the position that the mind is continually negating its own self-limitations, continually denying what it allows, or has allowed, validity. This standpoint springs easily from the Fichtian, if a greater value be attached to the empirical ego, relatively to the absolute ego, than Fichte attached to it. The true ego is, according to Schlegel, that of æsthetic sensibility and judgment. The true man is the artist, the genius; in him alone is true religion, true virtue.

---

[1] Noack, Zeller, Erdmann.

The genius is, as compared with the ordinary person, a god, and, like the gods of ancient Greece, occupies himself solely in the enjoyment of the free play of his own spontaneous energy. In creative activity he is governed by his subjective mood, expresses only his individuality; in moral action he knows nothing of conscience, of duty, of legality, or of conventional formality, but follows impulse. Since genius is above all institutions, marriage is to it not sacred, but is to be regarded as suited only to those incapable of true love, — love *aus einem Gusse*, or of one mould. Religion is the individual worshipping himself: "for what God can be worthy of honor to the man who would not be his own God?" Philosophy is poetry; the true philosopher is the poet.

(2) *Later Standpoint.* — Schlegel's later standpoint is described by himself as that of the science of experience, or the philosophy of life. According to this later view, a logico-genetic method — triadic in its movement — is an essential condition of sound philosophy; and the finite and infinite, instead of being one immediately (as in mere feeling), are so only in a process of becoming, or life (the finite ego being but a part of the infinite ego, itself continually becoming); and the individual finds his destination in surrendering himself to the universal, instead of clinging to and deifying his individuality. The world-ego, originally only infinite unity (without manifoldness), is "stirred by the feeling of this primal void to an infinite longing, which, extending itself on all sides, is nothing else than space. This longing, increasing with extension, becomes an active, mighty effort, a supernatural fire. In the painful conflict of this appetite, the world-soul remembers with distress and regret its lost unity, and from this arises time. Out of the conflict spring material elements."[1] This conflict appears in the finite ego as a discordance among its faculties, the restoration of which to primal harmony is the goal of life. The primary faculties are phantasy,

[1] Zeller.

reason (or the faculty of perceiving and combining distinctions), understanding (or the faculty of immediate inner perception of truth), will. These, when separated from their origin, and thus from one another, respectively become subjective fancy, sophistical ratiocination, a faculty of merely formal conceptions, a faculty of formal, arbitrary will. Through faith, love, and hope, they are preserved in harmony and in normal function. In normal understanding, and still more in normal will, we have immediate experience of the infinite ego. The four faculties, together with four subordinate ones — memory and conscience (belonging to reason), sense and impulse (belonging to phantasy) — are contained and combined in feeling, of which faith, hope, and love are the triadic manifestation. Language is a union of opposites, is a means of harmonizing the discordant powers. In history, as in the individual ego, is contained the process of the restoration of the lost divine image. The final salvation of humanity, the races of which may be characterized with reference to the faculties of man, is to be expected from science, which, far from depending upon the notion of the absolute, — whether Ego, Nature, or Idea, — must rest upon the recognition of the living God, and become a true philosophy of revelation![1] — Only the earlier doctrine of Schlegel has had any influence on German thinking. That, it is scarcely needful to add, is the philosophy of Romanticism.

§ 128.

Friedrich Daniel Ernst Schleiermacher[2] (1768-1834). — Schleiermacher was born in Breslau. He was educated in Pietistic Moravian schools at Niesky and Barby, and at the University of Halle, where he studied theology, philology, and philosophy. He occupied a number of important positions as preacher or professor at Halle, Berlin, and elsewhere. After 1796 he lived mostly in Berlin. In

---

[1] See Erdmann, § 315. 5.
[2] Noack, Zeller, Erdmann; Schleiermacher's "Dialektik."

1810, on the opening of Berlin University, he became professor of theology; in 1811, member of the Academy of Sciences; in 1814, secretary of the philosophical section of the Academy. His early philosophical training came through a study of the Leibnitzo-Wolffian philosophy, Kant, Spinoza, Fichte, Schelling, and Plato, and personal intercourse with the Schlegels and other "Romanticists." By both temperament and education, however, he was less suited to philosophy than to theology, for which he performed a service that has won for him the name of being the "great reformer of German Protestant theology."[1]

Works. — Perhaps the most important philosophical works of Schleiermacher are: "Vertraute Briefe über die Lucinde" ("Confidential Letters on Lucinde"), (1800), — a defence of the doctrine of love in Schlegel's Lucinde; "Reden über die Religion an die Gebildeten unter ihrer Verächtern" ("Discourses on Religion to the Cultured among its Contemners"), (1799) ; "Monologen: eine Weihnachtsgabe" ("Monologues," etc.), (1800); "Grundlinien einer Kritik der bisherigen Sittenlehre" ("Outlines of a Criticism of Previous Systems of Ethics"), (1803) ; "Der christliche Glaube nach den Grundsätzen der Evangelischen Kirche" ("The Christian Faith according to the Principles of the Evangelical Church"), (1821); "Entwurf eines Systems der Sittenlehre" ("Sketch of a System of Ethics"), (1835) ; "Dialektik" (1839); "Psychologie" (1862).

Philosophy: Doctrine of the Absolute and of Religion. — The highest conception, according to Schleiermacher, is that of the absolute unity of being, from which all distinction — even that of subject and object, thought and being — is absent. This conception represents nothing that can really be known, and is indeed not properly a conception, since knowledge begins where the distinction of subject and object, thought and being, enters. The absolute unity above the distinction, and even above the con-

[1] Zeller.

crete unity, of subject and object, is not characterizable by any terms of thought or being, whether *species* or *genus*, *matter* or *force*, *necessity* or *freedom*: it is unknown and unknowable. It is the ground of all being and knowledge, — that on which all things depend; and is apprehended most truly by us in the feeling of absolute dependence, or religion. As the unity of all things, it is revealed also in the feeling of love, — love, that is, which unites indistinguishably spiritual and sensual love, — whether love of a person of the opposite sex, or of the All. This absolute, unknowable being, the absolute unity of all things, cannot be distinguished from the world of phenomena, — except as its unity, — for then it would acquire definite character for finite thought. Its causality, therefore, is entirely within the world, or nature. It is the necessity of all things; and also the freedom of all, because it can only be self-determined. It is the unity of the finite and the infinite, and all things finite are in it infinite and eternal. As religion is our truest apprehension of the absolute, the philosophy of religion is the highest part of the whole system. Religion, as the feeling or intuition of the universe, is independent of all metaphysics and of all belief in the so-called personality of God. Along with the feeling of ourselves as finite and dependent, there goes that of the infinite and self-subsistent God. Religion is an infinite natural outlet for the superfluous energy in man, and restores the equilibrium and harmony of his nature with itself, and thus with the All. It needs no Bible as a condition to its existence, but makes its own Bibles. The highest, the only adequate, form of religion is monotheism; all others are only religion adapted to limited conditions of life, and but moments in the one complete totality. The only complete realization in human life, as a whole, is in a kingdom of God (a church), in which all parts are lost in a whole, and each also preserves an individuality. The peculiarity of Christianity as a religion is that in it every individual is related to the redemption, or reception into the God-consciousness of Christ, and is capable, though a natural being, of apprehending the supernatural and saving truth revealed in the person of Christ, in whom the infinite and finite were united in a special degree.[1]

Psychology and Dialectic. — In the sphere of true conceptions, or knowledge, the highest distinctions are those of being and thought, nature and spirit, sense and understanding. Since being and thought, and likewise nature and spirit, sense and understanding, though opposites, have their ground in the one Absolute, the problem of philosophy, as such, is the showing *how* being and thought, nature and spirit, sense and understanding, are united, — to realize the presupposition of their unity. Speaking psychologically, being and thought are represented in every act of consciousness. Those acts in which being preponderates are acts of perception; those in which thought preponderates are acts of thought proper; and all ideas may be ranged according to the relative degrees in which both sides of consciousness are represented in them. The highest conception is that from which all manifoldness of being or matter has vanished; the lowest, that which contains the mere manifold: between these are infinite degrees in the relations of matter and form in ideas. Space and time are not merely subjective, but forms of the existence of things. The forms of knowledge proper are conception and judgment. The processes of knowledge are deduction and induction, the former presupposing the latter. The highest conceptional knowledge does not attain to the identity of thought and being, which remains forever a mere presupposition or postulate of knowledge. — The union of subject and object reaches its highest known form in the conversation of men, — "dialogue" (whence *dialectic*), a form of consciousness which is not merely individual and subjective, but common and reciprocal. Conversation raised to an art is a "co-philosophizing," an exercise of the art of Dialectic. The theory of this

---

[1] See Noack in particular.

art, Dialectic, has two parts, — Transcendental (psychological) and Technical (methodological). Because of the twofold nature of consciousness (to give a few methodological distinctions), the sphere of knowledge has two primary parts, — the knowledge of nature, and the knowledge of reason. For a similar reason, knowledge may be speculative or rational, and historical or empirical. Combining these two distinctions in knowledge, we have — *natural science* (speculative doctrine of nature), *ethics* (speculative doctrine of reason), *natural history* (empirical doctrine of nature), and *history* (empirical doctrine of reason). The speculative sciences necessarily presuppose and depend upon dialectics; the empirical, mathematics, — and are truly scientific only in proportion to the mathematics they contain.

Ethics.[1] — Ethics (the only one of the four proper parts of philosophy systematically treated by Schleiermacher) is the speculative doctrine of reason in its relation to (*i. e.*, its action upon) nature, not the doctrine of the "blessed life" (or life of pure reason), nor the doctrine of reason in nature. The action of reason upon nature may be regarded with reference to the various sorts of union produced by it, the varied character of reason as the source of these, and the relation of reason to the unions, producible by it, regarded as laws of its action; and ethics accordingly falls into (1) the theory of goods, (2) the theory of virtues, (3) the theory of duties. (1) The action of reason in union with nature is either formative (or organizing) or significative (or symbolizing); it is also particular or universal. There are, therefore, four forms of the union of the two, — the formative universal, the formative particular, the significative universal, the significative particular, which may be designated respectively as Intercourse, Property, Knowledge, and Feeling. The relations of reason in or to itself (*i. e.*, of persons to one another) are respectively relations of Right, of Free Sociality, of Faith, and of Revelation.

[1] See particularly Professor Erdmann's treatment of this topic.

The relations of reason and nature in the sphere of ethical culture give, from the point of view of the formative activity, the sciences of gymnastics, mechanics, agriculture, collection of apparatus; from the point of view of significative activity, dialectic, mathematics, speculation, history, — as means of culture. Two extremes have to be avoided here, — (*a*) the assumption that knowledge is *only* for culture's sake; and (*b*) the opposite of this. Combining the distinctions " formative " and " symbolizing " with those of the " common " and " individual," we have, corresponding to intercourse, Division of Labor; to property, Domestic Authority and Hospitality; to knowledge, Discovery and Communication; to feeling, Religion and Art. Goods in the highest sense are persons, and, indeed, as communities. Of these, the original and germ of all the rest is the family. Out of it arise (*a*) the State, or the realization of the conception of right through the distinction of ruler and subject; (*b*) Free Society, the embodiment of the conception of property; (*c*) the School, the embodiment of that of knowledge; (*d*) the Church, the realization of feeling, having its highest manifestation in art. (2) Virtue in general is, in a formative regard, either Disposition or Skill. This distinction, united with that of knowledge and representation (which is a distinction in a significative regard), gives the four primary virtues: Wisdom and Love (forms of disposition as regards knowledge and representation), Discretion and Perseverance (skill in knowledge and representation). Each of these may, further, be viewed either in a " formative " or a " significative " regard, and shades of virtue thus be deduced. (3) Complete action of reason, or Duty, must have reference to both goods and virtue. Its primary law is, Act at every moment with thy whole ethical energy, and with the entire ethical problem in view. Subjectively stated, this becomes, Do always what thou feelest thyself vitally impelled to do; objectively, Do that which thou art required from without to do; subjective-objectively, Do always what can be most furthered by thee. Duty, distinguished with reference to the relations of society to self, and of the universal to the particular, is fourfold: Right (universal relation to society), Love (individual relation to society), Vocation (universal relation to self), Conscience (individual relation to self). "The ethical problem in general consists in our becoming ever more conscious of reason, and with conscious reason making ourselves ever more masters of nature, — in other words, in the realization of the universal end of reason to control the isolated in nature, making it an instrument, animating it until the entire surface of the earth is enlisted in the service of reason, and reason becomes the ruling soul of the universal body of nature, — a goal which will never be completely attained." The moral life is continuous with the natural, as reason is with nature.

Result. — It has been asserted: "The marked feature of Schleiermacher's thought in every department is the effort to combine and reconcile in the unity of a system the antithetic conceptions of other thinkers. He is realistic and idealistic, individualistic and universalistic, monistic and dualistic, sensationalist and intellectualist, naturalist and supernaturalist, rationalist and mystic, gnostic and agnostic." While there is a certain truth in the foregoing striking characterization, it is still a patent fact that Schleiermacher is a subjective idealist. For him reality, the absolute, is known only in mere feeling or bare intuition : it is in no sense comprehended, not an object of synthetic, constructive thought. — As followers of Schleiermacher (and Hegel) may be named Richard Rothe (1799–1867), professor at Bonn and Heidelberg; Johann Ulrich Wirth Leopold Georg (1811–1873), professor at Greifswald; Heinrich Ritter, the historian of philosophy, was a follower of Schleiermacher, but not of Hegel. — In this connection may be mentioned Friedrich von Hardenberg, otherwise known as "Novalis" (1772–1801), in a sense *forerunner* of Schleiermacher, as also of Schlegel and Schelling. For Novalis the supreme problem of thought and culture is "mastery of the transcendental self."

§ 129.

Friedrich Wilhelm Joseph von Schelling[1] (1775-1854). — Schelling, who was the son of a clergyman and Oriental scholar, was born in a small town of Würtemburg. After his early education, received partly in a Latin School, he entered, at the age of fifteen, the theological seminary of Tübingen, studying there, besides theology, philology and philosophy. He took his master's degree in 1792 with a thesis on Myths. Before 1796, in which year he went to Leipsic to study mathematics and the natural sciences, he had read Plato, Leibnitz, Herder, Kant, Reinhold, Schulze, Maimon, Fichte, Spinoza, and had become an enthusiastic follower of Fichte. In 1798 he was (through the influence of the poet Goethe) appointed *professor extraordinarius* of philosophy at Jena, where he lectured with brilliant success until 1803. During this period he wrote actively and published a number of volumes, and edited, with Hegel, the "Kritisches Journal für Philosophie." In 1803 he went as professor to Würzburg; in 1806 was made member of the Academy of Sciences in Munich, and afterwards General Secretary and Director of the Art Academy; from 1820 to 1826 he lectured at Erlangen; in 1827, was appointed professor of philosophy in the University of Munich; and in 1841 he received a call to Berlin as member of the Academy of Sciences. He availed himself of the privilege attaching to his position of lecturing in the university, — after having been, comparatively speaking, silent since 1806, though he had awakened great expectations by announcements of intention to publish to the world further statements of his philosophical views. He lectured but a short time in the university, and hopes which had been excited of his supplanting the Hegelianism then ruling

---

[1] See Schelling's "Introductions to the First Sketch of a System of Philosophy of Nature," and to "Transcendental Idealism," and "Lectures on the Method of Academical Study" (all translated in "Jour. of Spec. Philos."); Watson's "Schelling's Transcendental Idealism" (Griggs's "Philosophical Classics"); Zeller; Noack; Erdmann; etc.

powerfully in Prussian philosophical circles, were left unfulfilled. At Jena he was in intimate personal association with the members of the school of "Romantic" thinkers, and married Caroline Schlegel (divorced from her husband, August Schlegel, in order to become his wife), who is said to have influenced Schelling's thinking up to the time of her death in 1809.

Works.[1] — With a view to grouping properly Schelling's principal works, we may here, in a sentence, describe the general development of Schelling's thought. In so doing we may best follow a hint thrown out by Schelling himself. At first a Fichtian, he next asserted the co-ordinateness of nature with mind, and alongside the Fichtian Transcendentalism, Idealism (philosophy of spirit), placed the philosophy of nature as its polar opposite, the two together constituting philosophy as a whole; thirdly, he affirmed the indifference, or identity, of spirit and nature in an Absolute above them; and, finally, attempted to give a concrete and positive character to the Absolute, at first abstractly and negatively conceived. Works of the first period of the development are: "Ueber die Möglichkeit einer Form der Philosophie überhaupt" ("On the Possibility of a Form of Philosophy in general"), (1795); "Vom Ego als Prinzip der Philosophie, oder über das Unbedingte im menschlichen Wissen" ("On the Ego as Principle of Philosophy, or on the Unconditioned in Human Knowledge"), (1795); "Philosophische Briefe über Dogmatismus und Kriticismus" ("Philosophical Letters on Dogmatism and Criticism"), (1796); "Abhandlungen zur Erläuterung des Idealismus der Wissenschaftslehre" ("Essays in Explanation of the Idealism of the Science of Knowledge"), (written 1796–1797), — the work by which "Fichte's attention was first drawn to Schelling, and a way opened for Schelling to an academical chair." The most important of the foregoing works is perhaps the third mentioned, which by its very

---

[1] See Professor Adamson's article on Schelling in the "Encyclopædia Britannica."

title recalls the position taken by Fichte in his "First Introduction to the Science of Knowledge." A characteristic feature of his attitude in these works is a sharp antagonism to "Criticism" because of its alleged equivocal position (pointed out by Fichte) between Dogmatism (of Spinoza) and Idealism (of Fichte). Works of the second period (the first period of Schelling's independent philosophizing) are: "Ideen zur Philosophie der Natur" ("Ideas towards the Philosophy of Nature"), (1797),— in which an attempt is made to deduce *a priori* natural phenomena from two organically related forces, attraction and repulsion, and to explain nature dynamically (in the spirit of the Kantian Metaphysics of Nature), instead of mechanico-atomistically; "Von der Welt-Seele" ("On the World-Soul"), (1798), in which "Life [Soul] is treated as the essence of all things and the bond of organic and inorganic nature," and the world is the "active unity of positive and negative principles;" "Erster Entwurf eines Systems der Naturphilosophie" ("First Sketch of a System of a Philosophy of Nature"), (1799); "Einleitung zu seinem Entwurf eines Systems der Naturphilosophie, oder über den Begriff der speculativen Physik und die inner Organization eines Systems dieser Wissenschaft" ("Introduction to his Sketch of a System of the Philosophy of Nature, or on the Notion of Speculative Physics," etc.), (1799); "System des Transcendentalen Idealismus" (1800); "Allgemeine Deduction des dynamischen Processes, oder Kategorien der Physik" ("Universal Deduction of the Dynamic Process," etc.), (1800). Works of the *third* (second) period are: "Authentische Darstellung [Exposition] meines Systems der Philosophie" (1801),— Spinozistic in form and substance; "Bruno; oder über das göttliche und natürliche Prinzip der Dinge" (1802),— 2d edition of the "Ideen zur Philosophie der Natur" (1803); "Vorlesungen über die Methode des academischen Studiums" (1803); "Philosophie und Religion" (1804); "Darstellung des wahren Verhältniss der Naturphilosophie zur verbesserten Fichtischen Lehre" ("Exposition of the true Relation of the Philosophy of Nature to the improved Fichtian Doctrine"), (1806). Works of the *fourth* (third) period are: "Philosophische Untersuchungen über das Wesen der menschlichen Freiheit" ("Philosophical Inquiries into the Nature of Human Freedom"), (1809); "Denkmal der Schrift von den göttlichen Dingen des Herrn F. H. Jacobi," etc. ("Memorial on Jacobi's Work on Divine Things"), (1812); "Vorlesungen über die Philosophie der Mythologie, über die Philosophie der Offenbarung" (posthumous). — The periods in the development of Schelling's system are sometimes characterized by reference to those thinkers prior to and contemporaneous with him to whom he was especially indebted. These, in the order in which they affected his thinking, are: Fichte ("Science of Knowledge"), Kant ("Metaphysical Principles of Natural Science" and the "Critique of Judgment"), Spinoza ("Ethics"), Bruno, Plato, Steffens, Baader, Boehme, Kant ("Religion within the Limits of Mere Reason"), Hegel. The student of the history of philosophy will experience no difficulty in discovering for himself the kinship of Schelling's doctrines at the various stages with those of these thinkers.

Philosophy: — First Period: Philosophy of Nature and Transcendental Idealism (tending to Absolutism); Phenomenology. — Schelling begins to occupy an independent position in the history of philosophy when, as against the subjective idealism of Fichte, he maintains the (for thought) objectivity (as well as ideality) of nature. He finds a starting-point in the Kantian doctrine of the changes of matter as the product of the two forces of attraction and repulsion (see vol. i. p. 358), though he entirely repudiates the Kantian theoretical subjectivism. He attempts to deduce, by the aid of the conception of polarity borrowed from the phenomena of magnetism, the *necessity* of the unity of the two forces of attraction and repulsion in all bodies.[1] As Fichte had shown (pheno-

[1] See Erdmann, § 317, 1.

menal) mind to be the synthesis of opposing principles, Schelling will show nature to be a like synthesis, and, as such, to be relatively independent of mind; will show nature to be mind visible, and mind to be invisible nature. The Philosophy of Nature is therefore an independent branch, co-ordinate with Transcendental Philosophy, of the entire system of philosophy; and we have to inquire, not only, as the latter does, How, with mind as *prius*, we get to nature, but also How, with nature as *prius*, we get to mind. — To take the latter question first : the problem of the *philosophy of nature*. If we assume nature as a *prius*, we have to explain it by principles that are *inherent* in it; and we must carry the realistic explanation up to the very borders of mind,— must explain the ideal by the real, if possible. Only, if we assume mind as the *prius*, can we explain nature by principles lying outside it. These two modes of explanation ought, indeed, to harmonize, though they are not identical. Now, not nature as phenomenon and as mere product, is the object of *philosophical* inquiry, but nature as productive, as self-existent. And the only possible explanation of it is a dynamical one. Mechanically regarded, motion, instead of being self-subsistent, is a product of other motion, and that of other, and so on, *ad infinitum*. Dynamically viewed, motion arises not merely from motion, but from rest, so that there is motion even in the *rest* in nature, and mechanical motion is secondary and derivative. A philosophical explanation of nature must also be an *a priori* explanation, or an explanation from principles. Mere experiment can never get beyond the superficial *forces* of nature to its original productivity. There must therefore be speculative hypothesis employed,— which may properly be done if our presupposition be as involuntary and as necessary as nature itself, *i. e.*, carry its necessity within itself. The deduction of natural phenomena from an absolute hypothesis is a construction of nature. Though this construction may, and even must, be brought to the test of experiment, —

for philosophy is the explanation of experience, — the possibility of a speculative philosophy of nature depends upon that of such construction. Such an absolute hypothesis as our science demands is found in the very notion of nature as an infinite productivity, as self-producing, as both cause and effect, as organic unity. Nature, as productivity, is distinguished from its opposite, art, in that, whereas in art the idea passes over into the product and cannot be separated from it, in nature idea and product (which is an act), are contemporary and one. But an infinite productivity, which were merely such, would, in the infinite rapidity of its action, be nothing whatever for empirical perception. There must be fixedness, limitation. But if the ground of limitation lay outside nature, nature would not be absolute productivity. Determination, *i. e.*, negation, must be contained in nature itself and as a positive attribute. Nature cannot really be pure identity: it contains within itself a certain duplicity. But this duplicity, again, just because it is in nature, must be cancelled, and nature is thus a *process*, having three stages, of identity, antithesis, indifference, or rather struggle towards indifference, for antithesis cannot be wholly cancelled. This first deduction from the absolute hypothesis is the principle — not a result — of the physical explanation of nature. Now, pure productivity, by becoming permanent productivity (and only by so doing), becomes product; and, conversely, all subsistence is but a continual process of being reproduced. Every product is, therefore, merely the original productivity in a certain determination, or with a certain primal quality. In so far as each product is the result of a limitation of infinite productivity, it is finite; but in so far as it is just that infinite productivity, it is infinite: it is a finite subsistence in an infinite development (or, on the other hand, an infinite series or system gradually determining itself). Were these developing qualities of the infinite productivity finite in their development, then the primal product of nature would be an infinity of separate atomic productivities, — mechanical atoms. But as it is, they **are merely** potentialities, "entelechies," **or ideal ends of** productivity: they are not real, not in space. The true theory of nature, therefore, is *dynamical* (instead of mechanical) *atomism.* The first product of nature, as dynamical process, is **gravity (which is a** universal **active** tendency **towards** indifference, **a** result of which is matter without specific **form), with merely** difference of **weight and density. Gravity — the first potency, or power, — develops,** through **the stages of unity of product,** duplicity of product, **unity of the products, or thesis,** antithesis, synthesis, **into** magnetism, electricity, **chemical process,** which may **be** termed the categories **of the original construction of nature. The** limitation **of the inorganic** in its **highest power, or potency, gives, as product, the organic. The stages of the organic are** sensibility, **irritability,** reproduction. **As regards the relation of the inorganic and the organic, it appears that, phenomenally speaking, the former is second potency, may take its origin from simple factors, appears to have existed from all eternity, and arrives at indifference; whereas the organic is third potency, can originate from products only, appears as having been created, and never arrives at indifference, since "life consists in nothing more than a continual prevention of the attainment of indifference." " The most general problem of speculative physics, stated as the reduction of the construction of inorganic and organic products to a** common **expression, is incorrect, and therefore admits of no solution. The problem presupposes that the organic product and the inorganic product are mutually opposed, whereas the latter is only the higher** *power* **of the former, and is produced only by the higher power of the forces through** which **the latter also is produced. But the** difference between organic **and inorganic nature is only in nature** as product; **nature, as originally productive,** transcends both." **In the** organic, **as its highest power, nature** attains **to the borders of intelligence, and the deductions of the** organic completes the task of the philosophy of nature, which, as we have seen, was the showing how nature arrives at intelligence. — The converse task — the task of *transcendental philosophy* — has now to be taken up. Since nature and intelligence are, as object and subject, polar opposites, there must be an agreement in result between the transcendental philosophy and the philosophy of nature ; or, in other words, the transcendental philosophy is the reflection in the sphere of intelligence of the potencies of the philosophy of nature. As the transcendental philosophy " starts with the subjective as the only ground of all reality, the sole principle of explanation of everything else," it necessarily begins with universal doubt regarding the reality of the objective and the truth of ordinary prejudices. Transcendental knowledge is distinguished from ordinary knowledge in certain particulars : (1) For it the existence of external objects is a mere prejudice, which it ignores in order to find the grounds for it. "It can never be the business of the transcendental philosopher to *prove* the existence of things-in-themselves, — indeed, he has no means of doing so, since his only datum is the subjective,— but only to show that it is a natural and necessary prejudice." (2) The two affirmations, *I am*, and *There are things outside me*, which in the ordinary consciousness run together, are, in transcendental knowledge, separated, and the one placed before the other, with a view to demonstrating the fact of their identity and of that immediate connection, which in ordinary knowledge is merely felt. (3) In transcendental knowledge the object is cognized only indirectly, whereas in ordinary knowledge the object primarily is cognized, the act of knowing vanishing in that. "The nature of transcendental knowledge is in general as follows : In it that which escapes all other thinking, knowing, or acting, or escapes consciousness and is absolutely non-objective, is brought into consciousness and becomes objective, — in short, it is a continuous act of becoming an object to itself on the part of the subjective.

And the transcendental act, which unites the subjective and objective, consists in a readiness to maintain oneself in the duplicity of thinking and acting." Now, the parts of transcendental philosophy correspond in character and number to the original prejudices to be explained by it. First is the prejudice of the belief in things outside us, and in the agreement of our ideas with them, as being determined by them. Second, there is the prejudice of the belief that ideas, which spring up in us freely or without necessity, are capable of passing from the world of thought into the real world, and of arriving at objective reality. The solution of the problem how, by something merely thought, the objective may be altered, in agreement with that something thought, constitutes practical philosophy. But a contradiction arises here for thought: If the subjective is determined by the objective, how can it determine the objective? The solution of this contradiction is, though not the first, the highest task of philosophy. This solution is not given either in theoretical or in practical philosophy, but in a higher form of philosophy, which is both at once and a connecting link between them. How the objective world conforms itself to ideas, and ideas in us conform to the objective world, it is impossible to conceive, unless there exist between the two worlds — the ideal and the real — a pre-established harmony. And this pre-established harmony is not conceivable unless the activity, whereby the world is produced, be originally identical with that which appears in volition, and *vice versa*. The activity displayed in volition is productive — with consciousness; and we may suppose that displayed in the objective world to be the same activity, unconsciously productive. The absolute possibility for knowledge of such a twofold activity is shown by the fact of its existence in the ego, — the principle and starting-point of transcendental philosophy. Such an activity, in fact, is the activity, both conscious and unconscious, of genius in the creation of a work of art. "The objective world is only the primal, still unconscious, poetry of the mind; the universal organon of philosophy, therefore, the keystone of the whole arch, is the philosophy of art." The parts of transcendental philosophy are, then, theoretical philosophy, practical philosophy, and the philosophy of art. — "*Theoretical Philosophy.*" The source and organ of all transcendental thought is an original, unconditioned, intellectual intuition, at once perceptive and productive, consciously perceiving that which it unconsciously produces. The possession of the faculty for this is the peculiar genius of the philosopher. The first object and act of intellectual intuition is the pure, absolute ego, the eternal, non-temporal act of self-consciousness, which gives to all things existence and fills infinitude. In the ego is an activity directed outwards, infinite, limitable, constituting the objective in the ego; and also an activity which returns to the ego, is subjective and ideal, and is the effort of the ego to perceive itself in its outward infinitude. Conflict of these activities constitutes self-consciousness, which has its unity and totality not in any single act, but in an infinite series of acts or "powers" of the ego. The becoming conscious of these acts or potencies in their ideal order is a process, in which what is subjective (and unconscious) in any one state becomes objective to the ego in the succeeding or next higher. The history or development of self-consciousness is, in its chief stages, as follows: The ego, in its productive function, unconsciously sets a limit (matter) to itself, which is perceived by the intuitive ego as a sensation, the act of production and the sensation being (though not yet so perceived) organically correspondent aspects of the same single act of the ego as such. In sensations the ego, as subject, is immersed in ego, as object, and there occurs only a feeling of limitation as a real distinction. But the ego, as infinite (*i. e.*, as pure ego), transcends this state and distinguishes itself as feeling from itself as felt (subject from object), and so becoming cognizant of both, though *primarily* of the latter, which then it **perceives** instead of merely feeling it,— the **second stage of theoretical consciousness.** From the act of perception arises the consciousness of time, since the activity of the ego, both as object **and** as subject [?], produces **and is involved in, succession**; and along with it, by necessity **of contrast or** distinction, **that** of space; **and in consequence** the distinction **between inner** (merely temporal) **and outer (temporo-spatial) perception.** The consciousness **of the** object, **as in time and space, is an implicit consciousness of the unity of time and space, of** intension and extension, **which is force.** This, in its spatial (fixed) **aspect is perceived as substance; in its** temporal (changing) aspect **as accident.** The consciousness **of** substances and accidents, involving **that of cause and of reciprocity, is (as yet) indirect,** consciousness **being still in the stage of perception, in which object** *directly*, *self* **only** *indirectly*, **is before consciousness.** The direct **perception of the self, as having a determined object, reveals the hitherto hidden distinction of subject and object** as **such, and the categories, and constitutes the third stage of the theoretical consciousness, — the stage of** *reflection*. Reflection, **as a separation of subject and object,** is complete when **the** object **as such is entirely abstracted** from, and the subject **alone forms, the content of consciousness.** This absolute abstraction is possible only through the subject's recognizing, as its own unconscious work, all that had, in the stage of perception, been attributed solely to object as cause. Along with this is a recognition of object as self-determining, as organic, and as inwardly identical with subject. Consciousness of intelligence as its *own* product is real consciousness of it as productive,— *i. e.*, as will, which is precisely conscious production. (In intelligence, as such, production is unconscious.) With the consideration of will, we enter the sphere of practical philosophy. — *Practical Philosophy.* Will (or the free action of intelligence upon itself) is explicable only through the conception of a pre-established harmony, or reciprocity, among a multiplicity of intelligences (together with objects in which acts of intelligence may be objectified). Only by the fact that there are intelligences outside me is the world objective to me, and is there a possible sphere of objective effort on my part; for only effects wrought by other intelligences than myself upon the world of sense compel me to negate myself completely, and assume anything absolutely objective; and only through the perception of the identity of myself and the objective, *i. e.*, of the dependence of the satisfaction of my desires upon the external world, do I objectify my will; for will, as objective, is will seeking an objective satisfaction, — happiness, its only and highest good. As my will is bound up with other wills, happiness presupposes a moral order, and, consequently, an intelligence common to all intelligences. This can be in itself neither subject nor object, nor even both together, but is merely absolute identity,— unconscious, as containing in itself no distinction. It is the invisible root of all other intelligences, — which are merely " potencies " of it. Of it history as a whole is but a progressive self-revelation. It (God) *is* not; for if it (God) *were, we* should not be. But it continually reveals itself. Human history is a continual proof of the existence of God, — a proof which can be completed only by history as a whole. In the revelation of the (unconscious) Absolute there are three periods: (1) a period in which it appears as blind Fate, repressing freedom and destroying all that is noblest and grandest,— the period of the Past; (2) a period in which it appears as natural law, — the Present; (3) a period in which it is Providence, or God, — the Future. — *Philosophy of Art.* The infinite opposition and ceaseless movement which characterize the practical and the theoretical spheres, is resolved in the realm of art, which is just that unity of the conscious and the unconscious which the Absolute as the source of history and nature must be. In art, intellectual intuition, which is the spring and source of all development of intelligence, finds its true object,— returns to itself; and nature and science, as by a miracle, attain to perfection.

Philosophy of the Absolute,— the "System of Identity."— The standpoint of philosophy is that of reason, or the Absolute. In reason, or the Absolute, all things are; outside it, nothing: it is the All of things, the being of being. The highest law for the being of reason, and of all things as comprehended in reason, is the law of identity, — the identity of reason with itself in all things. This is absolutely certain: from it abstraction cannot be made. It is the only absolutely certain thing. In reason as identity, thought and being, subject and object, the finite and the infinite, all opposites whatever are one: reason is the absolute indifference of opposites. Knowledge of the absolute identity is a part of it (*not* outside it), flows directly from its being, belongs to the primal form of its being. Every particular thing is only the absolute, or reason itself, in a particular mode; in each thing, the opposites united in reason are also contained in union. What is called finite is also infinite: the finite as such does not exist in or for reason; philosophy, so far from deducing the finite or the particular as such, rather does the opposite, — *i.e.*, denies its existence. In Platonic phraseology, the finite has its truth and reality in an eternal Idea that is above the distinction of the finite and the infinite: merely as finite, a thing rather is *not* than is. In reason nothing originates or ceases to be; reason does not go out of itself; all that is or can be is already eternally in reason. Reason is the absolute totality of all distinctions. Things in reason are *relative* totalities; they are reason in certain degrees or potencies, which are in it contemporaneously. Existences differ owing and according to differences of quantitative relations of the objective and subjective moments of reason in them. The first relative totality is matter (containing the greatest quantity of the objective and least of the subjective, as such), which is relative totality in general, containing in possibility all other "potencies" or "powers" of reason. Absolute identity as ground of reality is mere force, which manifests itself as gravity, the first of the material potencies (potency A^1). The moments of gravity are attraction and expansion: these are in perfect equilibrium only in the infinite universe as a whole. All matter in itself is alike; and the so-called qualities of matter and the phenomenal immense in general are the result of a primal cohesional process, the first stage of which is magnetism, the second electricity, the third galvanism (chemical process), — the three together constituting the second general potency, Light (A^2). Light as distinguished from gravity, which is mere force, is *activity*, — a sublation of potencies through one another and a tendency to absolute indifference. The union of light and gravity gives the Organism, the third potency (A^3). The organism does not *absolutely originate* as a result of mere metamorphosis of the inorganic, so called; for it is virtually present in matter from the beginning. The inorganic as such does not really exist (see above, page 56). The organism as an end is the absolute identity as real or existent. The potencies of organic activity are reproduction, irritability, sensibility (compare statement made above, page 56). The highest product of organic activity is the human brain. The organic world, as a whole, has the two poles of plant and animal life: in its individuals, the poles of male and female. — As in the material potencies the objective moment of existence predominates, so the domination of the subjective moment produces the potencies of the ideal world. The potencies of the ideal world are, — *knowledge* (the potency of reflection, — including perception [sensation, consciousness, perception as such], thought, and real knowledge [conception, judgment, reasoning]), *action* (the potency of subsumption), and *art*, or reason (the unity of the two foregoing). "The ultimate ground and possibility of all truly absolute knowledge must rest in this, that precisely the general is at the same time the particular; and that which appears to the understanding as mere potentiality without reality, essence without form, just this is also reality and form." Philosophical knowledge, subjectively viewed, is an act of "construction" (not in *immediate* intuition, as in geometry, but) in *reflected* intuition, the object constructed being purely within the mind, thought, as such, — it is an act of self-construction of thought; objectively viewed, it is the science of Ideas, or the eternal archetypes of things. "The capacity for knowledge — pure intellectual intuition — is a capacity to see everything only as it is present in the Idea."[1] Philosophy as absolute knowledge is related to the special sciences, taken as a whole, as their internal organism; only in absolute archetypal knowing can those sciences have a solid foundation. "As philosophy is the harmony of universal and particular in the potency of knowledge, so in the potency of action are the State and the Church the unity of the two, — the former the real, the latter the ideal, unity." The State is in itself the harmony of the freedom of the individual with universal necessity, and in its historical development the unity of the finite with the infinite, and so the manifestation of Providence. Ancient history is a unity of finite and infinite, in which the former is dominant; with Christianity begins modern history, whose dominant idea is that of the infinite. The advent of Christ as God incarnate is the centre or indifference-point of history.[2] Art is a necessary and immediate image of the Eternal Archetypes or Ideas. According as its object is the real or the ideal, it is formative art (music, painting, plastic art, in each of which the others are involved) or poetry (epic, lyric, dramatic). The special matter of art is mythology, which is the ideas conceived as real; *i. e.*, as gods[3].

The Philosophy of Freedom and of Religion: "*Positive*

---

[1] See the "Method of Academical Study," Lectures iv. and vi.
[2] See Lecture vii. of the "Method of Academical Study."
[3] See Erdmann, § 318, 10.

Philosophy." — In the "System of Identity," as such, the possibility of the free existence of anything outside reason is, on the whole, unqualifiedly denied. But in the expositions of this system there incidentally occur distinctions having a different bearing, — the finite as such, it is declared, cannot exist *in* reason, and hence must exist by a certain self-determination, by a "falling-away from God," not explicable through the notion of the absolute as such. The development of this thought and the reconciliation of it with the principle of identity constitutes the third and last general stage of Schelling's (independent) philosophizing. The absolute cannot be mere identity, mere allness, mere necessity: there must be room for difference, particularity, freedom. The latter thought springs easily out of the former, and the more so the more the other is insisted on. *Mere* identity *is* nothing, explains nothing. But now, — to give Schelling's new view, — if there is anything in the absolute that is not just it, it must have as its ground something in the absolute which is not the absolute as such. We may therefore distinguish in the Absolute, — in God, — besides mere being, also the ground of being, and, further, the passage from one to the other; otherwise described, being as mere potentiality, being as actuality, being as transition from one to the other. The ground of God's *existence* — or actuality in God — is a nature inseparable, though distinguishable, from him. It is prior to him neither in time nor in nature. There is no first and last in God or the Absolute. Everything there presupposes every other thing. If the ground is in a certain regard prior to God as he actually is, it yet could not be ground unless God also existed. The ground is, as it were, the eternal yearning which the Absolute feels to bring forth, and (since the All, the One, is what is) to bring forth itself in an image, or copy. As the copy, again, is to and for the Absolute, the end of the bringing-forth is self-consciousness, or, finitely speaking, self-*revelation*. The yearning, in itself considered, is without understanding, and yet a yearning or desire for the content of understanding, — it is, without *perceiving* the understanding, controlled by it; *i. e.*, it is unconscious will. The presence of the yearning excites in the understanding (consciousness) a corresponding image in which the Absolute sees itself, and which, reacting upon the yearning, causes it to strive to become or produce the Absolute (in copy). Thus occurs a division of potencies in the Absolute, and free particularity — material forces and existences — results. Every being thus originating has a double nature, — one akin to the ground, another akin to the understanding; one "dark," the other "light." Since the process of origination just described takes place in one and the same unity, the dark principle is implicitly the light, and has it as its goal. The dark principle in each particular individual is his self-will, — his individual will; the light the universal will, which uses the other as its instrument, and raises it to the light, *i. e.*, to itself. This occurs, among known creatures, only in man. By virtue of his origin from the "ground" and of his particular will, man is independent of God as such, is free, and the subject of both good and evil. He is evil in so far as the dark principle, — particular will, — good in so far as the "light" principle, — the understanding, — rules in him. Evil is the subordination of the universal to the particular will; good is the reverse. (This subordination cannot occur in nature as such, but only in man.) The perfect union of particular and universal will is love, — which is not mere indifference, but the *organic* identity of opposites. What according to the "System of Identity" is abstract is here concrete; what was merely negative is here positive: what was mere hypostasis is here existence. Reason perceives only the *what;* the *that* must be known by experience, since spirit not merely is and is conceived, but *proves* its existence by its presence in experience as such. The system of Philosophy as a whole has two parts, — a negative, the function of which is the gaining the notion of the absolute; and a positive, which develops and realizes that conception in terms of concrete experience. The former includes the philosophy of nature and the "System of Identity" in all forms (even the Hegelian); the latter, a new form of philosophy, a "metaphysical empiricism," is primarily the philosophy of mythology and religion, which are *par excellence* the expression of the Absolute in its highest and true reality as spirit. Mythology and religion are not mere products of negative abstract reason; they are real, they are experimental facts in the process of the Absolute Consciousness. The mythological consciousness — the consciousness of heathendom — corresponds to that condition of the separatedness of the divine potencies which is signalized in nature. It culminates in the Grecian mysteries. It is a preparation for Christianity — like itself, a real fact — in which the moments separated in *it* are reconciled. The content of Christianity in its entirety is contained alone in the *person of Christ:* he is the particular in which the universal in the Christian religion is embodied, and that religion really existent; for the real is not the abstract and negative, but the concrete and positive. In him alone is the extra-divine existence (nature) brought back to the Absolute, and the divine potencies brought into organic union. The deed of Christ is valid for all time, and begins the religion of spirit and of freedom. In the past the kingdom of God has existed inwardly under forms of religion which may be designated as Petrine and Pauline: it must become eternal also, — Johannean. It will then introduce as a fact in the Absolute Consciousness philosophical religion, — the philosophy of religion.

Result. — Besides what has already been said or distinctly implied, and what will be brought out in connection with the study of Hegel, little need be said by way of characterizing the position of Schelling. The doctrine of Schelling may be described as objective idealism, with empiricism and intuitionism as subordinate momenta.

Schellingians. — More or less close followers of Schelling were, besides those specially treated below: (1) Georg Michael Klein (1776-1820), professor of philosophy at Würzburg; Georg Anton Friedrich Ast (1778-1841), professor in Landshut; Bernhard Heinrich Blasche (1776-1832); Adam Carl August Eschenmayer (1771-1852), professor at Tübingen; Gotthilf Heinrich Schubert (1780-1860), a practising physician; Carl Hieronymus Windischmann (1775-1839), professor at Bonn; Franz Joseph Molitor (1799-1860); Johann Jacob Wagner (1775-1821), professor at Würzburg; Ignaz Paul Vitalis Troxler (1780-1866), professor in Lucerne, Basel, and Berne, — all adherents to a greater or less degree of the "System of Identity;" (2) Hubert Beckers, sometime professor at Dillingen and Munich; Jacob Sengler (1799-1878), professor at Freiburg; Leopold Schmid (1808-1869), professor at Giessen; Martin Deutinger (1805-1865), professor at Munich and Dillingen; Wilhelm Rosenkrantz (d. 1874), — adherents of the Doctrine of Freedom and Positive Philosophy. — Requiring special notice here are a number of men, — Lorenz Oken, Henrik Steffens, Johann Erich von Berger, Carl Wilhelm Ferdinand Solzer, Franz Baader, — all of whom taught somewhat more independently than the foregoing of Schelling's theories.

§ 130.

Lorenz Oken[1] (1779-1851). — Oken studied medicine at Göttingen, and was *privat-docent* there (1802-1809). Speculative discoveries in biology won for him the position of *professor extraordinarius* of medicine at the University of Jena (of which Goethe was then rector). In 1812 he was appointed professor of natural science in the same institution. Having given offence to the government of Weimar, by publishing in a scientific journal edited by him censorious political comments relating to other German States, he was obliged to resign his professorship (or give

[1] See Noack, "Encyclopædia Britannica," Erdmann.

up his journal). Between the years 1819 and 1828 he lived in private. From 1828 to 1832 he was privat-docent and professor in the University of Munich, where Schelling and Baader were also lecturing. His naturalism gave offence here, and on the proposal to transfer him to some other institution in Bavaria, he resigned his professorship and went to fill the chair of natural history in the University of Zürich, where he remained until his death.

Works. — " Uebersicht des Grundrisses der Naturphilosophie und der damit entstehenden Theorie der Sinne " (" Synopsis of the Outlines of the Philosophy of Nature, etc."), (1803) ; " Die Zeugung " (Generation), (1805), — which propounds the cell-theory ; " Abriss [Sketch] des Systems der Biologie " (1805 ; " Beiträge zur vergleichenden Zoologie, Anatomie und Physiologie " (" Contributions to Comparative Zoölogy, Anatomy, and Physiology "), (1806) ; " Ueber die Bedeutung der Schädelknochen " (" On the Significance of the Skull-Bones "), (1807), — said to have been an "epoch-making" work in morphology; "Ueber das Universum " (1808) ; " Lehrbuch [Text-book] der Naturphilosophie " (1809–1811) ; " Isis " (1816–1848), — his famous journal ; " Allgemeine Naturgeschichte für alle Stande " (" Universal Natural History for Every Class ") (1833–1841), — his most widely circulated work.

Philosophy : God. — Philosophy, according to Oken, must be both speculation and empiricism, and is throughout the philosophy of nature, or the science of the world-becoming of God, or the disruption of the Absolute into phenomena. God is the All, outside which nothing is or can be. Becoming is not the origination of anything, but merely the passage of the ideal or inner totality into the real or outer and extended totality, — a going of the infinite idea out of itself into finitude. The real and the ideal are one and the same thing, only in different aspects. The real, or finite, is in and by itself nothing ; the only actual is the totality, the Absolute, God ; the finite has meaning only as the positing or affirmation of this. The finite is also only as sublated: it must cease, and give place to other finites. But since the Absolute, or God, is All, the cessation of the finite is merely its return to God. The totality of finite things is, necessarily, eternal equally with the finite. According to the foregoing, it follows that in the All are two inseparable moments,— that of self-position and that of self-sublation. As self-positing and self-sublating, God is self-consciousness. His self-positing in phenomena is his revelation of himself in sense; his self-sublation, his return to himself in thought. Things are the externalized thought of God. The highest of such thoughts of God is man, and that because he sublates and combines in himself a greater manifold of characters than any other finite existence. He is the finite God, — God become bodily.

Nature. — Since the All is, first, mere whole, then a plurality of individuals, and, finally, the union of two, the philosophy of nature has the three parts, — (1) Mathesis (theory of the whole); (2) Ontology (theory of individual existence); and (3) Biology (theory of individuals united into a whole). (1) As a mere whole, God appears first (viewed in a statical regard) as the monad, or unity, as many, and as self-consciousness; second (dynamically viewed), as rest, motion, and permanent time, or space; thirdly, as æther, or primal matter, in the forms of pure undetermined æther,— gravity; of æther under tension,— light; of æther extending itself in all directions, — heat. The material world (God as material world) is an infinite sphere of fire in which gravity, light, and heat are united. (2) The grand divisions of the realm of individuality, — *viz.*, the mineral, the vegetable, and the animal kingdoms,— depend upon, and correspond to, different combinations, — binary, ternary, quaternary,— of the four " elements," — which are all chemical compounds, — earth, water, air, fire. Rising through magnetism, electricity, and galvanism, the inorganic arrives at life and the organic, or the union of wholeness and individuality. Life originates from a primal slime, — a soft mass of carbon composed of "earth," "air," and "water,"— and in the form of the "cell," which, germinating on land, becomes the plant, in the water, the animal. The life of the plant is planetary; that of the animal, solar and cosmic. The classes of plants correspond to the essential organs of the plant; the classes of animals to the various senses in man, the animal being, as it were, dismembered man. Man, as the highest animal, is the eye-animal. (Man and other mammals constitute together the class *ophthalmozoa;* the "invertebrates" are "skin-animals," *dermatozoa;* fishes, "tongue-animals," *glossozoa;* reptiles, "nose-animals," *rhinozoa;* birds are "ear-animals," *otozoa.*) The soul of the animal is a function of the whole body. This has its lowest existence in the mollusk, the mentality of which is mesmeric; its highest in man, in whom dwells consciousness of self or of the entire (animal) nature,— universal understanding. In man nature attains her highest product: in the hero, or the individual of highest manhood,— highest, because all are united in war or the act of freedom, right, and peace, — nature becomes God. Man is a political animal, and the highest natural phenomenon is the State.[1] — According to Erdmann (and Blasche), Oken is the "perfecter of the [Schellingian] philosophy of nature."

§ 131.

Henrik Steffens (1773-1845). — Steffens was a Norwegian who studied medicine and the natural sciences, was greatly impressed by Spinoza's "Ethics" and Schelling's "Ideas for a Philosophy of Nature," and became an enthusiastic friend and follower of Schelling. He lectured at Kiel University, and held professorships at Breslau, Halle, and Berlin. His theories affected Schelling's thinking, and also that of Schleiermacher, with whom he formed a friendship in Berlin. Steffens was a mineralogist.

---

[1] Erdmann, § 325, 3 and 4.

Works. — Works of Steffens are: "Beiträge zur innern Naturgeschichte der Erde" ("Contributions towards the Inner Natural History of the Earth"), (1881); "Grundzüge der philosophischen Naturwissenschaft" ("Outlines of Philosophical Natural Science"), (1806); "Die gegenwärtige Zeit und wie Sie geworden" ("The Present Age, and the Manner of its Origin"), (1817); "Caricaturen des Heiligsten" ("Caricatures of the Holiest"), (1819-1821); "Anthropologie" (1822); "Christliche Religions-philosophie" (1839).

Philosophy. — The standpoint of Steffens may be described as the result of a combination of that of Schelling's "System of Identity" and his "Doctrine of Freedom," — of pantheism and individualism. He aims to be a Christian philosopher. Avoiding all empty metaphysical abstractions, his philosophy will begin with the concrete totality of things, — the All, — and end with personality, as the real principle of the universe. It points out, particularly in the mineral kingdom, that primal opposition which appears in personality as opposition of subject and object; sees in nature a course of development (running through six periods, corresponding to the "six days" of "Creation"); finds the principle and end of development in free individuality, and the highest reality to be that which combines in a single whole the greatest number of attributes; views the human race as the culmination and the salvation, the redeemer, of the created universe; discovers the ground of evil in a will opposed to the divine will, hence in a — though *non*-existent — personality; finds true salvation and blessedness in a mental act which is at once a surrender of self to God's consciousness and a reception of illumination and grace from the same, — *i. e.*, in a knowledge which consists in being known.

§ 132.

Johann Erich von Berger[1] (1772-1831). — Von Berger, who was a Dane, studied law in Copenhagen, philos-

[1] Noack.

ophy at Göttingen and Kiel, and also at Jena under Fichte and Schelling (1793). Returning to his home from the university, he spent a number of years on his estate, interesting himself particularly in the Schellingian school and its doctrines, and producing a philosophical work, " Philosophische Darstellung der Harmonie des Weltalls " (1808). After studying astronomy at Göttingen, he occupied the position of professor of astronomy at Kiel, and also, after Reinhold's death, of philosophy in the same university. He died as rector of the university.

Works. — His most important work, " Allgemeine Grundzüge zur Wissenschaft " (" Universal Outlines of Science "), appeared in four parts, as follows : I. " Analyse des Erkenntnissvermögens, oder die erscheinende Erkenntniss im Allgemeinen " (" Analysis of the Faculty of Knowledge, or Phenomenal Knowledge in General ") (1817) ; II. " Zur philosophischen Naturerkenntniss " (" Philosophical Knowledge of Nature "), (1821) ; III. " Grundzüge [Outlines] der Anthropologie und Psychologie " (1824) ; IV. " Grundzüge der Sittenlehre, der philosophischen Rechts- und Staatslehre und der Religionsphilosophie " (1827).

Philosophy. — Thought reaches its true goal and arrives at reason when, by natural dialectic, understanding makes the discovery that nature is its own creation and a complex of spiritual relations. From this point of view there are not two distinct natures, — an outer and an inner, — but one nature, which is both outer and inner. Spirit both creates and rises out of nature, and in it nature is one, — an interpretation of thought and matter. As such, matter is merely an abstraction : in reality, it is implicitly, as it were, spiritual, full of spiritual principles. Spirit, as such, rises out of matter, returning to itself. The human race could not — from a scientific point of view — have sprung from a higher race and have degenerated through " sin," but most probably had its physical beginning from the higher apes. Its earliest condition was that of simplicity and innocence; natural extravagance of **passion is** a sufficient explanation for its later condition of savagery, etc. There is but one virtue, — freedom, — which in its subjective aspect is wisdom; in its objective, justice and love; in relation to God, perfect knowledge. Right is relative to society, — there is no right *prior* to social relation. Public and private right are two aspects of one and the same thing. The original rights of men are: autonomy, developing itself according to natural law, equality, and mildness of right in the family; greatest possible freedom of dependent and serving members of society; security; inviolability of living personality; free use of thought, and its well-considered expression. All belong to the kingdom of mind, science, and art : the promulgation and teaching of truth are the highest institution. Immortality is probable, since eternal being postulates an eternal being-known. All spirits are harmoniously united in God, and in him are exalted above natural necessity. God is immanent in the world, — not a " beyond."

§ 133.

Carl Wilhelm Ferdinand Solger[1] (1780–1819). — Solger, after a gymnasial course, studied jurisprudence and philology in Halle, heard lectures of Schelling at Jena (1801–1802), and of Fichte in Berlin. A special study of the systems of Fichte, Schelling, and Spinoza was followed by his appearance at Frankfort-on-the-Oder as privat-docent (1809) ; later he was appointed professor of philosophy in the University of Berlin. Though he called Spinoza his real teacher, his close association with some of the leading " Romanticists " subjected him to influences which could not but powerfully affect his thinking.

Works. — His doctrines are contained in the works, — " Erwin " (dialogues on subjects in æsthetics) (1815) ; " Philosophische Gespräche " (" Philosophical Dialogues "),

[1] Noack.

(1817); "Nachgelassene Schriften und Briefwechsel" ("Literary Remains and Correspondence"), (1826); "Vorlesungen [Lectures] über Aesthetik" (1829).

Philosophy.—Philosophy is thought about the presence of essence in our knowledge and existence, or, in other words, about divine revelation. The presupposition of philosophy is the absolute fact that God reveals himself as unity of opposites,—a fact perceived by an act which is at once cognition and faith. In faith the reason underlying thought and life is directly present to us, and we apprehend the necessary laws of the universe. There is no real philosophy apart from faith as here understood: philosophy must surrender itself to the absolute fact. In so doing it does not yield to something foreign to its own nature, but what constitutes its own essence. In this act, whereby the absolute fact is apprehended, all contradiction and contrarieties vanish in the one essence. There is nothing outside God. Evil exists not in reality, but only for us as phenomenal beings. In revealing himself to us who are finite, and hence nothing, God sacrifices, annuls, himself. *We* should sacrifice our merely limited individuality, and view ourselves as mere particulars in the Idea, or him. Only by so doing are we, and do we perceive, ourselves as we are in God, or Essence. The perception, by the individual, of himself, and thereby the universe, in and through God, is the origin of religion: the perception of the external world, and thereby himself, in and through God, gives rise to art. In the work of art the divine creative power itself comes to existence. The essence of art is irony, wherein we perceive that our reality would not be if the revelation were not, but that just for that reason the Idea becomes null with this reality. Irony—as this certainty, that it is the fate of the beautiful to become nought—contains the consolation that even what is most excellent in reality, is nothing as compared with the Idea.

§ 134.

Franz Baader[1] (1765-1841). — Franz Baader, who was the son of a court-physician, was himself at one time a physician, but owing to his nervous sensitiveness — he had had for seven years when a child a peculiar brain disease — changed his occupation, becoming a mining engineer. While in this occupation he travelled through North Germany and spent several years in England, becoming a Director of the Bavarian Mining and Smelting Company. Meanwhile philosophical studies were pursued, and a wide range of philosophical reading was passed through, the Cabala, Kant, St. Martin, Boehme, receiving special attention. A peculiar mental constitution and peculiar mental struggles, in which supposed supernatural influences were present, to say nothing of the effect of a strongly religious early education, caused the domination in Baader's thinking of religious and mystical notions, and Baader himself to side with the Romanticist movement and to become an avowed champion of (Catholic) religious philosophy and the philosophy of the (Catholic) religion, in opposition to the anti-religious tendencies of the Enlightenment, and the Kantian and post-Kantian philosophy in Germany. Two years (1822-1824) were spent by Baader travelling through Germany in the interest of a practical reconciliation of philosophy and religion. In 1826, Baader accepted the position of professor of philosophy and speculative theology in the new University of Munich, having several years previously given up his occupation of mining engineer. This position he held — part of the time as colleague of Schelling and Oken — until his death. He was in close friendship with Jacobi and Schelling while at Munich.

Works. — " Beiträge [Contributions] zur Elementarphilosophie " (1797); " Ueber das pythagoräische Quadrat [Square] in der Natur, oder die vier Weltgegenden [World-regions]," (1798); " Beiträge zur dynamische

---

[1] Noack, Erdmann, Zeller, works of Baader, " Encyc. Brit.," etc.

Philosophie" (1809); "Fermenta Cognitionis" (1822–1825); "Ueber den Begriff der Zeit" ("The Notion of Time"), (1818); "Analogie des Erkenntniss- und Zeugungstriebes" ("Analogy between the Impulse of Knowledge and of Generation"), (1809 ?); "Ueber den Affect Ehrfurcht und der Bewunderung" ("On the Emotion of Reverence and Admiration"),(1804); "Ueber die Begründung der Ethik durch die Physik" ("The Basing of Ethics upon Physics"), (1813); "Ueber den Blitz als Vater des Lichts" ("The Lightning as the Father of Light"), (1815), — a criticism of the Kantian doctrine of the autonomy of the will; "Ueber das heilige Abendmahl" ("The Lord's Supper"),(1815), — treating of magnetic *rapport* with Christ; "Ueber den Urternar" ("On the First Ternary"), (1816); "Sätze aus der Bildungs- und Begründungslehre des Lebens" ("Principles of the Theory of Formation and Foundation of Life"), (1819); "Vorlesungen über speculative Dogmatik" (1828–1838).

Philosophy: Logic, Theory of Knowledge, or Transcendental Philosophy. — Philosophy begins, not with doubt, but with wonder and awe. Man cannot exist without an influence from above liberating him from what is below. All real consciousness is God-consciousness, or participation in the divine self-knowledge. The real knowledge of being must contain being as knower as well as the known. In perfect consciousness the divine is immanently present. In other forms of consciousness the divine element is present externally and in a necessary and constraining manner, or else as free impulse of knowledge (belief). To attempt, in the Cartesian manner, to get from mere self-certainty to the knowledge of God is absurd. The knowledge of God must be a participation in God's own knowledge of himself: we cannot find God without God. Instead of saying, with Descartes, "I think, therefore I am," we should say, "I think because I am thought; *i.e.*, because God by thought penetrates my thought, and I find myself as formed by him." This God-consciousness of God and of self is, on one side, faith in God, and on the other, illumination by him. Knowledge, in short, is ingenerated in us — as the child in the womb — by God; there is a strict analogy between generation and knowledge. According to the foregoing, God is self-manifestation. Now, this can be possible only as he is self-distinction. God *is* this self-distinction, being *and* becoming; activity, life. The divine activity is, first, activity in itself, or primal will, then activity going forth from itself as intelligible will, or manifestation, and, lastly, since it is a single activity, a returning to itself, spirit. The process thus described is not temporal, but eternal: God is in himself eternal self-distinction and self-identification (*cf.* Boehme, vol. i. page 34). This triplicity of activity in God, this "divine ternary," occurs or has its "place" in the divine idea or wisdom, which, with the three activities, constitutes the "divine quaternary." Besides the purely logical and immanent process there is also a real and emanent process by which God realizes himself or this process (since God is process) as tri-personality: God as quaternary or united will and idea, *i. e.*, as appetite or desire of himself ("Father"), distinguishes himself from himself, and becomes object to himself ("Son"), and sublates this distinction ("Spirit"). This process, like the foregoing, is a non-temporal or "non-historical" process. Still another process occurs, — an historical process, — depending, not on the activity of primal, unconscious will, nor on spontaneous (conscious) desire, but on God's free determination. His love and will are the process of "creation," whereby real existences outside of God — as angels, men, and merely natural existences — come into being, as images of God.

Philosophy of Nature. — In man, also, the process of a self-diremption occurs, — namely, in the "fall." This, like the "creation," is (was) a free act, and is susceptible only of an historical (not of a speculative) demonstration. The "fall of man" had as consequent the creation of the world of space, time, and matter, the destined end of which was to offer to man the means for returning to his original purity and harmony of nature as image of God; *i. e.*, for being redeemed. The whole significance of nature is contained in this fact. Nature is ascending potency or development, and because conditioned by a descent, the "fall." Nature must be born again: it reaches its true destination, that is to say, in giving birth to spirit. The Schellingian doctrine of a World-soul, the "first harbinger of an approaching spring, the first joyous expression of physics awakening from the death-sleep of mechanical atomistics," has rightly seized the duality and polarity of nature: it merely requires to be supplemented by the addition to the two ground-forces of expansion and contraction, (1) of the conception of the "upward and downward course in nature," and (2) of something external to the engine of nature setting it in motion and controlling it, which is the "breath from the all-animating principle of things." (These four principles Baader calls the "Four World-regions"). In every living thing there is as condition of its life and existence an intercourse, not only of members with each other, but of each and all with the ground and centre of the life of that thing. Continuance of life depends on the fact that the ground of life does not exhaust itself in it, but remains behind it in darkness. The fundamental law of life is that of regeneration.

Ethics. — If it is the destination of nature to give birth to spirit, it is on that account necessary that spirit, or the spiritual life, have its root in nature. On the other hand, since all human consciousness is a union with a higher than ourselves, the ethical life is also a religious life, or life of faith instead of pure reason. The (Kantian) so-called autonomy of will does not exist. Merely rational conscience, in truth, "neither gives a good disposition, nor takes away bad impulses; the approval of the moral law is in no way the power and the original motive force of will." The renunciation of all concrete ends (as required by the formal Kantian ethics) is self-contradictory, for self-denial means nothing unless there be really a "better, the evolution of which keeps pace with the involution of the bad life."[1] Instead of the merely formal will, we have given in "conscience with immediate certainty," the evidence of a connection with a fulness of life. The giver of the moral law is present with us as the fulfiller of it, provided that we with prayer and sacrament place ourselves in magnetic *rapport* with Christ, in whom pre-eminently the God-consciousness is realized. With the possession of this consciousness, which is salvation, immortality is attained, which, instead of being a quasi-temporal existence (as in the Kantian doctrine), is eternity itself, a being "*in*" time, but not "*within*" it. — Society exists only on the basis of the relation of ruler and ruled, with an inequality among the latter. It has the two forms of State and Church. The State is a contract, but with earlier and later generations as well as between individuals of one generation. It is a delusion that everything must be done by the government, and that the government, or ruler, should stand as one side over against the ruled as an opposite. The "Idea" should penetrate all classes alike. No bond between ruler and ruled is possible without religion: the true State is Christian. Transcending all nationalities, and universal in its importance, is the Catholic Church. The true Church aims to occupy the mean position between stagnation and revolution (Protestantism as such), and to this end it allies with it speculation: an "excommunication of intelligence would virtually be an excommunication from intelligence."[2]

Result. — Comment on the "system" of Baader, and its relation to the "system" of Schelling (*i. e.*, to the Doctrine of Freedom) is unnecessary. — Followers of Baader were Franz Hoffman (d. 1881), J. A. B. Lutterbeck (d. 1883), J. Hamberger (d. 1885).

[1] Ueber Kant's Deduction der praktischen Vernunft.
[2] See Erdmann, § 325, 9.

§ 135.

Karl Christian Friedrich Krause[1] (1781-1832). — Krause, born at Eisenberg, in the Duchy of Altenberg, was educated at a gymnasium and the University of Jena, where, after courses in theology, mathematics, and philosophy, he took the degree of doctor. He began teaching philosophy as privat-docent in the University of Jena in the year 1802, occupying a standpoint lying between the "*a-priorism*" of Fichte and Schelling (whose lectures had failed to satisfy him as a student) and the empiricism of Fries. (His own, final, standpoint he arrived at, as "by a sudden revelation," the next year.) In 1804, when the Government would have made him full professor, he left the university to devote himself to art-studies, being already himself a skilled amateur in piano-playing and in singing. He went to Dresden, pursued his studies, and supported himself and a family by private teaching. Thinking that he saw in the order, or brotherhood, of "Freemasons," of which he had become a member, the germ of a universal "league of humanity," he worked enthusiastically for it. An adverse criticism by him of the vowed secrecy of the order caused his dismissal from it, and involved him in a way that affected his entire after-career. He habilitated as privat-docent in Berlin University in 1814, and sought a professorship there; but failing to obtain what he desired, returned to Dresden, where he lectured. He habilitated at Göttingen in 1824, and had large and enthusiastic classes. The hostility of the "Freemasons" drove him from that place. It also followed him to Munich, where he habilitated at the age of forty-five as privat-docent, with the hope of rising to a professorship. Through the influence of Baader and others, Krause escaped banishment from Bavaria, and but for the opposition of Schelling would probably have been received

[1] Noack, Zeller, Erdmann.

into the Faculty of the University of Munich. He died suddenly of apoplexy.

Works. — Works of Krause are, — "Grundriss [Outlines] der historischen Logik" (1803); "Grundlage [Principles] des Naturrechts" (1803); "Grundlage eines philosophischen Systems der Mathematik" (1804); "Anleitung [Guide] zur Naturphilosophie, oder Entwurf [Sketch] des Systems der Philosophie" (1804); "System der Sittenlehre" ("Theory of Morals"), (1810); "Das Urbild [Prototype] der Menschheit" (1811); "Vorlesungen über die Grundwahrheiten [Fundamental Truths] der Wissenschaften [Sciences]," (1829); "Abriss des Systems der Philosophie, erste Abtheilung: analytische Philosophie" (1825); "Abriss des Systems der Rechtsphilosophie" (1828); "Vorlesungen über das System der Philosophie" (1825); "Die reine oder allgemeine Lebenlehre und Philosophie der Geschichte, zur Begründung der Lebenskunstwissenschaft" (1843).

Philosophy: Ground-Science. — Speculation must begin with what is absolutely, even though only subjectively, certain to every one, and thence rise to a principle of objective truth, on the basis of which philosophic science proper may pursue its objective "course." The ground-science, or fundamental part, of philosophy has accordingly two general divisions, — (1) a subjectivo-analytic, and (2) an objectivo-synthetic. (1) The first absolute certainty is the ego's consciousness of itself. It perceives itself as a unit, and as a union of soul and body, — as having an, in part, non-temporal, free, permanent, and, in part, temporal, necessitated, changing, nature; as possessing certain faculties and activities — *viz.*, perception, feeling, and will — working together as an organic whole. It perceives other egos (by inference from its own nature); sees its body to be a part of an external world, the mind to be a part of universal reason; rises through the perception of the limitedness of all these things, and of the opposition and duality of the ego as reason and nature, to the conception of a primal, infinite unity, essence, and ground of all things, before and above them all, — namely, God. God, as most truly conceived, is not *an* essence (among other essences), nor even *the* essence (*i.e.*, inner relation of reason and nature), but pure essence, since he is outside all relation, independent, absolute. As (our) knowledge (of him), he is immediate non-relative perception, — intuition, spiritual vision. (2) The perception of essence is the one fundamental perception, — unconditioned, and conditioning all others. It is necessary, and hence possible, to the finite spirit, which through it perceives not only its own self-perception, self-feeling, self-willing, but its being-in and intimacy-with God. Essence is as regards its "what," essentiality; as regards its "how," or "form," positionality (God, that is to say, is absolutely positive or affirmative). In essentiality we distinguish unity, selfhood, and wholeness (or self-subsistence and infinitude), which always presuppose one another, though their unity is only that of unitedness, not the primary unity of God. Positionality embraces (number) unity (corresponding to unity of essentiality), direction, or relation (corresponding to selfhood), comprehension (corresponding to wholeness). Essence and form, essentiality and positionality, combined, give existence, as regards which God is described as the unconditionally existent. Unity of essence and unity of form give unity of being, as regards which God is one and sole; selfhood and direction give relational unity, as regards which God is relation to himself and all else; wholeness and comprehension give unity of content, with reference to which God is content of himself and real content of all things; relation and content give unity of being. The foregoing essentialities, or categories, constitute in their unity and plurality the one "essentiality" of God. As every essentiality is just that which all others are not, and *vice versa*, the essentiality of God contains perfect contrariety; God is both contrariety and unity of essence. As such he contains and is the union of the two subordinate co-ordinate essences, spirit and nature, — the former representing his selfhood, the latter his wholeness. As unity of nature and spirit, he is humanity. As numerical unity, he is once-for-all the organic union of all essentialities: he contains all perfections, and subsists in and by himself. God is all, and in him are all things: the true philosophy is the philosophy of pan-en-theism. — The parts of philosophy as foreshadowed in this ground-science are, on the one hand, certain theories of essence, or material sciences, and, on the other, theories of form, or formal sciences. Material sciences are the science of primal essence, the science of reason, the science of nature, science of composite essence, or combined reason and nature, *i. e.*, anthropology (including the science of religion as its highest branch). Formal sciences — which are, however, rather disciplines than sciences — are mathesis (mathematics), logic (metaphysical as well as formal), the science of art, or æsthetics, ethics (including morals, rights, and politics). (To the foregoing should be added the philosophy of history, since Krause treated that in such a way as to make it a part — and indeed a most important part — of the system.)

The Sciences of Nature, Reason, and Composite Essence. — So far from being the work of blind necessity, nature is the constant revelation of an all-pervasive inner life, enveloped, it is true, in a permanent temporo-spatial matter. All its creatures live, and have their formation as a whole, from the whole, in the whole, and from within outward: all share the self-determination of the whole, and have also individual freedom. Organic nature attains its highest form, on this planet, in the human body; in worlds of a higher type than this it reaches a higher degree of perfection. Nature is a divine work of art, into which God has everywhere, even in its details, wrought his purposes. Nature therefore possesses an independent value in itself, and a value in relation to spirit with which it is in intimate penetration and harmony. The highest form of this interpenetration and harmony occurs in the individual beings composing humanity. Humanity is the totality of the composite beings, in whom the highest forms in nature (*viz.*, the most perfect organic bodies) are united the highest individual spirits. Humanity (comprising, not only the races of this earth, but those of all other worlds as well) is a constant whole: the number of individual souls (each of which is eternal, unborn, immortal) in it is unchangeable. The Idea of Humanity is, in a different manner, realized in every individual, and according to a divine providence. The destination of humanity, collectively and individually, is to realize in living the divine essentiality, and purely for the sake of that. And that every finite thing live the essentiality, in the essence and united with it, is the entire salvation of every finite essence. Every individual's plan of salvation — his plan of life — may and should agree with God's plan of salvation. Opposition to essence is evil. God is purely relative, and pertains to the finite as such: it is negated by God as essence. Essentially every finite essence is a co-worker with God.

Morals, Rights, Politics, Philosophy of History. — God is the good: life in and with him is the good life. The condition of the realization of the good in living is the right, or the "organic whole of all internal and external conditions for the perfection of life, depending on freedom." The right does not pertain to the individual as such and anterior to all possible relations to other individuals, but as a law "proceeding from God and embracing everything that must be performed by free action to the end of the realization of the purpose of the life of God and that of the life of infinite rational beings." The eternal demand of the right is that the entire good be realized by means of the whole of its temporal free conditions. The right attains a permanent being through social unions, — families, communities, art-unions, scientific unions, ethical unions, and, above all, the State. In the State the people, or the social person as the common life, is sovereign; and the republican form of constitution is the only one corresponding to the idea of right,— though other forms may be practically justifiable. The end of punishment is education and improvement; the death-penalty is irrational. The humanity of this earth constitutes a world-state. There are in the history of the earth-humanity three periods, corresponding to the unity, selfhood, and wholeness in essence; and each period may be divided into three parts. The first period of history is an age of innocence, of life in God as primal essence, nature, and reason, of unconscious union with higher powers in a sort of magnetic *rapport;* the second period is one of growth, conflicting selfhood, transition from polytheism to rational theism, from despotism to liberation from historical authority, from war to philanthropy, barbarism to culture; the third period is a period of wholeness, the outward manifestation in life of the essence, through the aid of the knowledge of the doctrine of essence as discovered by Spinoza and perfected by me. The social perfection of the earthly humanity is now only in its infancy: it will reach maturity only with the maturity of the entire life of humanity. "The foundation of the 'League of Humanity' was begun by Luther and scientific investigation, and completed by me in March of the year 1808 after Christ." My ground-idea of humanity, the life of humanity, and the league of humanity, should and will become the leading ground-idea in future ages. The earthly humanity is only a member of a higher humanity. Every man is an eternal member of the kingdom of God; his earthly life is only a part of a higher life-whole extending into the past and the future. Death is only a single event, a moment, of the eternal life, the germ of a new cycle of life, a liberating, purifying, exalting, restoring event. The finite spirit lives on after death as single and individual, when all suns that now exist shall have vanished into new-created suns.— Such is the life of essence and union with essence, of which, it must be said, the Church, which does not embrace even the whole of earthly humanity, is but a weak reflection.

Result. — Krause unites subject and object (of thought), in that he shows how the subject, beginning with mere subjective certainty, attains in an objective or systematic way to an intuition of object, which is not bare intuition of the absolute, but a concrete thought-intuition of it in its system (of categories). In this he advances beyond the Schellingian system of mere identity. But it should be noted that the intuition of being or essence in Krause's system is statical rather than dynamical; the categories, instead of developing and arranging themselves by an immanent self-movement, are dependent upon a certain external reflection; and it should further be noted that there is assumed without deduction the distinction between matter and form, as if that were something outside of, instead of within, the totality of things in general. Krause's system professes to be an organic blending of the real truths or principles of previous systems. Conspicuous in it is the attempt to unite the subjectivism of Fichte with the objectivism of Schelling. Krause, it has been well said, has drawn the logical consequences of the Fichtian theory of morals, but has undertaken to realize in the present that state of things which the doctrine of Fichte left to the future to realize. — Followers of Krause were: Heinrich Ahrens (1808–1876), professor at Brussels and Gräz; K. D. A. Röder; Hermann von Leonhardi (1809–1875), son-in-law of Krause, and professor at Prague; H. S. Lindemann (1807–1855), professor at Munich; Tcherghien, professor at Brussels; and others. Krause's doctrines are said to have been widely received in France and in the Romance countries of Europe generally.

§ 136.

Georg Wilhelm Friedrich Hegel [1] (1770-1831). — Hegel, born at Stuttgart, was the son of an officer in the civil service of Würtemberg, — a man of marked character and of probity. His mother was a woman of genuine intelligence, and at least learning enough to teach him the elements of Latin. He attended the gymnasium in his native place between the years of seven and eighteen, and then (1788-1793) took a philosophical course of two years, and a theological course of three, in the University of Tübingen. His tastes as a student inclined decidedly towards the ancient classics, but he was an industrious reader in various branches besides. He was in the habit of making copious extracts and annotations in the course of his studies and readings. Not precocious, — as was, for example, Schelling, who was a fellow-student, — nor even at all brilliant as a student in any direction, he gave no promise whatever in that branch of knowledge in which he is now generally recognized as one of the world's greatest masters. His teachers in the theological seminary were able to credit him in their certificates with only the possession of "fair ability, good character, and a passable knowledge of theology and philology," but no attainments in philosophy. He had, however, read Kant, Jacobi, and other philosophers. Receptive and companionable, he had friends, two of whom, Schelling and the poet Hölderlin, were of especial importance to him. The former largely governed his thinking on philosophical and political topics; the latter, his classical tastes: largely through the influence of the one, he became an admirer and enthusiastic defender of French ideas of liberty, and through that of the other, a worshipper of Greek art and life; through the influence of both, a sort of champion of the notion of the self-sufficiency

---

[1] "Hegel," by Edward Caird ("Blackwood's Philosophical Classics"); "Encyclopædia Britannica;" Noack; Zeller; Hegel's "Philosophie des Geistes," "Naturphilosophie," "Logik," "Propædeutik," etc.

of the individual. For several years his stated occupation was that of domestic tutor in Berne, Frankfort, his industry in reading and excerpting and annotating still continuing. Studies in history, politics, and theology were made, rather than studies in philosophy, though Hegel had, it seems, prepared the framework of a system before he left Frankfort, in 1799. The death of his father in this year, by which he came into an inheritance of a sum of money, caused a decision on his part to betake himself to Jena, — the chief seat of philosophical studies in Europe, — with a view to being near Schelling (with whom he had kept up a correspondence), and perhaps of preparing to habilitate, as he did in 1801, as privat-docent. He assisted Schelling, as co-editor of a " Critical Journal of Philosophy," in the promulgation of the doctrine of " Identity." In 1805 he became *professor extraordinarius* at Jena. Driven from his post the following year by the presence of Napoleon's army at Jena, he left Jena, and went to Bamberg to edit a political journal; two years later he was called to Nuremberg to take the position of rector of the gymnasium there. After eight years of fair success there, he became professor of philosophy at Heidelberg, and two years later at Berlin, where the remainder of his life was passed, with increased industry and activity on his part, and with steadily increasing influence and honor. He became the centre of a coterie of admirers and disciples, was decorated by royal orders, and was (in 1830) made rector of the university. A journal was established to promulgate his doctrines. He died suddenly of the cholera in November, 1831. As a lecturer, Hegel did not, it is reported, attract by grace in eloquence of speech and manner,— was, in fact, rather awkward, and stammered. He had few hearers at first, but by sheer force of thought gradually gained a respectable lecture-room following. His domestic and social relations seem to have been only felicitous. His personal character was markedly that of a man of profound thought, — his thought was himself.

Works. — The chief works of Hegel are : " Die Phænomonologie des Geistes " (1806) ; " Die Wissenschaft der Logik " (1812 and 1816) ; " Encyklopædie der philosophischen Wissenschaften im Grundrisse " (1st ed., 1817 ; 2d, 1827 ; 3d, 1830),— including " Logic," " Philosophy of Nature," and " Philosophy of Spirit ; " " Grundlinien [Outlines] der Philosophie des Rechts " (1821) ; " Vorlesungen über die Philosophie der Geschichte, über die Geschichte der Philosophie, über die Æsthetik, über die Religion," published by a company of friends of Hegel after his death, largely from notes of students, — a fact which should be taken into account in view of certain obvious defects, *e. g.*, want of proportion in the " History of Philosophy," in the form of the works. We may mention also the " Propædeutik " — an introduction to philosophical study prepared by Hegel for classes at the Nuremberg gymnasium — and the " Abhandlungen " (or Essays) ; " Glauben und Wissen " (" Faith and Knowledge "),— appeared in Schelling's and Hegel's " Critical Journal of Philosophy " (1802) ; " Differenz des Fichteschen und Schellingschen Systems der Philosophie " (1801) ; " Ueber das Verhältniss der Naturphilosophie zur Philosophie überhaupt " (" Relation of the Philosophy of Nature to Philosophy in General "), (1802) ; " Wer denkt abstrakt? " (" Who is the Abstract Thinker? ")

Philosophy : Deduction of the Principle. — In the beginning of his philosophical thinking, Hegel was without doubt somewhat of an Illuminationist. He was next an upholder of the Schellingian System of Identity. But already in his first-published philosophical essays (1801–1802) he sees that mere identity, or indifference, is in itself a comparatively barren conception ; that there must be in any conception, taken as the germinal principle of a system, the possibility of distinction and development ; and in the (preface to the) " Phænomenologie des Geistes " he points out the inability of the Schellingian system to get in a logical manner from its first principle to the assumed consequences of that principle. He also points out the fact that the first principle of the System of Identity remains underived, is a mere postulate. Broadly speaking, the philosophy of Hegel is an attempt to obviate these two fundamental defects. Hegel's proof, or, better, "construction," of his first principles (which is given in the "Phenomenology") is, very briefly, somewhat as follows. Required a principle possessing objectivity, universality, self-determination, its construction must be, as it were, a self-construction. Thought must, in the discovery of it, pass from its lowest stage in mere sensuous intuition to its highest stage in pure intellectual intuition, through all intermediate stages, and by a precise objective, or self-governing, movement. The earlier stages in a manner presuppose and are presupposed by the later; the last gathers up into itself all the foregoing, is their ideal totality : it is a spontaneous, objective, universal determination of thought, — an affirmation of the world-spirit as such. There are three main stages: Consciousness (of the "external world"), Self-consciousness, and Reason (the synthesis of two). The last-named comprises four main stages: (1) Certainty and Truth of Reason; (2) Spirit; (3) Religion; (4) Absolute Knowledge.[1]

Logic : Doctrine of Being. — When by its self-movement thought has determined itself *as such, i. e.,* as *pure*, in contradistinction to empirical, sensuous, or figurate, it turns to the problem of unfolding itself in its own element, displaying its organic constituents in their individual independence, their affiliations, and their totality. This is the sphere of logic (the doctrine of reason or thought as such), and, since thought is here its own object, and

---

[1] See Professor Wallace's brief, clear outline of the contents of the "Phenomenology" in the article on Hegel in the "Encyclopædia Britannica." For a more extended account, see W. T. Harris's "Hegel's Logic," chap. iv. ("Griggs's Philosophical Classics"), and article on Hegel's "Phenomenology" in "Journal of Speculative Philosophy," vol. vi.

thought and being are one, the sphere also of metaphysics (the doctrine of being as such). We have at the beginning of the development the mere fact, the mere being, of pure thought (or being). But *mere* being (being without any characteristics or determinations), is — to all appearances — just nothing. And yet if we compare these two, being and nothing, we discover a certain difference, consisting at least in a movement, or tendency to movement, from one to the other (which could not be the case if they were absolutely identical). They are, and yet are not, the same. The movement between them is (as their connecting link) their point of identity and difference, their synthesis, their "truth." Being and nothing prove to be nothing in themselves, but something in their interconnection, which, as it is a movement, is a becoming, or, rather, becoming in general. The notion *becoming*, as compared with *being* or *nothing*, is a concrete notion, a union of a "many." On the side of its multiplicity it is merely pure being and nothing; on that of its unity and totality, it is something *definite* (in general), — existence. Existence, as containing two factors, being and nothing (or not-being), and their union, is (1) *in itself*, or reality; (2) in (relation to) other, or negation (of itself); (3) being-for-itself, ideality. What a thing is in itself and in its relation to other is its quality. As in other, or as other, a thing is finite, *i. e.*, limited (by other); but the limit is not the mere ceasing of the being of a thing, but belongs to the thing in itself; and in it the thing, though changing, returns to itself, thus becoming being-for-self. Being-for-self excludes, and, just for this reason, at the same time has reference to, other; it repels and attracts (and there is no attraction without repulsion, or *vice versa*). The inner repulsion of being-for-self, which is all-inclusive, and, having no other, is one, produces many ones all alike, — or being-for-self, by virtue of the repulsion in it, reproduces itself; thus giving rise to quantity as such, which may be described as sublated being-for-self. Quantity, as compared with quality, from which it has sprung, is indifference, continuity; in itself it is discretion, discretion and continuity necessarily implying one another. As limited it is *quantum*, which, since limit contains *other* in itself, may be increased or diminished indefinitely. The limit of *quantum* as being-for-itself is intensive quantity; as externality (the opposite of being-for-self) is extensive quantity. *Quantum* ceases to exist as such when regarded as infinite, and has meaning only as the negation of a limit and the immediate negation of the negation, or the position of a new limit, *i.e.*, as the determination or quality of other *quanta*, — in other words, as measure, which is the synthesis of quantity and quality. Measure, as containing the dependence of one determination upon another, reveals a new form of thought or being, *viz.*, *Essence*, which is Being withdrawn *out* of its immediacy (for us) into itself (as it were).

(2) *Doctrine of Essence.*— In essence the determinations of being are only in so far as they are posited or thought: they are not "given," but are determinations of reflection. The first determination is essential unity with self, — identity $(A = A)$; the second, which is the negation of the first, is difference (including diversity, contrary opposition, and contradictory opposition); the third, the synthesis of the first two, is the ground, which is foreshadowed in the inseparable unity of the positive and negative. The principle of the ground in itself means that in every diversity there is an identity. The ground involves a thing grounded, the essence of which it is. Inner Essence, that is to say, develops through the ground into (outer) appearance, phenomenon. Appearance has first the form of a totality of existing determinations, — the Thing. But the Thing as a unity of properties is resolved into those properties, and what *was* Essence is now (definite) phenomenon: Essence necessarily *appears*, and because of the identity of the ground and that which

exists, there is nothing in the phenomenon which is not in the Essence, and *vice versa*. This interconnection of Essence and phenomenon is Relation, which may be defined as a "reference to one another of two things which have an indifferent subsistence as regards one another, but each of which is through the other, and in this unity of being determined." Relation is: (1) of whole to part; (2) of force to its manifestation (which contains all and no more than there is in force); and (3) of Outer and Inner. The terms of the relations whole and part, force and manifestation, outer and inner, are in turn mutually conditioning and conditioned, but the relations themselves as wholes are unconditioned; and through Relation, which is the last stage of Phenomenon, Essence in general becomes Actuality, in which the opposition of essence and phenomenon disappears. Actuality, as *mere unconditioned essence*, subsisting in and for itself, is substance. Substance as *e*xisting (appearing) has accidents, of which it is the totality and the inner power. Accidents taken in their separateness or in themselves are *possible*, in their relation through substance are *necessary*. Substance as manifesting itself in the becoming or change of its accidents is activity, or cause, which passes over into effect, and is identical with itself therein. Every cause is in turn effect, and *vice versa;* thus arise the *regressus* and the *progressus in infinitum* in series of causes and effects. In so far as cause must become effect, it is dependent thereon, and the two are in a relation of reciprocity, which is the truth of substance. (Substance is not in its truth mere inactive, dead existence, but self-subsisting interaction.) In reciprocity, since it is a return of substance to itself, substance becomes self-determining, free, universal.

(3) *Doctrine of the Notion.*— Here we leave the sphere of being, immediate and reflected (*objective logic*), and enter that of thought as such (*subjective logic*), the form of which is the pure, self-determining *conception*. In the sphere of

immediate being, thought is occupied with finite conceptions, conceptions merely marking a limit in being; in that of reflected being, or essence, thought is still occupied with finite conceptions, but conceptions which directly imply and are reflected by others as such; in the sphere of the pure conceptions, thought is occupied with conceptions which are purely self-determining, having the universal and self-determining as their object and content. Here present themselves, (1) the conception as such or in itself; (2) the conception in reference to its *realization* or objectivization; (3) the conception as *realized*, or objective, the Idea. The conception as such has the forms of the mere conception, the judgment, and the syllogism. Mere conception contains three moments: (1) that of the undifferentiated unity, or the identity of the notion, — universality; (2) that of the positive determination of the universal in its opposite, — particularity; (3) that of negative unity (excluding the opposite), or complete self-determination, — individuality. The universal *inheres* in the particular and individual, and *subsumes* them under itself. Conceptions stand in relations of co-ordination and subordination, of diversity, contradictory opposition (in so far as they have the same sphere in common, and one is positive and another negative, so that this negativity towards the first constitutes its nature), of contrary opposition (in so far as they are opposed in the same universal sphere, — or the one is positive in the same way as the other, and each can equally well be called positive or negative in relation to the other), and of opposition without relation to the distinction of positive and negative, etc. The exhibition of an object in the separate moments of the conception is judgment (which is not merely a subjective act of "thought," but a determination of reality as well). Judgments are distinguished by the manner in which, in the relation of subject and predicate, they reflect the nature of the conception, — *i. e.*, by the degree of ideal truth expressed in them as judgments. From this point of view judgments are: (1) those the predicates of which are immediate universals (sensible qualities), — *judgments of inherence* (*e. g.*, The rose is *red*), and are *positive, negative,* and *identical,* or *infinite,* the last two as not really containing the distinction of subject and predicate, being, however, not judgments proper; (2) those in which the predicate is some category of reflection while the subject returns to itself in its predicate, and which are therefore termed *judgments of reflection* (*e. g.,* This body is elastic), which are singular, particular, or universal judgments, the last-named of which foreshadow (3) those judgments in which subject and predicate are identical in content, and differ only as regards form, — *judgments of necessity* (e. g., *Gold* is a *metal*, — *i. e.*, metallity constitutes the substantial nature of gold), which are either categorical, hypothetical, or disjunctive; (4) those judgments of which the predicate expresses the agreement or disagreement of an existence with its conception, — *judgments of the conception,* or *notion* (*e. g.*, This action is good), which are assertorical, problematical, apodictic. The judgment, together with its grounds, constitutes the *syllogism,* which is the complete exhibition of the conception, or notion. The syllogism is: (1) syllogism of quality, or inherence (which differs according as its middle term is particular, individual, or universal); (2) syllogism of quantity, or reflection (in which the middle term is either the relation of mere identity or equality, — *mathematical syllogism,* or is all individuals embraced under a given universal, — *syllogism of induction,* or an individual assumed as universal, — *syllogism of analogy*); (3) syllogism of *relation* or *necessity,* which is categorical, hypothetical, disjunctive. A review of the forms of syllogism reveals that, (1) in the qualitative syllogism the moments are taken in their qualitative difference, and accordingly require a medium, which is their immediate unity, but falls without them; (2) in the quantitative syllogism, the qualitative difference of the moments, and hence also the relation of the "mean and the immediate," are matters of indifference; (3) in the syllogism of relation the *mediation* at the same time contains *immediacy*, whence results the notion of an *immediacy*, which is at the same time absolute *mediation*, — end and process, conception realized. The terms of the judgment and those also of the syllogism have shown themselves to be organically one; and so, instead of together determining the whole, are determined by it as end. The end is, (1) merely subjective conception; (2) a mediating transition; (3) objective existence: each of these being (since they are forms of the free notion) involved in the others (as the terms of the syllogism are virtually the entire syllogism). Realization or objectification is, then, of a syllogistic nature. In so far as the terms of the process are external to one another, and their union is accidental as regards them, the process is one of pure *mechanism*. In so far as they are virtually related as *opposites*, the process is *chemism*, the product of which, however, is merely a neutral one (or *mere* product, not also productivity). In so far as they can unite to form a self-determining and self-determined whole, — a product which is also productive, — the process is self-conservation. Self-conservation as the reality, or objective existence of the inner conception, is the Idea, which is just that actuality which does not correspond to any conception or notion outside itself, but is its own content or end. The Idea is an ideal in so far as it is (by abstraction) regarded as an existence conforming to a (subjective) conception; it is truth as regarded from the side of the conception (as conforming to an object). The Idea in its immediacy or phenomenal existence is Life, which is a whole such that the parts in it are nothing in themselves, but are through and in the whole, as the whole is in and through them, — an organic system. The Idea viewed as containing in separation the conception and the actuality is cognition and the good, — the former of which must receive determination and content from actuality, the latter from the former. Cognition is in general relation of the conception and actuality. It is first mere faith, or certainty of the identity of conception and actuality. Its successive forms are: *definition*, which determines the individuality of an object through its genus (universal) and species (particular); *division*, which displays the particular embraced under a universal; *analysis*, which unfolds a concrete object into its manifold, immediate, simple attributes; *synthesis*, which develops the reflected characters of an object, shows their necessary relations; and *construction* and *demonstration*, which are the instrumentalities of this synthesis. In mere knowledge there is but subjective agreement of conception and actuality (subject and object); in the good this agreement is objective. The good is, first, the good-in-itself, which has yet to be realized in a sphere that is foreign to it; then, the good as an absolute end, realizing itself in the world of existence and as the order of that world. It is thus the real identity of conception and ideality, — the Idea as truth and knowledge. Absolute knowledge is the conception which has itself as object and content, and is thus its own reality. The process or *method* of absolute knowledge is as well analytic as synthetic. The development of what is contained in the conception is the issuing forth of the various determinations which are contained in the conception, but are not as such immediately given, and hence are at the same time synthetic. The explication of the conception in its real determinations here proceeds from the conception itself, and what in ordinary cognition constitutes demonstration is here the return of the moments of the conception which have become separated into unity, which is thereby totality, — conception fulfilled and become its own content. The method, therefore, is not a mere outward form, but the soul and notion of its content. With this conception of method we reach that of absolute science, or the doctrine of the conception, *i. e.*, the science defines itself. The mediation of the conception with itself is not merely a process of subjective cognition, but also the real movement of the fact itself. In absolute cognition the conception is both beginning and result. We began with Being as in itself, or abstract; we now have Being as Idea, *i. e.*, as something in and for itself, or independent. Being as Idea, or Idea as Being, is Nature.

Philosophy of Nature. — Nature is the Idea in a form, the essence of which is otherness, externality, as such, so that its destination is to become other than, external to, itself, and thus become spirit. As realm of externality, it is not free, but subject to necessity throughout its parts, which, instead of being self-determined, are determined from without. It is to be viewed as a system of stages; but of stages which have only a logical existence: nature has no history, but is once for all. The philosophy of nature considers: (1) the ideal existence of nature, as space, time, and matter, in general; (2) inorganic nature; (3) organic nature,— is, accordingly, *mechanics* (including *mathematics*), *physics, organics*. (1) Space and time are externalized or existent abstractions, or pure form, pure intuition of nature; space being the externalized notion of mere diversity, time that of negative unity, or pure becoming. As externality in general, they are without limit, — infinite; but, as Ideas, they have their limitations and dimensions, whence the (synthetic) science of *geometry* and the (analytic) science of *arithmetic*, dealing with finite magnitudes, and the synthetico-analytic science of *calculus*, dealing with infinite magnitudes. The synthesis of space and time, as such, is place, while motion is the becoming of time and space, the one in the other; matter is the immediate identical *existent* (not merely abstract) unity of the two — filled space and time. Matter is perception passed out of its immediacy into being-in-and-for-self. By the mere temporal moment, or factor, of being-in-self (negative unity), matter would be a single point; by the spatial moment of being outside self, it would primarily be a multitude of mutually-exclusive *atoms*. But since these are, by virtue of the exclusion which they exercise, related to one another, the atom has not actuality; atomicity and continuity alike are merely possibilities in matter. The being-for-self and essential predicate of matter is gravity, which is the ground or cause of that union of space and time constituting motion. (2) Matter, as individualized and revealed in its qualitative differences by light, is concrete, or physical nature, — the subject of *physics*. The individuality of matter is either universal, particular, or total. Phenomena, falling under the first sort, are the heavenly bodies, the "four elements," meteorological phenomena; under the second, specific gravity, cohesion, sound, heat, etc.; under the third, the form (including magnetism), particular properties (including electricity), chemical process. The individualization and self-subsistency of bodies is also a reference of them to each other, an opposition and an impulse to activity and interaction, whence results a restoration of separate individuality to totality. This process coincides in animate nature with that of construction, whereby what, in one regard, is union is also separation, and a destruction of a neutral existence. (3) The sublation and higher truth of the chemical process is the organic, in which the parts do not determine the whole, but are the rather determined by it. Belonging to this sphere, though only conditionally, is the mineral kingdom. The first truly organic existence is the vegetable kingdom. The vegetable individual is lacking in complete organicity and unity, in that in it parts may themselves be regarded as independent individuals. Because of this deficiency in inner reality, they lack feeling, which belongs to the next higher stage of the organic, *viz.*, animal existence, possesssing, as it does, that subjective unity whereby all the parts are reduced to a single whole. There is in the animal an inner separation due to its irritability, or susceptibility to stimuli, whence results a feeling of want and a responsive *movement*, by virtue of which it stands in sympathetic relation to outward nature. The separation is overcome, and the unity of the animal restored, by the fact that the organism takes outward nature up into itself and assimilates it. Persistent presence of an unreduced foreign element in the organism constitutes disease (the science of which and its cure is medicine). Death is the natural cessation of the particularized individuality as such, and the transition to universality, — the passage from nature to spirit. The animal organism possesses, in a certain manner, universality, or self-determination and self-relatedness, in that it has power of movement, and is not subject to gravity, feels itself (in sensation), but is merely a particular individual, and not adequate to universality of existence, except as part of a higher whole, or genus, only the *genus* animal having an enduring universal *existence*. The sort of individual which is also genus, and so universal, is spirit. According to the foregoing, the logical goal of nature is to " destroy itself, to break through the rind of the immediate, sensible, to be consumed as a phœnix, that it may come forth out of its externality regenerated as spirit." This does not mean that spirit is a mere product of nature. As universal and self-determining, it is as much prior, as subsequent, to nature.

Philosophy of Spirit: Introduction. — Spirit exists (1) as issuing from nature and coming to consciousness of itself as free (subjective spirit); (2) as consciously realizing its freedom in a system of external forms (objective spirit); and (3) as completely self-determining and self-determined (absolute spirit).

Doctrine of Subjective Spirit. — Subjective spirit is (1) in immediate union with and dependence upon an organic body and its conditions, *i. e.*, a natural soul (the subject of *anthropology*); (2) subjective spirit also stands in relation as subject to another as object, or is consciousness as such (the subject of *phenomenology*); (3) subjective spirit is, finally, purely self-related (subject of *psychology*). — (1) *Anthropology*.[1] — As natural soul subjective spirit is

[1] Zeller.

merely the ideal unity of the natural life: it is not a particular substance that can be thought apart from the bodily life. It is as unreasonable to ask after the connection of body and soul as after that of universal and particular, essence and phenomena. Body, however, is not the more original, it is but a condition. As ideal unity of body, soul is subject more or less to bodily affections, dependent upon material conditions such as meteorological influences, climate, affected with peculiarities of race, disposition, temperament, character, and by ages in life, distinctions of sex, interchange of sleep and waking; it is a subject of feeling in various ways, — of obscure and confused feeling, purely passive states of feeling, self-feeling, habitual feelings. When in feeling it clearly distinguishes itself from outward existence and becomes object to itself, it is consciousness. — (2) *Phenomenology.* — Consciousness in general is the relation of spirit to an external world, and as such has three forms. (*a*) It is *first immediate sensible certainty* of external object. This vanishes through the fact that the object as such disappears in its qualities, which are "objects" of an *act* of the mind, and not of mere receptivity such as sensation is, namely, of a perceptive act. But the unity and essence of the qualities whereby they belong to an object becomes object of an inner act of thought, *i. e.*, of understanding, with its categories of reflection (identity, ground, force, phenomena, substance, cause, etc.). In simple, sensible consciousness subject is entirely determined by object; in understanding, object is an ideal creation of subject. The recognition of this fact by the subject is self-consciousness. (*b*) *Self-consciousness* is at first without special content; it is mere feeling of emptiness, want, *i. e.*, it is desire, which is virtually a relation between simple self-consciousness and a content with which it is to be filled. The satisfaction of desire gives to self-consciousness the felt realization of itself in itself and in its object. A higher realization of self-consciousness occurs when self-consciousness sees itself in other *selves* (in desire self-consciousness sees itself in selfless objects). In the consciousness of self in and through that of others a conflict occurs between self-consciousness as such and self-consciousness as consciousness of object, which (conflict) is resolved in the consciousness of mutual interdependence and essential identity of the two (as, *e.g.*, in the relation between master and slave). This last form of self-consciousness is universal self-consciousness, which is the intuition of the self as not merely a particular self different from others, but as virtually the single universal self. In this self-consciousness (which is the foundation of all virtues, all sacrifice, all repute, etc.), I know myself in others or as I am known. (*c*) The union of simple consciousness or cognition of the object, and self-consciousness, or cognition of self, is *reason*, which is the certainty that subjective determinations are also objective, or certainty of the self and of object in one and the same thought. What reason perceives is not something foreign to it, "given" to it, but something already penetrated by it, and in so far produced by it. Knowledge through reason is therefore not mere subjective certainty, but also truth, since truth is, precisely, the agreement or, rather, identity, of certitude and of being, or objectivity. — (3) *Psychology*. Psychology treats of the union of natural soul and consciousness. Intelligence begins with externality, not as its *principle*, which is itself, but as its condition. It is, in its immediacy, *presentation*, the content of which it elevates to *representation*, while as thought it purifies the content of contingency and particularity, raising it to universality. *Presentation* is (*a*) definite but perfectly simple affection (receptivity) of feeling, or sensation, whose content *may* be the most solid and true, or, just as well, the opposite in character, but has the form of mere particularity; (*b*) distinguishing *attention* (the *voluntary* activity in presentation); (*c*) *presentation proper*, which is the concrete unity of the two preceding, and contains the object as distinguished from subject. In sensation, reason as a whole is present;

though it is entirely erroneous to suppose that immediate presentation in any of its forms constitutes true knowledge. *Representation* is presentation withdrawn inwards (towards inner unity). In it presentation is sublated and sundered, — taken out of its spatial and temporal relations, and separated into its constituent characters, — and so universalized. Representation is (*a*) the subsumption of a presentation under another of like content that has already been sublated and universalized. In this act of subsumption there is, on the one hand, a perception of the identity of the content of the two presentations, and, on the other, the perception of my identity with myself, or an act of remembering myself, — *passive memory*. Representation is (*b*) the subsumption of a presentation under a former unlike content, and, as such, *imagination* in general. As recalling a past presentation without a present one corresponding to it, it is *reproduction*, or *reproductive imagination*. As combining preserved images and presentations in various ways not found in immediate presentation, — *i. e.*, as *associative imagination*, — it cannot properly be said to follow *laws* of association, but rather to be governed by more or less accidental connections, simultaneity, co-existence in space, similarity, contrast, relation of part and whole, cause and effect, ground and consequence. Among the creations of this reproductive imagination are dreams, the phenomena of somnambulism, mental derangement. As combining ideas not according to accidental conditions and determinations of the mind, but to ideals and the truth of mind in general, representation is the higher imagination, the poetic phantasy, *productive imagination*. Imaginative symbolization consists in the putting into sensible phemonena, or images, ideas of another sort than those they immediately express, which yet have relation of analogy with them. (Poetry, instead of being an imitation of nature, is more true than ordinary reality.) (*c*) As the active reproduction and combination of former presentations, representation is *memory proper*. It is first the power of recalling the meaning of a name or sign when either is presented, — *name-preserving-memory;* second, the employing of names as things, and connecting things with names without intervening presentation or image, — *reproductive memory;* third, the power of recalling at will a sign and the thing signified, however arbitrarily they may be joined, — *mechanical memory.* In mechanical memory intelligence is (in an external manner, it is true) the identity of opposites, and is thus the transition to thought. (The position and meaning of memory and its organic connection with thought are points that have hitherto been overlooked, and are the most difficult in the whole theory of spirit.) *Thought* is the activity of the spirit in its independent, identical simplicity, which draws its distinctions from itself, and places them in itself, — whereby they have the character of self-equality and universality. It is first purely formal, and is bound up in fixed distinctions, in mere being, essence, the qualities and laws of external things, — *objective understanding.* Second, it is the reference of a particular individual to a conception, the subsumption of the particular individual under the universal, — *judgment* (qualitative, reflective, real). Third, it is the perception of the universal as specifying and individualizing itself, the concrete union of all logical determinations, — *rational thought.* Here it is either *negative* or *dialectic,* in that it shows the passage of a distinction of the understanding as regards being into its opposite, *ratiocinative* in that it seeks the grounds of things, or *syllogizing* in so far as it unites the moments of universality, particularity, and individuality in an object. (Syllogizing reason is *formal* in so far as merely subjective, *teleological* as considering and proposing ends, *ideal* in so far as both subjective and objective, and so, fully self-determined.) Thought is free or universal (liberated from sensuous particularity) as regards both form and content. Intelligence, knowing itself as determining content, which is as much its own as it is objective, is *Will,* — *practical spirit.* The practical spirit, will, not only *has* ideas, but *is* the living Idea itself; it is spirit determining itself from itself, and giving its determinations external reality. In so far as it can abstract from all distinction in itself and remains in pure indeterminateness and self-equality, it is called *free will*. The will as at once subjective and objective is both action and act (by virtue of the former of which it is subject of guilt or innocence). As (*a*) *mere practical* feeling, which has as its content the practical legal and moral distinctions and laws, it is vague and affected with particularity, has yet to arrive at a definite consciousness of its content and become a totality as against it, is (*b*) the feeling of a contradiction to be overcome within itself, of an inner content to be realized, and so *impulse* and desire, which are the inner and the outward-looking sides of the same fact. In impulse and desire the practical spirit is not yet free, but dependent (on an outer object). (*c*) The satisfaction of impulse and desire is the restoration of totality and freedom in the will, and the beginning of the objective spirit.

The Doctrine of Objective Spirit:[1] *Rights, Morals, the State, History*. — Objective *spirit* is, (1) as immediate, and thus individual, person (which, with the externality which this freedom gives itself in *property*, is the subject of the doctrine of *Rights*); (2) as reflected in itself, so that it has its reality within itself, and is thus determined as *particular*, is a moral will (the subject of the doctrine of *Morals*); (3) as *substantial* will, its actuality conforming to its conception, is an ethical will, subsisting in the family, civil society, and the State (and subject of doctrine of *Ethics*). (1) The relation of abstract persons, or merely individual free beings, to one another is the *Right* (law). That action is contrary to right, by which man is not respected as person, or which is an infringement of the sphere of his freedom. The relation of right is essentially a *negative* relation, and does not require that one

---

[1] See Hegel's "Philosophy of the State and History," exposition by Prof. G. S. Morris.

should perform towards another any positive action, but only that one leave him unmolested as person. The external sphere of right and freedom is constituted by property, which is the subsumption of a thing without a possessor under my power and my will. Property has thus the two sides of possession, of arbitrary *seizure*, which constitutes mere *possession*, and of the being the expression of my will, which, as something absolute, must be respected by others. Property may be *alienated*, and *acquired, by contract*, which is a mutual agreement of two persons to alienate each his property, and turn it over to the other, and the agreement to receive it. As the sphere of my freedom contains my personality, and the reference of a thing to it, trespass upon that sphere may happen either through my personality as such not being recognized, or through the denial that the thing referred to it is mine. In trespassing upon my personality, another shows disrespect to his own: he does what is not merely individual, but universal in its content. What he has done in conception must be brought to actuality. The doing of this by the person injured is *revenge;* by and in the name of a universal will, is *punishment.* Right in relation to property is the subject of Common or Civil Law, or Right; in relation to personality, of Penal or Criminal Law. The principle of so-called *Natural Right* is not destroyed, but supplemented and truly realized in society. (2) The *right of the subject, will, or morality*, requires that each person respect *himself* and act from the determinations of his own nature and for their own sakes. (*a*) On its external side, his act is only *formally* his; his essentially is the inner side — the purpose — of his act. (*b*) This, viewed as merely *intention*, must be good in itself; but, (*c*) to be truly good, must in its content harmonize with the universal will. "Goodness" which is only individual, abstract, is only formally different from evil, which precisely consists in the willing of that which is in itself finite, limited,— null. What is called a conflict of duties is a collision in the individual will of limited would-be goods, not determinations of the universal objective will, which is in itself a harmonious, organic whole. This merely subjective character is the defect of morality. — (3) The content of the universal objective will is found in those necessary human relations constituting the essence of the family, the civil community, — the State. Filled with this content, the will possesses the character or attribute of ethicality,— which is perfection of objective spirit, and the truth of subjective and objective spirit. In ethicality, what, as duty, *ought* to be *is;* the disposition of individuals is the knowledge of the identity of all their interests with the whole; the attribute of personality is virtue (which, as regards the ethical world as a whole, is confidence, voluntary service to the same, and readiness to sacrifice self for it; as regards contingent relations with others, first justice, and then benevolent inclination). The ethical substance, or spirit, is : (1) as immediate, or *natural,* spirit, *the family;* (2) the relative totality of the relations of individuals, as independent persons, to one another in a formal universality, — the *civil society;* (3) the self-conscious substance as spirit developed into an organic activity, — *the State.* The basis of *the family,* as a natural society, is love and confidence. (*a*) The personalities here are united as one person, and to this end marriage is properly monogamous; (*b*) an ethical interest attaches to the property of the family, in view of the common relation in which the individuals stand; also to education of the children. (*c*) The family dissolves (and civil society arises) by the death of the parents, and the fact that children grow up and establish new families. *Civil* society — the State on its external side, or as government — embraces : (*a*) the satisfaction of human wants through the individual's labor, the division of labor, existence of classes, as " natural " (agricultural), " reflected " (industrial), and " universal " (intellectual); (*b*) the maintenance of justice through law administered (upon the rationality and abstract equality of persons); (*c*) police regulations and corporations, or unions of members of industrial classes, having the same trade. Civil society in its highest aspect — the police and the corporation — is still a formal universality, not fully self-conscious ethical substance. The *State* alone is, which is the synthesis of the principles of the family and civil society. The State is (*a*) as a self-related development, the *internal polity* or *the* constitution; (*b*) as a particular individual (State) in relation to others, external polity; (*c*) as a union of States, universal history. (*a*) The work of the State in itself is of a double character: first, the preservation of its members as persons, making right necessary reality, caring in a general way for the happiness of its members, protecting the family, and guiding civil society; second, to keep its individual members and its subordinated spheres immanent in the universal substance, or spirit. The laws express the attributes of objective freedom; are limits for the individuals, ends of their action, the embodiments of custom, or the ethos, of a people. The constitution of the State is the organization of the powers of the State. The categories of liberty and equality, so often misapplied, apply strictly only to the abstract person, not to the *natural*, but to the rational man. It is mere tautology to say that citizens are "*equal* before the law." A misconception of freedom, a viewing of it as mere arbitrary will, underlies the ordinary notion that each one must limit his freedom in relation to that of others, that the State is the condition of this mutual limitation and the laws the limitations. The laws are rather expressions of the positive characteristics of true freedom. The guarantee of a constitution lies in the spirit of the entire people and the real organization corresponding to this: it presupposes a consciousness of spirit. The living totality, the preservation, *i. e.*, the continual forth-bringing of the State, and its constitution, is the government. The powers of the State are the legislative and the executive,— the latter comprising the administrative and judicial powers; and inasmuch as the Idea is subjectivity and individuality, the first and highest, the all-pervading distinction in the organization of the State is, the administrative; only in it is the State *one*. The moment of subjective freedom (the consciousness of the subjects) is present through representation of classes in the legislative assembly, and trial by jury. The monarchical constitution is the constitution of developed reason; all others belong to lower stages of the development and realization of reason. The rational division of governments is that into democracy, aristocracy, and monarchy. The military class is indispensable to a State because of its relation to other States. (*b*) The polity of the State, as an individual, among others — the external polity — rests partly upon positive treaties, partly on the law of nations, whose principle is the recognition of the independence of other States, and partly upon morals in general. (*c*) The spirit of definite individual peoples is limited, and their independence a subordinate one; it passes over into the universal world history, whose events are the dialectic of the spirit of particular nations,— the world-judgment. The spirit of a particular nation is but a single moment and stage in the historical development of the world. The self-consciousness of a particular people represents the stage of development of the universal spirit at a given time, and the objective reality in which it places its will. Against this absolute will — absolute right — the will of other particular national spirits is without right. This people is for the time being the world-ruling people. But it in turn must yield to "fortune and judgment," and attain to universality only in the subjective form of fame. There have been in the development constituting the world's history four principal stages. (1) History begins in the East, and the history of the Orient is the first stage of universal history. In the Orient freedom has been realized, however, in only a very limited, abstract form; for there only *one* — the monarch — is recognized as free, all other wills being merely accidental to this one substantial will. Obedience to law is obedience, not to free self, but to something foreign to self. This generic character of the Orient appears most clearly in China, where all is governed immediately by external authority, custom, routine; and history has in consequence no development, but is mere chronology. In India the will is subject to an inner despot, in the shape of the sensuous phantasy: the Hindoo lives "as if in a dream," and does not distinguish himself from his dream; his mind is fantastic, and knows no universal inherent human rights and duties, but only numerous observances and customs and distinctions of caste. His sensuously imaginative apperception of the universal is that which distinguishes him from the Chinese, whose mind is prosaic. The Persians (including the Assyrians, Babylonians, Medes, Syrians, Phœnicians, Jews, and Egyptians), in contrast to the foregoing, possess a germ of historical development, and principle of opposition and struggle in the distinction of the light and the dark principles of the world, hypostatized good and evil. The Persians, indeed, are the first historical people. The ethical substance — the universal — is still, however, abstract (because divided against itself) in Persia. (2) In Greece, on the contrary, the universal receives concrete manifestation,— real freedom exists: the spirit — no longer submerged and hidden in the external as in China, nor in the sensuous internal, as in India, nor subsisting above the world in a remote "beyond," as in Persia — moves and works freely in the present natural life: the infinite is reflected in the finite, the universal in the particular, in Greek society, art, religion, and thought. Greece is the "home of spiritual individuality." (3) In the Roman world, the universal is abstract, — outside of and separated from the particular, but has a reflected (intellectual) character, is not a sensuous immediate. The Roman world stands in relation to the Grecian as reflective prose does to poetry. Its reflection and prosaic practical activity are the source of abstract civil and military forms and general rules of life, — the notion of abstract personality, of formal freedom. An element of subjectivity was introduced into the Roman world by the entrance of Christianity into it; but the principle of Roman civilization did not thereby become a concrete universal. (4) The historical concrete universal, the full synthetic union of the Christian principle of subjectivity and the Roman principle of objectivity, appears in the civilization of the Germanic nations, to whom it fell to make the principle of freedom contained in Christianity the organizing force of the ethical institution of the modern world. The German world has a consciousness of reconciliation between the finite and the infinite, which is conspicuously wanting in the ancient Roman world. — The history of the world, then, is the realization and embodiment of the logical Idea. The play of contingency in it is not to be denied, but may be explained as being, in part, only apparent, since reason realizes its ends by means, — *e. g.*, desires, wishes, fancies in men, — which are in themselves merely non-rational and in part natural and necessary; for no philosophy can "deduce" or "construct" the merely particular. On the whole, in history the real is rational, and the rational real. — The philosophy of history brings us to the limit of the realm of Objective Spirit, landing us at the threshold of Absolute Spirit.

Doctrine of the Absolute Spirit. — Subjective and objective spirit are ways by which there comes to exist a reality exactly corresponding to the conception of spirit, or an existence the consciousness of which is also immediately the consciousness of self. Spirit as at once this reality and its (conscious) conception is absolute spirit. Absolute spirit is, (1) as mediated in sensuous reality, — *art;* (2) as mediated by faith or subjective conviction that spirit is the reality of things, — *religion;* (3) as the *knowledge* of the identity of reality and spirit, — *philosophy.* — (1) *Art* is the realized harmony in sense of the finite and infinite, subject and object, freedom and necessity. It has as end, therefore, neither mere amusement or pleasure, mere imitation of nature, nor even moral perfection : pleasure is purely finite, the imitation of nature is determination by object and not by self; moral perfection is subjective, — not free, but involved in endless endeavor. The beauty, and in general ideality, of art as compared with that of nature is of a higher order in that art contains the fuller manifestation of the purely free activity of spirit. Real existences, whether natural or spiritual, are subject to given fixed relations, which constitute a sort of barrier to the subjective movement of the perfectly free spirit of art. And in general the work of art, as being the product of spirit, is higher than any mere work of nature. Owing to this character of freedom possessed by it, art is never mere imitation ; it, rather, " flatters " (idealizes) nature or the real. " A work of art represents the ideal by a determined situation, a particular action, in an individual character, and all addressed to the senses, and conforms to the same laws that are detected in the beautiful in nature ; *e.g.*, regularity, symmetry, conformity to law." And " however harmonious and complete a work of art may be in itself, it does not exist for itself, but for the public which contemplates and enjoys it ; forms borrowed from a foreign or a past civilization must be adapted to that of the now and here, — must be a conciliation of the objective and the subjective."[1] The work of art is, (*a*) the representation of the inner conception in an external, given material (including subjective images and presentations) so harmonized with it that no merely subjective limitation of artist or of material is allowed to appear, — *classical art*, the idea of which is *beauty;* (*b*) a representation in which the inner conception, itself more or less abstract and enigmatical, is embodied in a form relatively abstract, and hence inadequate, since the conception as spirit

[1] See Kedney's "Hegel's Æsthetics" ("Griggs's Philosophical Classics").

is concrete, — *symbolical art*, the idea of which is *sublimity;* or (*c*) a representation in which the inner conception appears in a form relatively subjective and also concrete, though not in itself perfectly harmonious, and not, as in classical art, perfectly adequate, — *romantic art.* Each of the individual arts may be characterized in any of its works by one of three different " styles : " the severe, which is the most elementary and contents itself with the substantial, or non-accidental ; the majestic, which is freely and harmoniously expressive ; and the graceful, which inclines to the addition to the interior content of charms which it does not really require. The individual arts are, in the order of their spirituality : *architecture* (symbolic, classic, romantic), which is fundamentally symbolic ; *sculpture* (symbolic, classic, romantic), which, inasmuch as in it the inner conception receives sensible concrete embodiment, is essentially classical ; *painting, music, poetry* (epic, lyric, dramatic), — romantic arts. Painting is the most romantic, music the most purely subjective, poetry the highest of the arts. Æsthetik, or theory of art, treats (as appears from the foregoing) of the idea of art, the development of the idea into the special forms of art, and the system of arts. — (2) *Religion* may be viewed as (*a*) religion as such ; (*b*) religion in various definite forms ; (*c*) absolute religion. (*a*) Religion as such is, first, the consciousness of a transcendent object, to which the individual has to surrender himself. But this is only the beginning. Every true religion strives to surmount this distinction between subject and object, the soul, or mere faith, and God ; for religion is absolute spirit. This it does, first, by means of so-called proofs of God's existence. In the nature of the case, these may either begin with being (phenomena), and end with the notion (God), or *vice versa ;* they are (1) cosmological and teleological, or (2) ontological. The cosmological and teleological proofs are conscious processes by which the contingent and particular resolves itself into what it virtually is, — the necessary and universal; and this latter thereby at the same time affirms its reality. The ontological proof is the "consciousness of that process in which the Absolute translates itself out of the mere conception into concrete reality." These "proofs" are the means by which the consciousness of the Absolute becomes identified with the absolute consciousness, or human consciousness realizes the thought that it knows God only in so far, and because God knows himself in it. They necessarily postulate what they attempt to prove, but are "proofs" in the sense that they demonstrate or show the existence of God in consciousness as its basis and truth, and hence also in the object with which consciousness is one, *i. e.*, in being or reality. (*b*) The consciousness of God as spirit, and not merely transcendent object, has various degrees; and hence the various "forms" of religion, or various religions, which, instead of being something merely accidental, are necessary stages in the self-development of religion. On the lowest stage, religion is *natural religion*, to which God is the immediate (nature). Next in order is the *religion of spiritual individuality*, to which God is a *subject*, but transcendent to or outside of the individual or human subject. In this form God is either exalted above the world, as in the Jewish religion (the religion of sublimity), or is clothed in sensuous, plastic forms, as in the religion of the Greeks (the religion of beauty), or is viewed as the self-realizing end (the religion of conformity to end). (*c*) Last of the forms of religion is *revealed religion*, in which there is complete reconciliation of the subject and object, finite and infinite, contingent and absolute, human and divine consciousness. Such is the Christian religion, which is therefore the *absolute religion*. In absolute religion God is (1) in himself, or essence ("Father"); (2) in the world, or manifestation ("Son"); (3) in communion with himself and all finite creatures ("Spirit.") In God is contained a process of creation ("fall") and redemption, which, however, instead of being, as represented by the ordinary consciousness, a historical process, is an eternal one. Man must "sin," or "fall away" from God, and must be redeemed; *i. e.*, must lose his mere innocent will-less consciousness, and become a conscious, rational self-determination. Evil is merely a stage in the self-realization of the good. The good, even as religion, is realized only in the life of the State. The common consciousness which absolute religion is, involves a church and a creed as its manifestation and symbol. In these is the pure surrender of the human to the divine, and the reception of the divine into the human, self-consciousness, which is God-consciousness, and *vice versa*. — (3) The inner substance and truth of art and religion, freed from its finite and merely relative forms, and viewed as it is in itself and in a form entirely adequate to itself as conception, or thought, is *philosophy*, — the *self-thinking* Idea. In this thought of the self-thinking idea philosophy realizes its conception, and returns upon itself, since this thought is just that with which philosophy began, only it is now self-determined as well as self-determining. In a syllogism of which the middle term is nature, the universality of the Idea has been demonstrated. Taking spirit as the middle term of a syllogism whose extremes are Nature and the Idea, we have Nature mediated with the Idea as its presupposition as well as its consequence. Likewise by a syllogism the middle term of which is Idea, Spirit is mediated with Nature as its presupposition as well as result. Idea, Nature, and Spirit thus prove to be organic parts, each involving the whole of the same totality; at the same time *logic*, the *philosophy of nature*, the *philosophy of spirit*, are shown to be the necessary organic parts of philosophy as a whole. The result thus reached by philosophy in itself appears also from its history, the various systems of which are but successive momenta in the absolute philosophy. "The philosophies of the Eleatics, of Heraclitus, and of the Atomists correspond with pure being, becoming, and being-for-self, or independent being; the philosophy of Plato corresponds with categories of Essence; Aristotle's, with the Conception; the philosophy of the Neo-Platonists, with thought as the totality, or the Concrete Idea; and the philosophy of modern times, with the Idea as spirit, or the Self-knowing Idea. The Cartesian philosophy occupies the standpoint of consciousness, the Kantian and Fichtian philosophies occupy that of self-consciousness, and the newest philosophy (Schelling's and Hegel's) occupies the standpoint of reason or of subjectivity as identical with substance in the form of intellectual intuition with Schelling, and that of pure thought or absolute knowledge with Hegel. The principles of all previous systems are contained as sublated *momenta* in the absolute philosophy" (Ueberweg).

Result. — The system of Hegel is, like that of Krause, an attempted sublation and reconciliation of the truths of previous systems in general, and of the Fichtian and Schellingian in especial. As we have seen, Hegel attempts to supplement Schelling by grounding and systematically developing the principle of the System of Identity. He does this with the help of the Fichtian method. The result is a self-determined organism of conceptions, objective as well as subjective in their significance. Hegel makes an advance upon Krause in that his system of categories is determined from within rather than from without, is speculatively rather than reflectively evolved. All things considered, it may with truth be said that Hegel, more adequately than any of his predecessors, combined the tendencies of thought which from Kant onwards it had been the almost universally avowed task of German philosophers as such to combine. Hegel is a rationalist to whom empiricism and intuitionism have meaning, but only as subordinate moments of a self-determining — *i. e.*, a self-distinguishing and self-identifying — reflection. The rationalism of Hegel is (as all German rationalism, from Kant onwards, inherently tended to be) a not merely formal, but also material, rationalism: it asserts and everywhere strives to show that reason is the substance, as well as the shadow, or show, of all things whatsoever; that the rational is real, and the real is rational ("Was vernünftig ist, das ist wirklich; und was wirklich ist, das ist vernünftig").

§ 137.

Hegelians.[1] — Hegel's teachings have had a very large following, — larger, by universal admission, than those of any philosopher of this century. His followers may be divided into two classes, — the "conservative" and the "radical." The conservative class, as might be expected, includes some who are more moderate in their conservatism than others. The earlier conservatives are the more conservative. Of the conservatives we mention Andreas Gabler (1786-1853), successor of Hegel at Berlin; Wilhelm Hinrichs (1794-1861), professor at Breslau and Halle; Leopold von Henning (1791-1866), for twenty years editor of the Berlin "Jahrbücher für wissenschaftliche Kritik," — the literary "organ" of the Hegelian school; Ed. Gans (1798-1839), principal founder of the "Jahrbücher;" Karl Daub (1765-1836), professor at Berlin, and (according to Erdmann) founder of Protestant speculative theology; Carl Friedrich Göschel (1781-1861), a particularly successful (non-professorial) expounder and defender of Hegel's system; Heinrich Gustav Hotho (1802-1873), professor in Berlin, and writer on esthetics in particular; Heinrich Theodor Rötscher, writer on esthetics; Karl Friedrich Rosenkranz (1805-1879), perhaps the most generally accomplished of the German Hegelians; Johannes Müller (1801-1858), the physiologist; K. Th. Bayrhofer; Theodor Fischer (1807-1887), writer on æsthetics; and the well-known historian Erdmann (1804-   ); Schwegler (1819-1857), and Michelet (1801-   ), who, however, is sometimes regarded as a radical Hegelian. The

---

[1] Erdmann, Noack.

"radical" Hegelians may be divided into two general groups, — one comprising those who sought to develop or to modify the Hegelian teaching in a " theistic " direction; the other, those who developed and modified in pantheistico-naturalistic and individualistic directions, — both classes having realistic leanings. Theistic were Christian Hermann Weisse (1801–1866), professor in Leipsic; Friedrich Julius Stahl (1802–1862), professor in Berlin; Christlieb Julius Braniss (1792–1873), professor at Breslau; Bruno Bauer (1809–1882), docent at Berlin and Bonn; Wilhelm Vatke (1806–1882), professor at Berlin; K. Conradi: pantheistic were, Ludwig Andreas Feuerbach (1804–1872); Friedrich Richter; David Friedrich Strauss (1808–1874), author of the epoch-making work in Christology, "The Life of Jesus:" individualistic were Arnold Ruge (1802–1880), Theodor Echtermaeyer (d. 1842), editors of the " Hallische Jahrbücher," an organ of Hegelianism (?); Edgar Bauer; Bruno Bauer (whose views altered); Feuerbach; Max Stirner; Friedrich Daumer (1800–1875). Of these "radicals" we select for special mention Weisse and Feuerbach.

§ 138.

Christian Hermann Weisse (1801–1866). — Weisse was born and educated in Leipsic. In 1828 he habilitated there as privat-docent; in 1832 he became professor extraordinary; and in 1847 ordinary professor, after having lived some years in private.

Works. — The most important works of Weisse are: "Ueber den gegenwärtigen Standpunkt in der philosophischen Wissenschaft " ("On the Present Standpoint of Philosophical Science "), (1829); " System der Æsthetik als Wissenschaft von der Idee der Schönheit " (1830); " Ueber das Verhältniss [Attitude] des Publikums zur Philosophie um den Zeitpunkt von Hegel's Abscheiden [Decease]," (1832); " Grundzüge der Metaphysik" (1835);

"Das philosophische Problem der Gegenwart" (1842); "Idee der Gottheit" (1833).

Philosophy. — Weisse attempts to modify the, to him, too rationalistic doctrine of Hegel by the insertion into the Hegelian logical system of certain "real" categories (space and time), and into the Hegelian doctrine of God of a personalistic element. He contends that it is impossible to get from the mere (logical) forms of being to concrete or real being merely by thought, and that "experience" must be appealed to for the explanation of the real, and that, in order to avoid pantheism (the error of the Hegelian doctrine of God) and its opposite, extreme Deism, and so get at the truth, it is necessary to maintain, upon a speculative basis, the Christian doctrine of the Trinity. Weisse eventually (as did others of the above-mentioned "radicals") became strongly anti-Hegelian in his views.

§ 139.

Ludwig Andreas Feuerbach[1] (1804–1872). — Feuerbach, a native of Landshut, Bavaria, studied theology at Heidelberg (1822–1824), philosophy (under Hegel) at Berlin, and the natural sciences at Erlangen. At Erlangen, in 1828, he habilitated as privat-docent, lecturing one year only. He lectured there again, several years afterwards, for a single year. His well-known "atheistic" (pantheistic) views blocked the way to his promotion, and he retired to private life, living for many years in straitened circumstances and almost unnoticed. Shortly before his death contributions from friends and certain societies were made to his financial support.

Works. — Works of Feuerbach are: "Gedanken über Tod und Immortalität" (1830); "Geschichte der neuern Philosophie von Baco von Verulam bis Benedict Spinoza" (1833); "Darstellung, Entwickelung und Kritik der Leibnizschen Philosophie;" "Das Wesen des Christenthum" (1840), his best-known work; "Unsterblichkeit vom

[1] Noack.

Standpunkt der Anthropologie" (1866); "Grundsätze der Philosophie der Zukunft [Future]."

Philosophy. — The philosophy of Feuerbach is a movement from pantheism through subjectivism to anthropologism; or, as it has been said, "Feuerbach's first idea was God, his second reason, his third, and last, man." In the "Thoughts on Death and Immortality" he asserts that the individual human being is at death resolved into the infinite by an inner law of its nature and in consequence of a natural inner longing. The individual attains after death to an intuition of and immersion in God, who is the All; he is in the embrace of the all-creating and all-destroying love, which (before death) only the genuine pantheist understands. Life beyond death is life in "religion, art, science, and the experience of humanity as a whole," in that which is an end-in-itself, past individuality being realized only in memory. When (and only when) man realizes that death is real, and not merely apparent, absolutely closing the existence of the individual as such, will he have the faith to begin the new and true life of making the infinite the purpose and content of all that he does. — In the "Essence of Christianity" the position is taken that all that lives finds satisfaction only in its own element or nature, and that man, if he is to find satisfaction in God, must find God in (and as) himself. What is really divine in religion is merely the human purified, — freed from what is merely individual, — and then viewed, and worshipped, as a nature different from man, — hypostatized. God is our prayer, our love, our ideal realized in a world beyond; theology is merely anthropology. There is no God. — In the "Principles of the Philosophy of the Future," it is declared that philosophy is the knowledge of things as they are, and is merely "universal empiricism." Empiricism denies theology and that so-called philosophy which is but its abstract expression, *viz.*, the Hegelian. Real being is the unity of mind and nature; the real Idea is the invisible or visible man, man as presented to himself in sense. Truth, sensibility, and reality are identical. In sensation are hidden the deepest and highest truths; the feeling of love is the ontological proof of the existence of God. The new philosophy is the complete and absolutely incontrovertible resolution of theology into anthropology.

§ 140.

Arthur Schopenhauer[1] (1788-1860). — Schopenhauer was the son of a Dantzic banker who had married an authoress twenty years younger than himself and of temperament and tastes incompatible with his. Schopenhauer while a youth spent two years and a half in France and England, learning the languages of those countries and receiving impressions which were life-long influences with him. He was educated for and entered upon a commercial career, in accordance with, though not entirely in consequence of, his father's earnest wish; but upon the death of his father he abandoned the occupation he found himself engaged in, in order to gratify a natural taste for knowledge and culture. He began his studies at Gotha; but, dismissed from school on account of self-will and over-fondness for satire (directed against one of his teachers), he went to Weimar, whither his mother had gone after the death of her husband to find surroundings congenial for a person of literary ambition. Schopenhauer studied privately with the Greek scholar Passow, and, as it appears, made good progress, acquiring a taste for and a real proficiency in the knowledge of the ancient classics, which never left him. Friction between the tempers of himself and his mother caused him, in 1809, to take his portion of the patrimonial estate and leave Weimar. He went to Göttingen to study medicine. He heard lectures in physiology by Blumenbach, and in philosophy by G. E. Schulze, — "Aenesidemus" Schulze, — who advised him to study especially Kant and Plato. University studies developed in him a certain latent morbidity of temperament (his father had before his

---

[1] Works of Schopenhauer; Noack; Zeller; "Encyclopædia Britannica;" Erdmann, etc.

death shown symptoms of insanity), and he became the victim of pessimistic fancies and anxieties (keeping always by his bedside loaded weapons). In 1811 he went to Berlin to hear Fichte, but left the university, disgusted with Fichte and his "Wissenschafts*leere*," and with university life generally. After taking a doctorate at Jena in 1813, he returned to Weimar, there exciting the interest of Goethe (whose theory of colors he studied), and, what is more important, acquiring, through the Orientalist F. O. Meyer, a knowledge of and taste for Hindoo literature that powerfully affected his thinking afterwards. A disagreement with his mother again caused him to leave Weimar. He went to Dresden, and there, between the years 1814 and 1818, was occupied with the composition of his chief work, the inspiration for which came especially from the reading of Kant, Plato, and the sacred books, of the Hindoos. Owing, as it is said, to the birth of a natural son, a visit to Italy was made (1819). After a year of gayety and even sensuous extravagance (with English companions), Schopenhauer settled in Berlin, and, on passing the requisite examination, began lecturing as privat-docent (1820). Nearly ten years of effort and expectation failed to realize anything answering to his ambition to become a professor of philosophy; he got a hearing, in fact, for but a single course of lectures. Leaving Berlin in mortification, he settled, after a year of hypochondria, in Mannheim, at Frankfort-on-the-Main, which continued to be his place of residence until his death. The passion and melancholy of his earlier years visibly diminished with increasing age, and the prospect of a longed-for fame, which had been denied him for thirty years, began to be his. After a few years of enjoyment of coveted renown he died. He died (not slowly, by self-starvation, as his own theory would have required, but) suddenly one morning after (an ordinary) breakfast, presumably of "apoplexy." When asked shortly before his death where he should be buried, he replied, "It's no matter; men will find me."

Works.—The principal works of Schopenhauer are: "Ueber die vierfache Wurzel des Satzes vom zureichenden Grunde" ("On the Fourfold Root of the Principle of Sufficient Reason"), (1813),—his doctor's thesis; "Ueber das Sehen und die Farben" ("On Sight and Colors"), (1816); "Die Welt als Wille und Vorstellung" ("The World as Will and Idea"), (1819; 2d edition, with a volume of additions to the nearly unaltered 1st edition, 1844); "Ueber den Willen in der Natur" (1836); "Die beiden Grundprobleme der Ethik" (1841); "Parerga und Paralipomena" (1851).

Philosophy: Theory of Idea (or Knowledge).—The foundation of all science is the postulate, Everything has a ground, or sufficient reason. This principle has hitherto been imperfectly understood; it has been supposed to be fully comprised in the two principles of the ground of knowledge, or *ratio cognoscendi*, and the ground of change, or becoming, *ratio fiendi*. But the principle of the ground, or sufficient reason, has, in reality, a fourfold root: besides the two sorts of ground just mentioned, there is a ground of being in space and time, *ratio essendi*, and a ground of action, *ratio agendi*. The familiar *ratio fiendi*, or cause of becoming, has the three forms of mere mechanical cause, stimulus, and motive. Corollaries of it are the laws of inertia and of the persistence of substance. The application of this principle is direct, not syllogistic. By it we obtain the notion of objects, there being no object that is not subject to it. The *ratio cognoscendi* is the criterion of truth, and has application as regards (1) abstract conceptions, (2) sense-perceptions, (3) the pure forms of the understanding, (4) the fundamental conditions of all reasoning (laws of identity, contradiction), etc. In result this application is truth, which, in accordance with the foregoing division, is material, logical, transcendental, or metalogical. By the use of the principle of *ratio essendi* we derive the being of things in time and space (whence the sciences of number and figure). The *ratio agendi* is the *ratio essendi* in the inner world of phenomena, the law of motivation, which is necessary instead of free. The principle of ground in its fourfold root comprehends in itself all the Kantian categories. It has meaning only as regards phenomena; by it we can never get at things-in-themselves, which, accordingly, we have no right to assume as scientifically known.

Theory of Will (or Being). — And yet the Kantian distinction of things into phenomena and noumena is correct, — self-evident even. We have an immediate intuitive knowledge of something not made known to us by our faculty of presentation. We know, for example, our bodies, not only as "given" in presentations of sense, or as idea, but as force and subject of pleasure and pain, *i. e.*, as will. Will, therefore, is the non-phenomenal in us, our in-ourselves; and just as, qualitatively speaking, our body as phenomenon is to body-in-itself, so the world as phenomenon is to the world-in-itself. The world-in-itself must also be will; and both phenomenal body and world are objectivizations of will. To will as the inner essence of ourselves and the world must of course be assigned attributes the negative of those of phenomena: it is individual, not plural, — eternal, not temporal; free, not subject to the law of causality; unconscious, not conscious, hence not affected with the distinction of subject and object; it is throughout simple, everywhere the same, is in every act all that it can be, and is inseparable from its exercise. Because of the identity in essence of man and the world in general, as will, the former may be regarded as the microcosm, the latter the macrocosm; and we may justifiably draw inferences, by the principle of analogy, from one to the other. They differ, however, in being different stages of the objectification of the will. In neither occurs an absolute objectification of the will. This occurs only in the Eternal Ideas, or immutable species of things. The lowest stage of the objectification of will is inorganic matter, which is the product of will as mere necessary or blind force. Next higher in rank is organic existence, vegetable and animal. In these three stages — of inorganic existence, plant life, and animal life — will differs as acting blindly or in response to stimulus or as a result of motives. The highest objectification of will in nature is the human brain, of which cognition and the world as idea are a mere function. The stages maintain their positions by a struggle and a conflict, — hence the unrest of nature, — a mastering and an assimilation to themselves of beings in other stages; according to their power to master and assimilate do they objectify the Idea. All mere individuals perish in the process; only the Idea persists. In the conflict and arrest of will there is everywhere pain.

Theory of Art. — The Idea obtains a relatively complete realization in Art (and philosophy) in the creations of genius. While ordinary cognition is merely subservient to the ends of mere living, or is purely relative, æsthetic and philosophic cognition are ends in themselves, and reveal the pure idea, since they show the immediate essence or nature,— the " what,"— and not merely the mediate nature, — the " why," or relative causes of things. In such cognition the individual subject and the individual object are lost in the universal; all limited interest, all impulse towards finite objectivization, all will to live, all conflict and pain, cease. Accompanying this cognition, which is mere contemplation, there is a disinterested pleasure. In the series of arts constituting a series of objectifications of the Idea, architecture contains the idea of mere blind force; sculpture and painting, respectively, of organic (human) form and action; poetry, of historical development; music, — the highest of the arts, — of the inner essence of things.

Theory of Ethics. — Art and philosophy are only a passive and negative negation of the will to live, and afford only a temporary elevation above all conflict and pain; for the will to live is the cause of all strife and misery. A positive negation and a quietive of the will to live is found only in the will itself, *i. e.*, as will not to live, asceticism. Asceticism comprehends not only poverty, complete chastity, and resignation, but tranquillity and sympathy, the way for which (last) is prepared by the negation of purely individual appetite and interest. By this quietive, also, is the way prepared for the objectification of the notion of eternal justice, which not merely aims to prevent the doing and suffering of wrong, as imperfect human justice does, but is positive kindness, *i. e.*, philanthropy, or practical love of humanity. By the willessness of asceticism we attain to that " intelligible " primal nature in ourselves (which it is the immortal merit of Kant to have demonstrated, in contradistinction to the merely empirical nature), and so to the haven of the soul's peace,— the Nirvana of the Hindoo. The asceticism of Christianity, it must be observed, is imperfect, since it is vitiated by the Jewish will to live ; in Brahminism alone is the doctrine of willessness. The extreme of asceticism is suicide by starvation, against which there is nothing to be said.

Result. — Since the real is for Schopenhauer outside consciousness, it is not in any sense the ideal, and he is to be classed as a realist (although at the same time a subjective idealist). He is, of course, an intuitionist, as holding the real to be the object of intuition (but empty intuition). On the question of Schopenhauer's originality, about which there seems to have been doubt, we may quote Professor Adamson's remark (article on Fichte in the " Encyclopædia Britannica ") that " it will escape no one . . . how completely the whole philosophy of Schopenhauer is contained in the later writings of Fichte." Schopenhauer, it will be remembered, professed to find the *Wissenschaftslehre* of Fichte a " Wissenschafts*leere* " (*empty* science of knowledge). — Followers of Schopenhauer were Julius Frauenstädt, Julius Bahnsen, and O. Lindner.

§ 141.

Johann Friedrich Herbart[1] (1776-1841).—Herbart was the only son of a counsellor at the court of justice at Oldenburg. He received his early instruction from a private tutor, then at a private school and in a gymnasium, where he studied the philosophies of Wolff and Kant. In the year 1794 he entered the University of Jena to study law. He had no taste for the subject, and turned to philosophy. He heard the lectures of Fichte on this subject. Greatly impressed by the enthusiasm of Fichte as a teacher, he became a Fichtian. But the spirit of criticism before long took possession of him, and a breach with the Fichtian philosophy occurred in his thinking. Herbart is said, however, always to have regarded Fichte himself with the highest admiration, and to have regarded him as a pattern of scientific precision and strictness in thinking. After several years spent in private teaching in the study at the same time of the art of teaching (particularly as taught by Pestalozzi, whose acquaintance he had made at Berne) and in the study of the natural sciences, mathematics, and psychology, he habilitated as privat-docent at the University of Göttingen. In 1805 he was made *professor extraordinarius* there in philosophy and pedagogy. From 1809 to 1833 he occupied the chair earlier occupied by Kant at Königsberg. Here he did important work in pedagogy (as well as in philosophy proper), in a *Seminar* founded by him. For the rest of his life after 1833 he was professor at Göttingen.

Works.—The following are regarded as his most important works: "Hauptpunkte der Metaphysik" (1808); "Lehrbuch zur Einleitung [Introduction] in die Philosophie" (1813); "Psychologische Untersuchungen über die Stärke einer gegebenen Vorstellung als Function ihrer Dauer betrachtet" ("Psychological Investigations on the Strength of an Idea, regarded as a Function of its Duration"), (1812); "Ueber die Möglichkeit und Nothwendigkeit der Mathematik auf Psychologie aufzuwenden" ("The

---

[1] Noack, Zeller, Herbart's "Einleitung," etc.

Possibility and Necessity of applying Mathematics to Psychology"), (1822); "Psychologie als Wissenschaft neugegründet auf Erfahrung, Metaphysik und Mathematik" ("Psychology as a Science newly founded on Experience, Metaphysics, and Mathematics"), (1824–1825); "Allgemeine Metaphysik, nebst den Anfängen der philosophischen Naturlehre" ("Universal Metaphysics, together with the Elements of the Philosophical Theory of Nature"), (1828–1829); "Allgemeine praktische Philosophie" (1808); "Kurze Encyklopaedie der Philosophie aus praktischen Gesichtspunkten entworfen" ("Concise Encyclopædia of Philosophy from Practical Points of View"), (1831); "Analytische Beleuchtung des Naturrechts und der Moral" ("Analytical Explanation of Natural Right and Morals"), (1836). Of these the "Allgemeine Metaphysik" and the "Psychologie" are the most important; the "Einleitung" gives the best view of Herbart's system in outline.

Philosophy: Introduction.—There is contained in ordinary consciousness the germ of a science which has to do with truth and error as such, *viz.*, philosophy. Philosophy has in common with ordinary knowledge and the lower sciences the circumstances that it presupposes a definite method of settling disputed questions and a necessary progression in thought; further, it deals with the same objects with which they deal (it is not, however, limited to any one class of objects, as the separate sciences are), though it has an independent way of treating them. Philosophy begins where, with regard to the knowledges contained in the other sciences, there arises the question as to their meaning and value,— it begins, that is to say, with reflection upon given *conceptions ;* has nothing whatever to do with *perceptions* as such, and is, in fact, precisely the elaboration, or development, of the true content of given conceptions by the method of reflection. Reflection begins with doubt, but does not there end: a persistence in scepticism is a consequence and evidence of immaturity of thought. Inasmuch as reflection deals with what is *given* (by perception and in conception), and the given, just because it *is* given, is essentially real and true for us, philosophy is realism. The parts of philosophy result naturally from the various forms which reflection assumes. First, it has to attend to clearness and distinctness in conceptions, and their union into judgments and syllogisms, and is the science of *logic;* second, it is required to transform and supplement certain conceptions of a self-contradictory nature, — as space, time, inference, causality, the ego, each of which involves, in some form or other, the unity of a manifold of parts, properties, states, etc., — the conception of one as many, and *vice versa*, in which case it is *metaphysics;* third, it has to deal with (certain) conceptions as containing, along with a definite idea, a judgment of approval or disapproval, — *æsthetics*.

Metaphysics. — Metaphysics is either *universal* or *applied*. *Universal Metaphysics* is the doctrine (1) of principles and methods, — *methodology;* or (2) of the elements being, change, inherence, — *ontology;* or (3) of the *continuum* or intelligible space, — *synechology;* or (4) of phenomena, — *idolology*. Applied *Metaphysics* falls into the three parts, — *philosophy of nature, psychology, natural theology*.

Methodology. — If we have given a conception A, containing contradictory attributes M and N, it is required just because the conception is "given," not to deny or explain away either of the attributes, but to discover a point of union between them. This we do by an analysis of M (say), whence it may appear that N is contained in it as a consequence of a certain relation between its parts. This method of resolving contradiction is the *method* of *relations*. Belonging to methodology is also the "methodic expedient of contingent aspects" (to be noticed later).

Ontology. — Phenomena alone are the "given;" with them, therefore, investigation must begin. Phenomena are not, as such, the real, and yet, in a certain sense, they *are;* for otherwise they were not phenomena. As existent, they require us to posit being, — " as much appearance, *so much being.*" What, now, is Being? Being is, first, something positive, excluding negativity and relativity; second, simple; and hence, thirdly, non-quantitative, since the quantitative is composite, — has parts; though, fourthly, it may be plural; fifthly, it is self-subsistent. To explain the unity of the manifold, either as change or as inherence of attributes in substance, it is required, according to the methodological rule, the " method of relations," to regard them as relations of the real, or being; whence it appears that being must be conceived as a plurality of real existences, and phenomena as products of the interrelations of these. The interrelation of " reals," or separate beings, is possible through the possession by them of certain " contingent aspects " (not *necessary* characters, since beings are simple, positive, absolute), the discovery of which by analysis is the " methodic expedient of contingent aspects." " Contradiction " in the real is thus reduced to a merely phenomenal phase of it, which, as a *relation* of the real, is merely its reaction against other reals, and its act of preservation of its positive character against their disturbing influence.

Synechology. — The interrelation of the reals requires the assumption of what by analogy may be termed " intelligible space,"— " intelligible," because the " reals " are by nature outside sensible space. Between any two reals may be conceived a series of reals, forming an " intelligible " line. The " intelligible line," as a pure and independent line, consists of a definite number of distinct, fixed points, and is necessarily discrete. (Continuity is a fictitious conception, which surreptitiously presents itself when lines are viewed in certain relations, — such, for example, as that between the side and the diagonal of a square, or the base and the hypothenuse of a right-angled triangle. The two lines in such relations being incommensurable if regarded as discrete, we resort to the conception of the divisibility of the points, and so their *overlapping* [whence the notion of continuity], in order to explain the "given" relation of the lines. In like manner, from a series of time-points we feign continuous succession in time.) Imperfect connections of the real in such interrelation, or, in other words (since such interrelation is merely phenomenal or in and for intelligence of some sort), confused relations in intelligible space, have as consequence the phenomena of ordinary space and time. Such imperfect combinations of the reals occur when many of them tend to enter at the same time into a real which cannot maintain itself against them. In such a case there is an overlapping and incomplete mutual interpenetration, in consequence of which they occupy a non-mathematical point, and constitute together a molecule, or mass of phenomenal matter. This, in so far as the reals tend to interpenetrate or to have a common centre, contains the force of attraction; in so far as they conserve themselves against one another, that of repulsion. With matter, ordinary space is given. The change of matter with reference to space is motion, which, since matter and space are phenomenal, is itself phenomenal, though not merely subjectively so.— With Synechology are given the *a priori* data for a philosophy of nature, Synechology being, in fact, the link between the philosophy of nature and ontology. Natural phenomena receive their explanation, for the most part, from the imperfect interpenetration of the reals. The primary phenomena of matter — fixed or solid matter (and its fundamental attributes), heat-stuff, electricum, æther (including light and gravity) — respectively correspond to four principal relations of the elements to each other, as follows: (1) a relation of strong and equal, or nearly equal, opposition; (2) one of strong but very unequal opposition; (3) one of weak and equal opposition; (4) one of weak and very unequal opposition. Impenetrability and action at a distance are unscientific conceptions.

Idolology. — There is required, as a means of transition from metaphysics to the science of the particular mental phenomena, or pyschology, a theory of the data of such science. This, since it has to transform the false conceptions, εἴδωλα, relating to the ego in general, may be termed *idolology*. The ego as a knowledge of knowledge, and as the ideality of subject and object and of various faculties, is obviously a self-contradictory conception, and must be transformed. The soul in itself is real, perfectly simple, and the distinctions in it have to be explained as consequences of its relations to other reals: all mental phenomena are results of its efforts to conserve itself against disturbances from without. Ideas — or the soul's acts of self-conservation — may be compatible or incompatible with, and may, accordingly, combine with or arrest, each other. When ideas belonging to different *continua* (*e. g.*, ideas of different senses) meet, they arrest each other, forming a "complication;" when ideas belonging to the same *continuum* meet, they combine, forming fusions. The arrest of ideas creates a state of tension among them; some being forced out of, or "below the threshold" of, consciousness, others, already below the threshold, having a tendency to rise above the threshold. In every instance the idea holds its own as far as possible. In this state of tension the ideas obey certain statical and mechanical laws, and there is a *statics* and *mechanics* of mind.

Psychology: Synthetic and Analytic. — The statics and the mechanics of mind form the first, or *synthetic*, part of *psychology*. Mental statics, as the name indicates, treats of ideas in a state of equilibrium; mental mechanics treats of the movements of ideas, their rising and falling above the threshold, their revivability, etc. In the statics two things have to be determined, — the sum of arrest, and the manner in which this is distributed between or among the opposing ideas. The sum of arrest equals the intensity of the weaker idea, and the arrest is distributed in inverse ratio to the strength of the ideas. An important mechanical law is that, in case of the meeting of more than two ideas, the amount of arrest distributed to the weaker idea may drive it below the threshold of consciousness, where it subsists as a mere tendency or effort to think. Another important law of mental mechanics is that an idea rising anew into consciousness after suppression tends to draw after it, according to mathematically demonstrable laws, other ideas combined with it. Perfect equilibrium of ideas in consciousness never exists. The statical and the mechanical relations of ideas, as above indicated, are susceptible of mathematical expression, — a fact which excites the hope that psychology may be reduced to a branch of mathematical metaphysics. A mathematical psychology would enable us to answer the all-important question, not answerable by idealistic metaphysics, as to how it is possible to think things as outside and after one another. — The *analytical* part of *psychology* treats of the soul's so-called faculties and its identity. From the behavior of ideas, as the soul's acts of self-conservation, are (as has been indicated) deduced the various so-called faculties. Memory is the tendency of ideas to return into consciousness and bring with them associated ideas; the understanding is the total effect of the ideas generated in response to external stimuli; reason, the "coincident operation of several complete series of ideas;"[1] feeling is a general resultant and accompaniment of the arrest of ideas in consciousness; desire, an idea entering consciousness in spite of opposition, and determining other ideas in accordance with itself; volition is desire accompanied by the idea of the attainability of the object (freedom of will is forbidden by the law of causality); thinking, as distinguished from feeling, desiring, and willing, occurs when an idea remains in consciousness because "resting in itself;" self-consciousness is to be explained as the immediate consequence of the fact that a part of our ideas is apperceiving and a part apperceived. The entire knowable ego, or the ego of consciousness, is merely a complex of ideas and feeling and desires, which, having begun with the bodily

---

[1] See Ueberweg.

feelings as a nucleus, attained (gradually) to its fulness of content through processes of appropriation, association, and transformation of influences received from without, the exerting of outward-going activities, the distinguishing of past and present, of outer and inner, etc. It is not merely theoretical, — the knowledge of knowledge, — but the equilibrium of the theoretical and the practical, — of knowledge, on the one hand, and feeling and desire, on the other: it is both self-assertion and self-surrender, — the former in knowledge, the latter in sensation. The ego of consciousness, this product of the soul's acts of self-conservation, presupposes a non-phenomenal bearer and substrate of its faculties and ideas. This, because it is non-phenomenal, *i. e.*, not an idea or an aggregate of ideas, or not in consciousness, — is not known by self-observation, and is known at all only as a necessary pre-supposition. It must be thought of as an individual, once-for-all fully existent, personality, — as a metaphysical real. The transformed conception of the ego is, then, that of, on the one hand, a metaphysical real, and, on the other, a complex of mere ideas, or acts of the real, variously related under mathematical laws.

Æsthetics. — Æsthetics, as the science of conceptions in so far as they excite a judgment of approval or disapproval, includes practical philosophy, or the theory of the morally beautiful. Beautiful is whatever calls forth immediately, or without reflection, a feeling of disinterested pleasure or an approving judgment of taste. Æsthetics has, first of all, to discover the simplest *relations* (of being) that please unconditionally; there is no single ultimate principle from which all others are deducible. The practical relations, or relations of the will, that please, and please unconditionally, so that it would be absurd to inquire "why," are comprised in the ideas of (1) inner freedom (depending on the agreement of will with judgment); (2) perfection (depending on right relations of quantity — intensity, variety, concentration — in effort); (3) benevolence (aiming at the satisfaction of the will of another); (4) right (harmony of wills in so far as to prevent strife); (5) equity, or retribution (right relation in doing and suffering good and evil). The application of these to society gives four derived ideas, — civil right (flowing from right), a system of rewards and punishments (flowing from equity), a system of administration (flowing from benevolence), a system of culture (flowing from perfection). In a true society these ideas interpenetrate and constitute a single animating social soul of all. Ethical ideas are not "imperatives," but ideals; morality as mere duty is "arrested morality." The perfect accordance of the will with them is virtue. *Applied Ethics* is moral technology, or theory of virtue. Its branches are pedagogy and politics. The object of education is moral culture. The State has its origin in social need, and has as its end the sum total of the ends of the combined societies of right, the system of rewards and punishments, administration, and culture. It subsists as a psychological necessity rather than as a legal institution; is a union of personalities rather than the embodiment of formal conceptions. The form of the constitution is not a matter of primary importance.

Religion. — Religion is based in part on practical philosophy, in part on the philosophy of nature. It is an ethical need, and has a certain support in physico-ethical teleology, in that this approves to rational feeling, though not exactly to scientific reflection, the idea of the most excellent being.

Result. — It should not escape notice that Herbart's "realism" becomes idealism in the process of the development of it: the "reals" are the purest possible creations of subjective reflection. — The followers of Herbart, like those of Hegel, have been legion (see Ueberweg's list of the names of them, "History of Philosophy," vol. ii. pp. 308–312). "Indisputably the most important" of these (according to Erdmann) is Moritz Drobisch (born in 1802). We mention also Theodor Waitz, the anthropologist, G.

Hartenstein, editor of Kant's works, Volkmann, the psychologist, Zimmermann, writer on Æsthetics; Strümpel, psychologist, Lazarus, psychologist, Lindner, psychologist, Exner, psychologist, Steinthal, philologist. Next to the influence of Hegel, that of Herbart has been the most extended among those of the post-Kantian philosophers.

§ 142.

Eduard Beneke[1] (1798-1854). — Beneke, who was born in Berlin, took a course in the Gymnasium Fredricianum there, and attended the universities of Halle and Berlin as a student of theology. Having become, through the effect of the instruction of certain of his professors, especially interested in psychological investigation, he gave up the study of theology for that of philosophy. He made a study of the leading English and Scotch philosophers (especially Thomas Brown), and of Kant, Jacobi, Fries, Schelling, Herbart, and Schopenhauer; and qualified as privat-docent in Berlin University in 1820. Prohibited (through the influence of Hegel) from continuing his lectures there, on account of his peculiar views, he habilitated in 1822 at Göttingen. Some years afterwards he obtained permission to return to the University of Berlin. After the death of Hegel (who stood in the way of his receiving promotion) he was appointed *professor extraordinarius* (without salary); and so remained until his death, in spite of indefatigable, varied, and, in a certain sense, outwardly successful activity as lecturer and author. Mental depression, due to ill-health, as it is supposed, caused his sudden disappearance and drowning in March, 1854.

Works. — The following are among the more important of his works: " Erfahrungsseelenlehre als Grundlage alles Wissens in ihren Hauptzügen dargestellt " (" Empirical Theory of the Soul as Foundation of all Knowledge, etc."), (1820); " De Veris Philosophiæ Initiis " (1820);

---

[1] Noack, Erdmann, " Encyclopædia Britannica."

"Grundlegung zur Physik der Sitten" ("Basis for the Physics of Morals"), (1822); "Neue Grundlegung zur Metaphysik" ("New Basis for Metaphysics"), (1822); "Psychologische Skizzen" ("Psychological Sketches"), (1825-1826); "Das Verhältniss von Seele und Leib" ("Relation of the Soul and Body"), (1826); "Kant und die philosophischen Aufgaben unserer Zeit" ("Kant and the Philosophical Problems of our Age"), (1832); "Lehrbuch der Psychologie als Naturwissenschaft" ("Text-book of Psychology as Natural Science"), (1833); "Erziehungs- und Unterrichtslehre" ("Theory of Education and Instruction"), (1835-1836); "Grundlinien [Outlines] des natürlichen Systems der praktischen Philosophie" (3 vols., 1837-1840); "System der Metaphysik und Religionsphilosophie aus den natürlichen Grundverhältnissen des menschlichen Geistes abgeleitet" (1840).

Philosophy: Introduction. — Metaphysics, with its so-called knowledge of the supersensible and its *a priori* method, is a remnant of effete Scholasticism. The real basis of all philosophy, as regards both matter and method, is empirical psychology, as the science of inner experience according to the method of self-observation. All philosophical conceptions are phenomena of the human soul; the logically correct and incorrect, the æsthetically beautiful and ugly, the ethical and unethical, right and wrong, and whatever else can be a problem of philosophy, are only various psychical forms of action; even the inner forces and grounds of external things, so far as we are able to know them, we can apprehend only in analogy with our own soul-nature, which in general we can apprehend in its truth and inner character, — all the rest of philosophy is merely "applied psychology." The supersensible we can only approach in belief and presentiment; the only sort of theory possible of it is such as merely answers to subjective need.

Psychology. — Man's inner life and experience is a product of certain innate primal capacities acting in response to external stimuli. The fixed "faculties" and the single simple metaphysical entity called the soul, of ordinary psychology, have no scientific warrant, are mere hypotheses of general classes of phenomena. The real soul is a changing nature, constantly losing and acquiring powers according as the outward stimuli of its activity and the combinations of its acquired powers change. The primary processes of soul-development are as follows: *First*, is that of the appropriation of stimuli; *second*, is that of the formation of new faculties to succeed worn-out faculties. (This process is not a conscious one, but is inferred from the fact of faculties observed to come into being. These faculties are formed from the continuation of stimuli and already existing powers in the soul.) A *third* process is that of the equilibration or transference of "movable elements," *i. e.*, of stimuli and "of 'faculties,' whereby in so far as certain formations lose a part of their elements, they become unconscious or continue to exist as mere 'traces;' but in so far as those elements flow over to other formations, these latter, in case they were unconscious, are excited to consciousness." A *fourth* process consists in the fact that mental formations attract one another in proportion to their likeness. Besides these four ground-processes is the general process by which the secondary faculties, or phenomena, of the soul are formed; *viz.*, the combination of "traces." In the trace is contained the condition or occasion for the reproduction of the formation (or image). As mere unconscious trace, it exists in the soul as a tendency or effort. It is nowhere; is connected with no bodily organ. The primary faculties in themselves contain no separation of thought, desire, and feeling (which are merely secondary powers), but each such faculty is capable of becoming either of these, according to the conditions of its development or the relations of its combination. If the addition made by "stimulus" to the primary faculty be just such as the faculty calls for, there arises a representation; if the faculty is not adequate to the stimulus, there occurs a sensation of pain; if the faculty is surcharged by the stimulus, but not to excess, there results a feeling of pleasure, — if to excess, of pain; if there is a gradual surcharging to excess, the result is satiety. The transference of stimulations from traces to traces produces, according to circumstances, consciousness or unconsciousness in ideas. Attention is the relation of excited "traces" to stimulations. Memory is the persistence of ideas in the psychical being after having passed out of the condition of excitedness; it is not a faculty in the ordinary sense. Every psychological element has its memory. Desire is the upward striving or tending towards satisfaction, — due to a lack of stimulation. Desire becomes volition when the thing desired is represented in idea as realized. Desires differ only phenomenally from ideas; in every idea there is a striving, as in every desire there is an image. Understanding and comprehension result only when ideas attract one another on account of likeness (*i. e.*, under the fourth law); and ideas formed into one act by the combination of like elements are conceptions. The relation to the particular, contained in a conception, is judgment. Syllogisms are formed when the individual members of a united group or series of ideas enter into the relations of necessarily combined ideas. The idea of the ego is not simple and innate, but a highly composite group of ideas formed by the blending of acts in themselves more or less composite. Only gradually does it become the nucleus for all our thought, feeling, and striving. The difference of egos is a difference merely of degree of comprehensiveness and clearness; the greater the clearness and comprehensiveness of consciousness, the greater the spirituality of the ego.

Metaphysics. — Directly and immediately we know only one thing as it is in itself; namely, our psychical being. Our knowledge of other existences must be derived by analogy from our knowledge of this. The knowledge possible for us of other beings decreases in proportion to their likeness to us. We can conceive our bodies only as consisting ultimately of forces differing only in degree from those of our souls. Other beings than ourselves we come to know only as we conceive them as in closer or remoter analogy with our souls, and, finally, corporeal existence as such. By like analogical reasoning we apply the categories of the understanding to external reality, having first discovered in ourselves an embodiment of them, *i. e.*, that *we* are substance, cause, attribute, etc. Of immortality and the existence of God we can know nothing; but we are not therefore confined to the materialistic view of these questions. "It is quite possible that, owing to the energy of our primal faculties, our souls may exist in a new sphere," as the "plant continues to grow in new soil to which it has been transplanted;" and the visible incompleteness of the known requires the hypothesis of a higher complementary existence to which we must attribute qualities analogous with those which we already know either in ourselves or nature, or being in general. The philosophy of religion can be only a doctrine of a psychical phenomenon.

Practical Philosophy. — Practical principles arise when there is added to desire the conceptions of the objects desired, which are formed by abstraction. The direction of effort, undisturbed by outer circumstances, and of activity to one end, is character. The value of things is estimated according to the transitoriness or permanence of the enhancement or depression of our psychical condition dependent on them. Of this enhancement we form our notion in practical matters by means of the imaginative representation of ourselves and others, judging others by ourselves. Our judgment of values may be vitiated by a too manifold accumulation of sensations of pleasure and pain of the lower sorts. When the enhancement of psychical condition is combined with the group of ideas constituting our ego, our estimation is selfish, otherwise unselfish. The correct estimate manifests itself in the feeling of duty, or obligation, which is rooted in the essence of the soul. When ethical feelings of like sort unite with one another, there are formed ethical conceptions; and if to these be added, as predicates, estimations and conations, there result ethical judgments. We arrive at the universal moral law by progressive development of thought from the more special judgments; rational morality is therefore not innate; Kant's "categorical imperative" is of a highly abstract and derivative nature.

Result. — In the philosophy of Beneke we have a reaction from the method of the great idealists towards that of scientific empiricism, — a reduction of philosophy to a branch of natural science; and of course a consequent "throwing of metaphysic to the dogs." In this Beneke is faithful to his Scotch masters, if not to his German master, Herbart; for it is to be noted that Herbart's "reals" are metaphysical entities. — As followers of Beneke may be named Johann Gottlieb Dressler (1799-1867), director of a teachers' seminary; Friedrich Ueberweg (1826-1871), professor at Königsberg and historian of philosophy; and in part only, Carl Fortlage (1806-1881), professor at Jena.

§ 143.

Gustav Theodor Fechner[1] (1801-1887). — Fechner, born in Lower Lusatia, studied medicine and the natural sciences at Leipsic University, where he habilitated as docent, and in 1834 became *professor ordinarius* in physics. On account of a malady in the head, and particularly in the eyes, he gave up physical studies in 1839, and took up the philosophy of nature, anthropology, and æsthetics. He won an enviable reputation as a humorist and a poet, as well as a philosopher.

Works. — Works of Fechner are: "Ueber das höchste Gut" (1846); "Nanna, oder über das Seelenleben der Pflanzen" (1848); "Zendavesta, oder über die Dinge des Himmels und des Jenseits" (1851); "Ueber die Seelenfrage" (1861), — gives the "best general view of his the-

Erdmann; Fechner's "Ueber die Seelenfrage."

ory;" "Die Drei Motive und Gründe des Glaubens" (1863); "Einige Ideen zur Schöpfungs- und Entwickelungsgeschichte der Organismen" ("Ideas on the History of the Creation and Development of Organisms"), (1873); "Vorschule der Æsthetik" (1876); "Elemente der Psychophysik" (1860), — regarded as his chief work; etc.

Philosophy. — According to Fechner, philosophy is, as method, speculation on the basis of what experience and calculation have established as data. All that can be known is what is found in consciousness,— either our own or a higher. What is not in some sort of consciousness does not exist. The real is simply the permanent element in consciousness,— the laws of conscious (*i. e.*, phenomenal) existence. All questions as to cause, therefore, are answered by pointing to the laws of phenomena. Phenomena are of two classes: one class comprising all that which appears to itself; another, that which appears to other natures only,— *i. e.*, souls, or spirits, and corporeal substances. To each individual only one fact is there that is absolutely certain; namely, that of his own soul's existence, — an existence which is self-manifest. All other things are matter of inference and faith. Bodies are apprehended by the outward senses; other souls than ours are known by analogy with our own. Corporeal existence is, as the undulatory theory and the doctrine of heat prove, atomic in constitution. The atom is not a thing-in-itself (since no thing-in-itself exists), but only the simplest possible phenomenon in "consciousness." Atoms have position without extension,— they are "real" points, which are found as the absolutely discontinuous in the absolutely continuous, *viz.*, space and time, by means of which they acquire relations and forms. As the atom is a determination of consciousness, it is in no way a cause, outside of consciousness, producing changes in consciousness; soul, that is to say, is not a product of body. Soul and body constitute a solidarity, a single substance, and are mutually conditioned. "There is no human thought without a brain, no divine thought without a world." On the other hand, there is no body without a soul. The soul is the uniting bond of the body, having its seat in brain, spinal cord, and nerves. Bodily and psychical processes are functions of one another; their relations are formulated in the law, — that within certain limits constant differences in the intensities of sensations correspond to constant quotients of the intensities of the stimuli (Weber's law); " that when the susceptibility for two stimuli changes in a constant ratio, the sensation of their difference remains the same;" that for each sense there is a "threshold value" of the stimulus, or "a value corresponding to the least distinguishable sensation of that sense" ("law of the threshold"); etc. Analogy assures us that animals and plants, as well as man, have souls. Plants have sensation and instinct bound to the present; animals have presentiment and after-feeling, together with representative association. There are souls above, as well as below, that of man,— angels, an earth-spirit, a spirit of humanity, spirit of planetary system, spirit of the world (God, which is the all-embracing consciousness). In all things there is a tendency to stability, which controls and determines all things for the best. In the material world this tendency is manifested in a movement of the organic to the inorganic (but not *vice versa*), in the spiritual world as the realization of the end. It is this principle, together with that of the organic relations of the conditions of existence, — instead of the so-called struggle for existence,— that determines the evolution of life-forms in the universe,— an evolution in which the lower forms do not perform the office of giving rise to the higher, but are merely off-shoots from the same principle of life with them.

Result. — Fechner, like Beneke, makes philosophy a natural science, discarding metaphysics as the doctrine of the supersensible; but Fechner aims at a thoroughgoing (sensualistic?) idealism, while that of Beneke is subjective idealism merely. Fechner " reconciles " idealism and realism by treating the material and the spiritual as two sides of the same *conscious* substance.

§ 144.

Materialists. — The (partial) occupation of the German mind during the last half century with investigations in natural science has had as one consequence the revival of the French materialism of the last century — the materialism of D'Holbach and Lamettrie — by, in particular, Karl Vogt, Jacob Moleschott, and Louis Büchner, and the setting-up of newer forms of materialism by Feuerbach, Strauss, and Heinrich Czolbe. The materialism of Strauss, not like that of D'Holbach, crudely mechanical, contains elements of a dynamical and evolutionary view of things, *e. g.*, the law of the conservation of energy and the (Darwinian) theory of natural selection. It does not deny real order in nature, but does deny teleological connection. Czolbe advocates a changing doctrine, at no time, however, recognizing the supernatural in any form. He taught, first, that there are eternally existent atoms and certain eternally existent forms, or species, that are the source of life and consciousness; then, that there is, besides atoms and species, a "world-soul," in which sensations, in themselves eternal, remain dormant, until awakened by cerebral activity; lastly, that space is the source of sensuous qualities and sensations. He explained all teleological phenomena on mechanical principles. — Materialism has historically far less importance in this most recent period of philosophy than either subjective or phenomenalistic idealism on the one hand, or "ideal-realism," on the other.

§ 145.

Friedrich Adolf Trendelenburg[1] (1802-1872).— Trendelenburg, who was born at Eutin, in Lübeck, attended,

---

[1] Noack; Erdmann; "New Englander." vol. xxxiii. (art. by G. S. Morris); Trendelenburg's "Logische Untersuchungen."

after an unusually liberal and thorough preliminary training in the gymnasium of his native town, first the University of Kiel, and afterwards the universities of Leipsic and Berlin, with the view of carefully preparing himself for an academic career in philology and philosophy. At Kiel he heard Reinhold and Von Berger, at Berlin, Hegel, Schleiermacher, and Steffens. A careful and conscientious effort, motived by the conviction that "one must have a philosophical system, just as one must have a house," to find for himself a philosophical ποῦ στῶ, resulted in a positive preference for ancient over modern thinking. His doctor's thesis was a Latin essay entitled " Plato's Doctrine of Ideas and Number in the Light of Aristotle's Criticisms; " and for years after his graduation, as well as for some time before, he " occupied himself very particularly with Plato and Aristotle and the history of ancient philosophy." After seven years spent as private tutor, he entered the faculty of Berlin University as privat-docent. Soon after, he received the appointment of *professor extraordinarius* of philosophy, and four years later (1837), that of full professor of philosophy and pedagogy. In 1846 he became member of the Academy of Sciences, and in the following year permanent secretary of the philosophical section. He was also member of the scientific commission for the examination of gymnasial instructors, and as such, exercised a very important influence.

Works. — Trendelenburg's principal works are, — " Elementa Logices Aristoteleæ" (1837); with " Erläuterungen [Explanations]," (1842); " Logische Untersuchungen [Investigations]," (1840), — his chief work; " Logische Frage [Questions] in Hegel's System " (1843); " Sittliche [Moral] Idee des Rechts [Law] " (1849); " Ueber Herbart's Metaphysik und eine neue Auffassung [Conception] derselben " (1853); " Historische Beiträge [Contributions] zur Philosophie" (i. 1846; ii. 1855; iii. 1867); " Naturrecht auf dem Grunde der Ethik " (1860; 2d ed. 1868); " Lücken im Völkerrecht " (" Lacunæ in the Law of Nations "), (1870); " Kleine Schriften " (1870, 1871).

There should be mentioned also the celebrated edition of the " Psychology of Aristotle."

Philosophy: The Conception of Philosophy. — Philosophy, far from being merely an *a priori* subjectivistic and arbitrary *creation*, is an objective *growth*; it is a real historical product, and is dependent in every age on the state of the other sciences in that age. The foundations of philosophy were laid by Plato and Aristotle in their organic view of the world. Upon these foundations must the superstructure be erected, from materials provided by the history of thought, the highest results of the sciences, and original reflection. In its relation to the other sciences, philosophy is merely a higher empiricism. Like them, it may begin with the particular, and yet feel confident, from its necessary postulate of the organic unity of all things, that it will arrive at the universal. It does not deal with other objects than they deal with, but with the same from a different point of view and by a different method. The different sorts of being with which they occupy themselves have their limits in higher kinds of being, which they necessarily imply as their presupposition, and through these, being as such, which is the object of philosophy. The methods governing them imply a universal method, which, again, it is the business of philosophy to deal with. All sciences, in short, postulate logic and metaphysics, — the two necessary and interwoven branches of the science of sciences.

Mathematical Philosophy: Motion. — It is contained in the postulate of the organic unity of things in general, that thought and being are essentially one. The *proof* of the unity of thought and being is found in the conception of motion. Motion is universal in the external world; even rest is but the equilibrium or counterpoise of motions. And there is in thought a motion corresponding to (though unlike) the motion of the external world, for how otherwise could we be conscious of that external motion? The fact of this internal motion is reflected constantly in language, and especially in such terms as *whence, whither, for what end, ground, causality, finality, combining, distinguished*, etc. The activities of both sense and understanding are inconceivable apart from motion. Motion is, further, original, or non-derivative; all attempts to derive motion presuppose its existence. Motion arises always from a previous motion, so that motion is ultimate. It is not merely an effect of force; on the contrary, the conception of force is empty without that of motion. Again, motion is simple: instead of being (as is often asserted) a product whose components are time and space, it is rather their source. It is finally indefinable; is really presupposed by every conceivable "definition" of it. If motion is common to both thought and being, it is possible to understand, not only how thoughts can represent the external world, but also how thought can go out of itself, and can anticipate — as, *e.g.*, in mathematics — motion in the external world, *i.e.*, can have *a priori* validity in relation to the external world. Time and space, *e.g.*, which, as inner, are certainly products of motion, cannot (as Kant taught) be merely inner or subjective, but are also outer, or objective; and as a matter of fact, space is the external product of motion, and time the inner measure of it.

Physical Philosophy: Matter. — As regards matter, motion is an essential factor of it; but there must be something that moves, — a substrate and bearer of motion. Even if this be resolved into motion, another rises behind the last motion, and so on; so that matter cannot be entirely resolved into motion, though form and the attributes of matter are the products of motion. In and through motion are realized the categories of thought, which, since motion is universal and objective, have objective and universal application. Motion as productive and product is, (1) *cause* (formal as well as real) and effect, which as permanent is (2) *substance.* Substance as in motion and having effect is *quality;* as mathematically regarded, it is *quantity. Inherence, reciprocity,* etc., easily flow from the foregoing. The categories, it is to be observed, are discovered *a priori*, or in ourselves, by the observation of the inner motion.

Organic Philosophy: the Organism. — The category of final cause is not, so far as we can now see, to be deduced from motion, and we are warranted in assuming it as a new category, distinct from the mathematico-physical categories derived from motion. It is possible that upon closer investigation of the efficient cause, the end, or final cause, may reduce itself to mere appearance. Until, however, this is proved to be the case, the final cause remains as a distinct category. At present the insufficiency of purely mechanical causes to explain the harmony and precision of activity of organic existence is an indirect proof of final causes. The only doubt regarding the end in nature arises from our inability to determine the precise point at which it enters into and takes control of motion. We do know that thought is, through motion, one with being, and acts upon it; and we know that finality is an apparent fact in the world. Granting the category of finality, the mechanical categories take a place below it as subservient to it: efficient cause becomes *means;* substance, organism, or *machine;* inherence, the *relation of members to organism:* quality, the *activity of the organism,* etc., — the mechanical categories hereby acquiring a higher meaning in thought. The mechanical categories are reflected in the understanding, as such, in the notions of *conception* (corresponding to substance); *judgment* (corresponding to causal activity); *ground of knowing* (corresponding to cause). An exact correspondence of the ground of knowing with the external cause constitutes real knowledge; and hence the true definition is the genetic definition, and absolute knowledge is a knowledge of and through causes. Knowledge of causes from effects is but an indirect cognition and inconclusive, though it possesses a certain value nevertheless.

Ethical Philosophy : The Will. — With the union, which occurs in human nature, of free consciousness with the notion of the end, we step from the merely organic to the ethical sphere of existence. The end here assumes the form of will, or "desire permeated by thought." Will is in essence free (from mere mechanical control), and the more so the more it contains of the self-determining idea of its own nature, or the nature of man. In the form of desire it possesses a merely formal freedom. As merely formally free, it is merely individual and selfish, and is governed by the notion of pleasure, and that, too, of the mere individual. It possesses a higher value when ruled by the idea of the pleasure of other individuals; a higher value still, when governed by the intelligent conception of one's own material advantage ; and yet higher value when actuated by the idea of the welfare of all. But all these values are still inferior to that of the harmonious union of the individual and the totality of individuals, — which is the ethical ideal. The ethical problem is, as regards the individual, a strengthening and furthering of individuals by and for individuals. Society is a means to this end. As it is *only* this, there is no legality distinct from morality. The realization of the idea of humanity is the end of both individual and State.

The Philosophy of the Unconditioned and the Philosophical Standpoint. — In the four spheres of the mathematical, the physical, the organic, and the ethical is comprised the entire realm of the conditioned and positively knowable. Of the unconditioned we possess only an indirect knowledge ; it forever remains for us an ideal (of thought and action) rather than an object of knowledge. "God alone can comprehend God." Our ignorance in this regard does not (however) land us in materialism ; as, on the other hand, it does not warrant a dreamy idealism. The real, as "given," points directly to the ideal, and the ideal is (particularly in the ethical and organic realms) clearly manifest in the real, so that the only logically consistent standpoint for speculation is that of ideal-realism.

Result.— Trendelenburg, instead of "reconciling" idealism and realism, by reducing them to the same level, by placing them both under a single, abstract "method," reconciles them by making the stages of the one, realism, lead up to those of the other, which in turn sublate in themselves the stages leading up to them. The system of Trendelenburg, therefore, rises above that mechanical character which too purely governs the systems of Beneke and Fechner. It is a system of ethical ideal-realism. The system of Trendelenburg is peculiar among all the systems of the present century, or Third Period even, *viz.*, in that it bases itself so largely upon ancient conceptions.

§ 146.

Hermann Ulrici[1] (1806-1884).— Ulrici studied law at Halle and Berlin, and began the practice of it; but soon gave that up to pursue studies in history, poetry, and philosophy. After four years spent in these studies, he habilitated (in 1833) in the University of Berlin. The next year he went as professor to Halle, where he remained until his death. From the year 1847 on, he was editor, with I. H. Fichte, of the "Zeitschrift für Philosophie." He is noted in the purely literary world as a profound Shakespearean critic and interpreter.

Works. — Works of Ulrici are: "Ueber Princip und Methode der Hegel'schen Philosophie" (1841); "Grundprincip der Philosophie" (1845); "System der Logik" (1852); "Glauben und Wissen, Speculation und exacte Wissenschaft" (1858); "Gott und die Natur" (1862); "Gott und der Mensch," etc., (1866; 2d ed., 1874); "Allgemeine grundlegende Einleitung [Introduction] und das Naturrecht" (1873).

---

[1] "New Englander," vol. xxxiii. (article by B. P. Bowne); Erdmann, vol. ii. (iii.).

Philosophy. — Ulrici arrives at his peculiar standpoint partly by way of reaction against Hegelianism. He charges that the system of Hegel is purely subjective, formal, and anthropologistic, and sees the remedy for what he deems Hegel's one-sidedness in a sound empiricism, taken as the basis for idealistic speculation. Every system of philosophy presupposes a certain fact: there is no presuppositionless philosophy. This fact is the fact of human thought, the explanation of which is the chief business of philosophy. All thought implies distinction, differentiation: thought is a distinguishing activity. It exists only as distinguishing, or in distinction: there is no (Hegelian) "pure thought." It distinguishes objects one from another, according to the law of identity and contradiction, which its very activity creates; it distinguishes subject from object under the law of causation, which also exists for it only as created by it. Besides these two modes of distinguishing, there are no others. As a distinguishing activity, thought is also a comparing activity. But distinction and comparison imply the existence for thought of points of distinction and comparison. These points of comparison it possesses are the categories of thinking, which may be regarded as just the "universal points of comparison, according to which the soul unconsciously, but necessarily, proceeds in that differentiation whereby it comes to knowledge." The categories are not ideas present to the mind, nor even "forms" (in the Kantian sense), for the reception of a given manifold of sensation, but norms of activity, expressions of the inner nature of mind. They are not things originated by abstraction, but make possible the existence of objects for us. This they do by the necessity which they possess for our thought. We are compelled by the law of causation to refer sensations of which we are conscious that we are not the cause to something outside us as cause. And not merely are "we forced to admit external objects, but also to admit that these objects are differentiated from one another, for the effects produced by them are different, and by the law of identity and contradiction we are forced to assume that unlike effects spring from unlike causes; and they differ in ways which may be determined by reference to our points of comparison,— the categories." Thus by thought we determine the nature of things. And the things are not mere thought, but real objects. "The laws and forms of mind prove to be laws and forms of nature also." Nature is a product and an expression of intelligence. This fact may be proved in another way. As different from one another, things are related to one another. All things — even the so-called atoms, which, to be real, must possess definite differentiating attributes — stand in relation, are not independent and original. The "relativity" which lies in the notion of difference compels us to conceive the differentiation of external objects as the work of a Power which proceeds according to mental methods, *i. e.*, we must view this differentiation as originated and established by a Rational Mind. Hence the categories have a metaphysical or objective as well as a logical value, although they still remain mere thought-forms. Of the categories there are four classes,— " primary categories, categories of simple nature, categories of relation, categories of order." To the first class belong the notions of being, activity and act, space and time; to the second, the categories of "quantity and quality, with their subdivisions." These two classes are the conditions of knowledge in general. The third and fourth are categories of scientific knowledge. The first two classes of categories are categories of things as well as thoughts. The last two are not certainly such, but they are at least subjective necessities, — *i. e.*, necessary in relation to things in so far as science is necessary. Without science or system in knowledge, the world is a chaos for us, — contradicts our consciousness of ourselves. We naturally and inevitably assume nature to be subject to law, and as naturally apply to it such conceptions of law as we find in ourselves. We attribute to nature an activity like that in ourselves, *i. e.*, a purposeful and organic activity. There is no science without the notion of an all-controlling idea. The objectivity of this notion is practically proved beyond doubt by scientific fact, — the (definite) order of nature as known to intelligent observation and reflection. The same fact proves the existence of natural classes in things, — the inorganic, organic; minerals, plants, animals; gold, lead, iron, copper, etc. Thought is the prius and goal of all things. The order of nature, in atoms as well as in visible forms, presupposes an intelligent personal absolute. Thus, upon the basis of realism we arrive by scientific conviction, or faith, at idealism, and discover true philosophy to be neither realism nor idealism alone, but ideal-realism. Scientific faith, it must be observed, is distinguished from " purely subjective opinion, from personal conviction, and from religious faith, in that when reasons *pro* and *con* are of equal value, the first gives its assent simply in accordance with its wishes; the second because one side of our personality demands a decision; the third, because the whole and particularly the ethical personality makes this demand,— while scientific faith rests on an objective preponderance of reasons." According to this doctrine of scientific faith, the prevalent physical theories are as much religious as anti-religious; to scientific faith atoms presuppose a God, who is their author, and of whose thought our thought is an after-thinking. But, further, scientific (logical and physical) categories presuppose ideal and ethical, and so refer us back to a creator through whom nature is made the workshop of ethical Ideas, the means of attaining to living fellowship with God. The fact that man possesses ethical ideas and is an ethical nature is *proved* by the fact that we have the inexpugnable feeling that we ought to do this or that, which feeling is a product of freedom united with a presupposing consciousness. And it appears from a consideration of the ethical categories, — the true, beautiful, good, — in themselves, that all truth is knowable only because its nature is ethical. The highest of these categories and the foundation of the rest is truth. Its origin is not to be found in sense, and it aims always and everywhere at law and order,— pursues the ideal. Knowledge is not complete philosophy, not the highest philosophy, where this fact is not recognized. Hence ideal-realism is the only really conceivable standpoint.

Result. — The system of Ulrici (like that of Trendelenburg) is a system of ethical ideal-realism.

§ 147.

Karl Robert Eduard von Hartmann (born in 1842). — Von Hartmann, son of a military officer, received, after a gymnasial course, a military training in the army and in a school of engineering and artillery. He afterwards held a position as artillery officer. Owing to a bodily infirmity contracted in service, he was obliged to give up military life; and since 1865 has devoted himself to literary and to scientifico-philosophical work.

Works. — Von Hartmann's principal (as well as most noted) work is "Die Philosophie des Unbewussten" ("The Philosophy of the Unconscious"), (1st ed. 1869; 9th ed., — including a volume of *addenda* and *corrigenda*,— 1882). Of hardly less importance and note is the " Phaenomenologie des sittlichen [Moral] Bewustsseins [Consciousness] " (1879). Other works are: " Das religiöse Bewusstsein der Menschheit im Stufenfolge [Successive Stages] seiner Entwickelung [Development]," 1882 ; " Die Religion des Geistes " (1882), — with which (latter) are connected " Die Selbstersetzung des Christenthums und die Religion der Zukunft " (1874), and " Die Krisis des Christenthums in der modernen Theologie " (1881) ; " Ueber die dialektische Methode " (1868) ; " Schelling's ' Positive Philosophie ' als Einheit von Hegel und Schopenhauer " (1869) ; " Das Ding-an-Sich und seine Beschaffenheit " (1871), or " Kritische Grundlegung des Transcendentalen Idealismus " (1875) ; " Wahrheit und Irrthum im Darwinismus "

(1875). Many of his works are polemical productions, called forth by criticism of his principal work.

Philosophy:[1] *Scope and Method of the Philosophy of the Unconscious.* — By "the Unconscious" are to be understood: (1) united unconscious will and unconscious idea; (2) the identical subject of unconscious psychical functions; (3) the one absolute subject. The idea of the Unconscious has formed the core of all great philosophies, — the Substance of Spinoza, the Absolute of Fichte, Schelling's Absolute Subject-Object, the Absolute Idea of Plato and Hegel, Schopenhauer's Will; and the Philosophy of the Unconscious embraces in itself all that is valid and valuable in these and all true systems in the history of philosophy. The present system has mainly for its object the elevation of Hegel's unconscious philosophy of the Unconscious into a conscious philosophy of the Unconscious. The method of philosophy at the present historical juncture, when there is demanded a reconciliation of a variety of views, can properly be neither the dialectic method of Hegel, nor the mathematico-deductive method (alone), nor the inductive method of the natural sciences. The first is unintelligible to ordinary comprehension; the second by itself does not explain the real; the third never arrives at a principle. The true method seems to be a combination of deduction and induction: all speculation is baseless which contradicts the clear results of empirical investigation; and conversely, all conceptions and interpretations of empirical fact are erroneous which contradict the strict results of a purely logical speculation. The theory of the Unconscious naturally divides into the two main parts: (1) the *phenomenology of the Unconscious;* and (2) the *metaphysics of the Unconscious.* The former subdivides into (1) *the manifestation of the Unconscious in bodily life;* and (2) *the Unconscious in the human mind.*

[1] This account is based upon the translation of the "Philosophie des Unbewussten," by W. C. Coupland (1884).

The Phenomenology of the Unconscious: The Manifestation of the Unconscious in Bodily Life. — Scientific observation and experimentation (upon decapitated frogs and birds without cerebral hemispheres, as subjects) demonstrate the presence of unconscious will in the independent functions of the spinal cord and ganglia. Many actions and functions have been shown to be regularly performed without a co-operating activity of the organ of bodily consciousness, the cerebrum, or even, in some cases, without a nervous system at all (*e.g.*, the polyp). What occurs in such cases is not always explicable by the theory of mechanical reflex action, but frequently must be referred to an immanent unconscious will. The execution of voluntary movement is satisfactorily explained only when a middle term of unconscious ideation is hypothetically inserted between the unconscious *idea* of the movement and the movement itself. So intricate is the operation connecting idea and movement, and yet so direct and infallible, that no mere mechanism, no possible relation of muscular feeling or association resulting from habit, can suffice for the purposes of intelligible explanation,— nothing, in fact, but the unconscious idea both of the positions of the nerve-endings corresponding to the idea of the movement, and of the movement itself. Instinct, or purposive action without consciousness of purpose, or a conscious willing of means to an unconscious end, is not — since instincts are, not uncommonly, quite unlike where bodily organizations are alike, and, not uncommonly, the same where bodily organization differs — merely a result of bodily organization. Nor, since instinct never hesitates, and is found in animals bred in solitude (hence without chance of learning from others), can it be resolved into reflection. Nor can it be resolved into the action of a mechanism standing outside the animal. It belongs, in fact, to the inmost nature and character of the animal, its own individual activity. Frequently the knowledge of the purpose of the action to be performed by the animal is not at all ascertainable through sense-perception, but must be due to a clairvoyant intuition such as we have a feeble echo of in presentiment. The presence of an unconscious non-mechanical principle in reflex action is demonstrated by the fact that any section or cutting of the spinal cord of an animal which, though interrupting old paths of the nerve-current, leaves opportunity for the possible formation of new ones, does not destroy reflex action. It is also strikingly shown by the rapidity and ease with which movements of the body are unconsciously adapted to changing positions, — as, for example, in preserving one's balance. The reparative power of nature — especially in the lowest forms of animal life — is an instance of the working of an unconscious non-mechanical principle, a " physical power which, aided by the unconscious representation of the type and the means requisite for the end of self-preservation, brings about those circumstances in consequence of which the restoration of the normal condition must ensue according to general physical and chemical laws." In the indirect influence of conscious psychical activity, — conscious will and conscious ideation, — in organic function, again, the unconscious comes to the surface : the mere exercise of will affects the vegetative function ; the conscious idea of a definite effect can, without the conscious will, excite movement of muscles, etc. Finally, we have to admit a "clairvoyance" of the Unconscious in the manifest purposiveness of the creative impulse, as, *e. g.*, in the production of organs before there is use for them (as the eyes and the lungs of the unborn child), in propagation, nutrition, maintenance of constant temperature, etc. The conception of a mechanism is defective, because the performance of a mechanism always leaves over something (not explicable by rule) to be immediately performed by psychical action ; and, further, the fitness of the mechanism itself would have to be accounted for.

The Unconscious in the Human Mind. — An unconscious element is manifested in the instinctive feelings of aversion (particularly in fear of death), shame, disgust, purity, modesty, maternal love, sympathy, etc. Sexual love finds its adequate explanation only in the hypothesis of a principle providing for a "constitution of succeeding generations corresponding as far as possible to the Idea of the human race." This principle is undoubtedly the same as that which governs organic formation in general, the principle operating here with reference to procreation. Pleasure and pain receive due explanation as being respectively the satisfaction and the unsatisfiedness of an unconscious will (resulting from the perceptions and feelings of lower nerve-centres and from obscure sensuous perceptions). The deeds and outward characters of men have to be referred to something underneath — far below — the surface of conscious reflection and so-called conscious volition, — hidden psychical processes, the results only of which appear in consciousness. There cannot, *e. g.*, really occur in the will as such that hesitancy so often attending on a so-called choice of will. In æsthetic judgment, again, we have the operation of a principle acting instinctively, and determined neither by an *a priori* intellectual ideal of beauty, nor by an empirically acquired sense of the agreeable and fit, nor by ordinary conscious reflection ; in other words, what is called artistic genius is but the spontaneous intuition and working of the Unconscious. Language, which is prior to distinct consciousness, has its source in the Unconscious. The common or general notion is the reaction of the Unconscious to the stimulus of interest excited. The association of ideas is too complicated a process to admit of our regarding it as a result of conscious activity. To speak of sense-perception, space may be viewed as a spontaneous creation of the Unconscious in response to stimulation. (*Time* is, as regards origin, a perception, rather.) And all sensible qualities are reactions of the Unconscious against stimuli ; and the elaboration of these falls mostly within the domain of the unconscious. The characteristic conditions of mysticism, such as clairvoyance, inspiration, presentiment, intellectual intuition, refer us at once to the Unconscious. In history the Unconscious manifests itself in the movements of masses of people — migrations, crusades, revolutions — and in the unexpected appearance of genius at a critical juncture, or when needed most. Society has its origin in three instincts, — the sexual instinct, the social instinct, and the instinct of the enmity of all to all. Historical development everywhere points to unconscious will and a clairvoyance of unconscious representation, which are as necessary as any "Fate" and as unerring as any "Providence" could be.

The Metaphysics of the Unconscious: Brain and Ganglia as Conditions of Animal Consciousness. — In attempting to derive from the Unconscious consciousness and the conscious or known universe, we at once encounter a fundamental proposition of materialism: All conscious mental activity can come to pass only by normal functioning of the brain. This proposition is irrefutable, and must be accepted. (And, in general, only a philosophy which takes account of the results of the natural sciences and accepts without reservation the perfectly legitimate point of departure of materialism can hope to make a stand against materialism, if at the same time it fulfils the condition of being universally intelligible, — as the philosophy of Identity and absolute Idealism is not.)

Origin of Consciousness. — Consciousness originates from the meeting of mind in its original unconscious state and matter in motion; in this meeting the will is impregnated. The idea acting upon the will as a stimulus evokes an act which has for its content or object the negation of the idea, — whence consciousness. Were the excited will related affirmatively or positively (instead of negatively) to the idea, there would be no consciousness, because no opposition (consciousness being an opposition of subject and object). Consciousness, it thus appears, does not belong to the idea as such, but comes to it as it were from a foreign source. (This is the first and most important result of our investigation.) The comparative weakness of the will in relation to the idea, preventing its accomplishing in full the negation aimed at, produces dissatisfaction of will, and pain is the result: every process of becoming conscious is *eo ipso* a process accompanied by pain. This is, as it were, the vexation of the unconscious individual at the interloping idea, which it must endure and cannot get rid of. We can conceive material changes as affecting will only by supposing matter to be in its essence merely unconscious mind, whose representations or ideas are limited to spatial attraction and repulsion of uniformly varying intensity, and whose volitional manifestations consist in realizing this limited ideational province. Consciousness would then be a consequence of the clashing of the atomic will, or will in the matter of the brain, and the psychical will, whereby the latter becomes objectified to itself (and so becomes conscious of itself) in the will (like itself) entering its sphere. Merely psychical wills do not clash, and thereby become directly conscious of one another, because they can have no common sphere. In all cases of common thought we have to do with cerebral vibrations, which affect the individual mind and compel it to uniform reaction. Why consciousness should result from the meeting of unconscious will and unconscious idea, it is unreasonable to demand, — as unreasonable as it would be of the physicist why aërial vibrations should cause sound. The becoming conscious of *pleasure* is an *indirect* process. Consciousness pertains to pleasure as soon as consciousness is compelled to acknowledge the external condition of success, and therewith satisfaction as something partially or wholly conditioned from without. Will can *never* become conscious, because it can never contradict itself, cannot, since it is one, apprehend itself as foreign to itself and react against itself, etc. So-called conscious volition is merely the conscious conceptual representation, "I will." One knows what he wills only so far as he possesses the knowledge of his own character and of the psychological laws, the sequence of motive and desire and the strength of different desires, and can calculate beforehand their struggle or their resultant will. Consciousness as such has no degree, — there may be degree in the content given to consciousness. Unity of consciousness we can speak of only with reference to its empirical side. There could be unity in essential consciousness only in so far as there is unity of nerve-structure. Consciousness as such belongs to plants as well as animals; the difference between the vegetable and animal consciousness being merely of content and intensity.

Matter as Will and Idea. — The principle which produces the material world is the sundering into a polar dualism of corporeal and ethereal atoms distinguished by the, respectively, positive and negative direction of their forces or, rather, motions. The true theory of matter and force lies between mere mechanical atomism and the Kantian dynamism, which asserts but does not prove the origin of the higher material forces from attraction and repulsion. Matter being but a complex of atomic forces, there exists no use for the conception of *substratum* in relation to it. If we compare force and will in themselves and their places in the universe, we find that we may, without doing violence to thought, extend the notion of will to include that of force, — though the latter does not include the former: will is the appropriate term to express the *essence* of what are called *forces, e. g.*, muscular force. Accordingly, matter, as force having certain directions and forms, may be resolved into will and idea. Hereby is the (supposed) radical distinction between matter and spirit abolished; their difference being only a difference of degree of manifestation of the same essence, the Eternally Unconscious; and materialism and idealism are done away with.

Individuality. — From the foregoing emerges the fact of the individuality of the Unconscious, which is, indeed, as we shall see, the strictest individuality we have any knowledge of. The individual is that which is essentially indivisible. That which unites in itself all possible modes of unity, *i. e.*, as space-unity (unity of form), time-unity (continuity of action), unity of cause, unity of purpose, unity of reciprocal action of parts (so far as such are present), is the highest individual. Individuals may be classed as material and spiritual; spiritual individuals as consciously spiritual and unconsciously spiritual. What in any given sphere (*i. e.*, of plants) constitutes an individual, is not always easy of determination. The lowest individual is the immaterial functional atomic force, which is a continued single act of will. Atoms, if conscious, are the lowest conscious individuals. The cells of plants and animals are in different ways conscious individuals, those of animals being of higher order, possessing a consciousness as compared with which that of plant-cells is evanescent. The distinctive unity of organic life in general is that of reciprocity. Material individuality is a condition of, but not a sufficient reason for, conscious individuality, which presupposes a certain mode, strength, excellence of conduction.

The Unconscious as an Individual. — The Unconscious is the inseparable unity of Will and Idea. This unity is that of an end (instead of mere reciprocity, as in the organism) of time, and, indirectly, also that of space. There is One Unconscious, the Absolute Individual. *That* the One Unconscious is the cause of all finite individualities — is sundered into substance and phenomenon (and why, if the soul of the animal be simultaneously present and purposively efficient in all organs and cells of the animal organism, should not an unconscious world-soul be simultaneously present and purposively efficient in all organisms and atoms?) — is not a distinction of individuality. The Unconscious itself is the source of the differences that appear in it, — has unity of cause in relation to them. It is not in space, hence contains no spatial difference; it *originates* time-distinctions, and is not subject to them. We have arrived at a result which has been represented as the culminating point of the speculation of modern times, *viz.*, Schelling's " individual which is all being;" but we have reached it by the *a pos-*

teriori inductive highway accessible to all, instead of by a speculative *a priori* by-path.

The Unconscious as the Supra-Conscious. — The intelligence of the Unconscious appears from our inductive investigation a clairvoyant intelligence, though never aware of its own vision, and unable, without the mirror of individual consciousness, to see the seeing eye. It is infallible and infinite, transcends all forms of reflective consciousness. Only a formless consciousness, indistinguishable from unconsciousness, could belong to it. The sole content of the absolutely formless consciousness of the Unconscious is absolutely indefinite pain. Ethical and ideological distinctions are entirely foreign to it. To attribute consciousness to it, as Theism does to God, would be to degrade it. A consciousness over and above the individual consciousness, whose source it is, would swallow up and cancel those individual consciousnesses.

Generation. — From the standpoint of the universality and unity of the Unconscious the phenomenal world is a product, not of "a creative act" in the vulgar sense of that term, but of evolutional generation. The world of organic beings is the result of the action of the unconscious on organic matter. Spontaneous generation may have existed before the mechanism of sexual generation could be brought into existence; but in the present stage of existence it would cost the Unconscious infinitely more trouble to produce by spontaneous generation an egg possessed of all the characters of a higher species to be newly created than either to evolve an individual of the new higher species from an ovum containing the characters of the new higher species in an ovary of an individual of lower species, or, lastly, to make use of both expedients at the same time, — *i. e.*, to develop an ovum particularly constituted in view of the new species both in the ovary of the inferior individual, as well as after quitting the same, with the modifications necessary for attaining the higher species. The Unconscious follows the path marked out by circumstances already existing, and offering least obstacles; it creates new and higher species as far as possible from those species in which only new characters are to be added, but the fewest, or no extant positive characters are to be destroyed, *i. e.*, from the *relatively imperfect* species provided with few specific characters affording much scope for further development, but not from species already highly developed, *strongly differentiated*, and endowed with many and definite characters. (The assumption of the Darwinian theory does not suffice to show why the higher forms come the more readily from the more imperfect of the lower; why the conversion into a new order takes place only when within the previous order the abundance of perfect forms is exhausted.) The Unconscious sometimes, in preference to endeavoring to overcome existing material difficulties, sends monsters into the world.

Individuation. — Individuals are willed-thoughts or will-acts of the Unconscious, the unity of essence of the Unconscious remaining unaffected by the plurality of individuals, which are only activities (or combinations of certain activities) of the One Essential Being. In the Unconscious, individuals are distinguished immediately by intuitive imagination, without thought of spatial relations, just as one recognizes by perception, without aid of conceptions, the right glove as right; but the *principium* (or rather *medium*) *individuationis* is (in case of atoms) the combinations of space and time (in case of organic life), of matter. This combination is independent of the conscious perceiving subject; so that plurality, while mere appearance of the One Essence, is not mere subjective appearance. Individuality in persons is, not transcendentally innate and entirely fixed once for all, nor innate in respect to type, and further determinable, but a product of the individual constitution of the brain (produced by former impressions), and the action of the Unconscious upon it. Every human being, according to the law of heredity, brings the main part of his character with him into the world: in this sense only is character innate; in a similar sense only are ideas innate.

The Supreme Wisdom of the Unconscious and the Perfection of the World. — In virtue of its absolute clairvoyance, the Unconscious can never err, nor even doubt or hesitate; it is always in absolute possession of the required ideas, or of the required knowledge of ends, near and remote; its interpositions and action in the world of organic matter are always adapted to the peculiarity of the case. Mechanical contrivances it everywhere employs, but these can and do not do away with its continual direct interposition; they merely cover homogeneous cases, leaving over always a remnant of work which falls to the direct activity of the Unconscious. As soon as the expenditure of force needed for the construction of a machine would become greater than the saving force attained by the mechanism (which is the case in all combinations of circumstances which by their nature occur but seldom), or where for other reasons a mechanism can be constructed only with difficulty, then, of course, the direct activity of the Unconscious must display itself without hesitation. "If now, according to this, we cannot avoid attributing to the Unconscious, first, absolute clairvoyance (which answers to the theological notion of omniscience); secondly, an infallible and indubitable logical concatenation of the included data, and the most appropriate action at the most suitable moment (in theological language, 'omniscience' united with 'supreme wisdom'); and thirdly, a ceaseless intervention at every moment and at every place (theologically, 'omnipresence,' — one must add, omnipresence at all times); if we further consider that, at the first moment when the Unconscious became active thus, at the moment of the first positing and disposing of this world, just the same ideal world of all possible conceptions, thus also of possible worlds and world-goals and world-ends, and their possible means, rested in the Unconscious, — if, lastly, we take notice that the chain of final causality cannot, from its very nature, be conceived interminable like that of bare causality, but must terminate in a final end, because every preceding link of the chain in final causation must be conditioned by the following, — we may with justice confide that the world is contrived . . . and guided as wisely and well as is possible; that if among possible ideas that of a better world could have lain in the omniscient Unconscious, certainly the better one would have come to pass instead of the present one; that the unerring Unconscious neither could have been deceived, in positing this world, as to its value, nor that in the omnitemporal omnipresence of the Unconscious a pause in its action could ever have been possible, since by such a remissness in the government of the world the better grounded world would have of itself deteriorated." The doctrine here expounded agrees closely with the Leibnitzian optimism. This latter, however, is incorrect as to the nature of evil: evil is not merely a less degree of good, but is something positively inherent in the world as a world of individuals. All birth of the Unconscious into individual consciousness is necessarily attended by pain or suffering, which as such is evil: evil must exist as long as the world exists. So essentially is evil as suffering a part of the world that the solution of the problem of pain and its opposite is the ultimate end of the world-process, the ideas of morality and justice having no meaning except in reference to this, — no application to the unindividualized, painless Unconscious.

The Misery and the Irrationality of Existence. — It is natural that the Unconscious, if it wills the misery and evil of existence, should for its own ends also will that conscious beings should be subject to illusion regarding this misery and evil. There are three stages of this illusion. First, it is supposed that happiness has been actually attained at the present stage of development, and is accordingly attainable by the individual to-day in his earthly life; second, happiness is conceived attainable by the individual in a transcendental life after death; third, happiness is relegated to the future of the world. As regards the first of these stages of illusion, it appears on reflection that such "goods as health, youth, freedom, a competence, contentment, are merely privative; equal in value to non-existence would be only the absolutely contented life, — which does not exist; the misery attending hunger (and most of the thirteen hundred millions of earth's inhabitants have only a scanty and unsatisfying nourishment), love (consider the pains of child-bearing, the torments of love prior to marriage, the consequences of betrayed love, adultery, the disappointing nature of sexual love), compassion (which is harrowing to refined natures), religious edification (the mortification of the appetites, fear of one's own unworthiness, anxiety concerning future judgment), immorality (the essence of which is the infliction of pain), attainment in science and art (the difficulty of them, the disappointment of unsuccessful aspirants), troubled sleep and dreams, the acquisitive instinct, and love of comfort (how frequently disappointed), envy, jealousy, chagrin, pain, and lamentation for the past, repentance, vindictiveness, anger, hope, — the actual misery in the world attending these things considerably outweighs the pleasure they cause. Even if it lay in the nature of the will to produce as it were, in gross, an equal amount of pleasure and of pain, yet the net result of pleasure and pain would, in general, be modified unfavorably to pleasure by the fact that nervous fatigue increases the repugnance to pain, and diminishes the effort to pleasure, thus increasing pain of pain and diminishing the pleasure in pleasure; that the pleasure which arises through the cessation or remission of pain cannot by a long way balance this pain, — and of this kind is the largest part of existing pleasure; that pain thrusts itself on consciousness, which must feel it, whereas pleasure must, as it were, be discovered and inferred by consciousness where the motive for its discovery is wanting; that satisfaction is short, and quickly fades, while pain endures so long as it is not limited by hope, so long as desire exists without satisfaction (and when does not such exist?); that equal quantities of pleasure and pain united in a consciousness are not of equal value, do not compensate one another; but pain remains in excess, or the exclusion of every sensation is preferred to the questionable union. As to the second stage of Illusion, hope of happiness after death is a delusion, since there is no immortality. The relegation of happiness to the future of the world is a mistake, because however great the progress of mankind, it will never get rid of, or even diminish, the greatest sufferings, — those of sickness, age, immorality, dependence on the will and power of others, want, discontent, etc. Disease increases faster than medical skill; cheerful youth is always in a minority; immorality does not decrease, but increases; pleasure in scientific production is becoming ever less; the ideal of happiness recedes with progress, — in short, the capacity for misery increases, rather than decreases, with the progress of civilization, and will continue to increase; and the old age of the world will be like that of the individual, — the least happy of all; it will feel the vanity, as well as the wretchedness, of existence, will recognize the folly of volition, and long for absolute painlessness, nothingness, — Nirvana.

The Goal of Evolution and the Significance of Consciousness. — Can a world of utter misery have its real end in its own evolution, in freedom, or even in self-consciousness, which may be regarded as the proximate end of the will's activity? Mere evolution is not an end; freedom is merely privative and formal; consciousness, or self-knowledge, would in such a world of misery be like the preying on one's own vitals. The only thing possessing absolute value — and hence capable of being an absolute end — is happiness. The endeavor after happiness is the most deeply rooted impulse, — the very essence of the will itself seeking satisfaction. As positive happiness is unattainable in a world of volition (since all volition is essentially painful), the end to be striven for, namely, that which most nearly approximates positive happiness, — *i. e.*, painlessness, — can be attained only by the negation of all volition. The negative of Will (as we have already seen) is contained in the Idea (and only in that), since Will and Idea are the only factors of the Absolute. The ceasing of Will to be mere Will and its becoming its opposite, Idea, have as attendant condition (as we have also already seen) the fact of consciousness. The end of existence may, therefore, be formulated as the Emancipation of the Idea from the Will; which can be brought about by cosmic universal negation of the Will, and in a *temporal* act, since otherwise it would be an endless process, and never really be accomplished, — an act *after* which there will be no more volition. As practical principle, — and, indeed, the ground-principle of practical philosophy, — there follows from the foregoing principle of the emancipation of idea from will the principle of the complete devotion of personality to the world-process for the sake of its goal, the general redemption of the world from the misery of volition; which becomes, if the Unconscious be recognized as identical with the Conscious, except in not being conscious, the making of the ends of the Unconscious ends of our own consciousness.

Ultimate Principles: The Unconscious as Will. — After its "redemption," its return to pure potentiality, — for only as volition is the will actuality, — the will is again what it was before all volition; and since the unconscious has no memory, there is the possibility that will may again become volition, and the unhappy world-process be repeated. "If there is nothing at all that determines volition or non-volition, it is, mathematically speaking, *accidental* whether at this moment the potentiality wills or does not will, — *i. e.*, probability $= \frac{1}{2}$. Only when the probability of each of the possible cases $= \frac{1}{2}$, only where absolute chance comes into play, only there is absolute freedom conceivable. Freedom (pure potentiality of will) and chance are, as absolute notions, — *i. e.*, notions deprived of all relations, — identical. Now, were the potentiality *in time*, the probability would, as time is infinite, be $= 1$, — *i. e.*, certainty, — that the potentiality resolve in time once again to become actual; but as this potentiality is *outside* time, which the actual first created, and this extra-temporal eternity is not at all distinguished in temporal reference from the moment (as great and small are not distinguished as regards color), so is also the probability that the potentiality determines itself to volition in its extra-temporal eternity equal to this, that it determines itself thereto instantaneously,—*i. e.*, $= \frac{1}{2}$. It follows from this that the redemption from volition can be regarded as no final one, but that it only reduces the pain of the volition and being from the probability 1 (which it has during the world process) to the probability $\frac{1}{2}$, thus always affords a gain not to be despised in practice. Of course the probability of future events cannot be influenced by the past (the Unconscious having no memory); consequently the coefficient of probability of $\frac{1}{2}$ for the repeated emergence of the willing from potentiality cannot be thereby diminished that the latter had once before resolved to will; but where one *a priori* considers the probability that the emergence of volition from potentiality repeat itself with whole process n times, it is manifestly $= \frac{1}{2}n$, just as the *a priori* probability of throwing heads n times in succession with a coin, since with the end of one world-process time ceases till the beginning of the next time, there is *no time pause;* but the state of affairs is precisely the same as if the potentiality had at the moment of annihilation of its former act externalized itself anew to act. It is, however, clear that, n increasing, the probability $\frac{1}{2}n$ becomes so small that it is practically sufficient for consolation.

The Idea. — The Idea (we have seen) receives actuality from an act of the Unconscious as will. It is non-existent, super-existent, and indeed not even, as is the mere will-in-itself, a potentiality, but only pure passive possibility, or form, being unable to get out of itself, as the will does. The principle of the Idea is only to determine the *what* of things, — the *that* being determined by the will. As self-identical it determines that all things shall centre in one thing, — *i. e.*, have an end, — and that there shall be law, or necessary order of succession, among things in general, or that there shall be an efficient cause for everything; that is to say, in the Idea are contained together, and as two aspects of the same thing, final and efficient causes, the latter depending on the former, as the higher. Finally, all necessity, causal, final, deterministic (by motive), is necessity only because it is logical.

The Identical Substance of both Attributes. — Will and Idea cannot really be conceived as independent ultimate substances. So conceived, they are without the possibility of influencing one another; they must be viewed as attributes of a single substance, — which has been denominated the Unconscious. Such an inner dualism in the absolute substance as thus results is not impossible, but an indispensable condition to its having existence (for consciousness). An Absolute One could exist only as absolutely rigid, identically self-persistent, not a principle either of being or of knowledge in relation to any process, such as the phenomenal world presents to us; it could be only empty volition. That an actual process may come to pass, there must be, besides the commencing factor, at least *one* other that encounters the former, and indeed in the double sense of the term of succoring and opposing; for only from the co-operation and counteraction of at least two moments can a process result. The Unconscious is then both one and many, — primarily the former. The problem of the Oneness of the Unconscious as a substrate of Will and Idea is insoluble; philosophy has to state it, rather than to try to solve it.

The Possibility of Metaphysical Knowledge. — Will and Idea can exist in unity only if (instead of being distinguished as they are in consciousness, as such) they are really brought together, which can be done only by the will, which alone gives reality to all possibilities. As will in itself lies outside consciousness, there is a possible foothold for scepticism in regard to our knowledge of ultimate reality. So far as experience goes, we are warranted in attaching a high degree of probability to our supposed knowledge of it, — a probability sufficient in relation to practice, not only in life, but also in science. We may state the case as follows: If there is a knowledge of the Absolute, it must rest in the material identity of Thought and Being, is therefore also to be found in immediate experience (affection of thought by being), and the logically correct inferences from the same; the inferences from experience establish the material identity of Thought and Being; hence the possibility of the knowledge of the Absolute.

Result. — The system of Von Hartmann is an ideal-realism, consisting in an attempted combination of the Idea of Hegel and the Will of Schopenhauer. In so far as it subjects efficient and final causes to logical causes, it is a logical ideal-realism. But in so far as the relation of will and idea is a mechanical one (will acting only as *stimulated* in some inexplicable way by idea), it is a merely *mechanico*-logical ideal-realism. Though Hegel may have attached insufficient importance to the *real* element of things (which natural science has made so one-sidedly prominent in the last half-century), it can hardly be said that Von Hartmann's emphasis of it has brought him nearer the truth than was Hegel, — rather, he falls behind Hegel here. Von Hartmann's advance upon Schopenhauer is chiefly in the employment of recently discovered scientific truth as illustration of his doctrine. The *Unconscious*, as such, can never *explain* anything; to maintain that it can, is a contradiction in terms.

§ 148.

Rudolph Hermann Lotze (1817–1881). — Lotze, born at Bautzen, in Saxony, was educated at the gymnasium of Zittau and the University of Göttingen. The son of a physician, he went to the university primarily to study medicine, but instead studied philosophy and the natural sciences. His philosophical studies were guided by C. H. Weisse, originally a Hegelian. In 1838, four years after entering the university, he took the degree of doctor in both "philosophy" and medicine, and in 1839 qualified as docent in both at the University of Leipsic. In 1844 he went to Göttingen as professor of philosophy. He was called to the

University of Berlin in 1881; he died shortly after beginning work there.

Works.— Of Lotze's numerous valuable works perhaps the most important are: "Allgemeine Pathologie und Therapie als mechanische Naturwissenschaften" (1842, 2d ed. 1848); "Allgemeine Physiologie des körperlichen Lebens" (1851); "Medicinische Psychologie, oder Physiologie der Seele" (1852); "Mikrokosmus, Ideen zur Naturgeschichte und Geschichte der Menschheit" (1858); "Geschichte der Aesthetik in Deutschland" (1868); "System der Philosophie" (vol. i., "Logik," 1874; vol. ii., "Metaphysik," 1878; vol. iii., "Praktische Philosophie, Aesthetik, Philosophie der Religion," — unwritten); "Grundzüge [Outlines] der Philosophie (Logik und Encyklopädie, Metaphysik, Psychologie, Praktische Philosophie, Aesthetik, Philosophie der Religion)". Here should not be overlooked entirely articles in Wagner's "Handwörterbuch der Physiologie" on "Lebenskraft" and "Seele und Seelenleben." Lotze published a "Metaphysik" in 1841, and a "Logik" in 1843.

Philosophy:[1] *Problem, Method, and Divisions.* — In relation to ordinary consciousness, philosophy is not a mere intellectual luxury, nor a thing appealing to mere curiosity, but an earnest and systematic attempt to discover a solution for "those riddles by which our mind is oppressed in life, and about which we are compelled to hold some view in order really to be able to live at all." In relation to the sciences, philosophy has the task of determining the "claims of the principles underlying the different sciences (*e. g.*, freedom and necessity underlying ethics and physics respectively), and the circuit within which they are valid, and to establish a universal view of the world possessing indubitable validity." Philosophy necessarily makes two presuppositions, *viz.*, that there is a universal object of cognition, or truth, and that we are in a condition to apprehend in some

---

[1] The following account is based on Professor Ladd's translation of Lotze's "Grundzüge" (Ginn & Co., Boston, publishers).

real way this object or truth. It has at the outset to meet doubt in three forms, — (1) that of wanton scepticism, (2) that of scepticism with a *motif*, (3) that implied in the so-called "criticism" of the faculties. Merely aimless scepticism can never be satisfied. Legitimate scepticism has to be dealt with in the regular course of the investigations of philosophy. "Criticism" is a superfluous and meaningless task, since the trustworthiness of the faculties must be assumed if the "criticism" shall have any validity. Such criticism, further, has to make certain presuppositions concerning the nature of things cognizable, of the cognizing spirit, and the kind of reciprocal action that takes place between them, etc. Philosophy has, then, to begin with confidence in reason, — with the principle "that all propositions which remain, after the correction of accidental errors, as always and universally necessary to thought, are put by us at the foundation of everything as confessedly true, that according to them must our views concerning the nature of things be determined, and from them alone must a theory of cognition be obtained." — Since we cannot assume ourselves to be already at the "centre of things, or to be able to divine the one principle from which all things are to be deduced," our *method* cannot be the ambitious *a priori* method; which is adapted to the purpose, not of discovery, but of exposition of the known. The search for truth must set out from many "points of attachment that lie near each other," and be limited only by the laws of thinking; it may employ in the freest manner all possible means, direct or indirect, of getting behind the truth. The most general problems of philosophy are the two problems of What exists? and What different values do we attach to the existent? Philosophy is, accordingly, theoretical and practical. Theoretical philosophy is philosophy of nature, philosophy of the soul, and metaphysics, the last of which is preliminary to the two former. Practical philosophy is æsthetics, which treats of the ideal as such, and ethics, which has to do with the ideal as a source of obligation or thing obligated. There is conceivable a science which should be preliminary to æsthetics and ethics, as metaphysics is to the philosophy of nature and the philosophy of the soul. A "common conclusion for both theoretical and practical investigations" is given in the philosophy of religion. Philosophy concludes with an unattainable ideal; it can never be such an "unchanging science" as to be able to deduce from one principle all its results in uniform sequence, but will always be separated into the three parts which have to do, respectively, with the universal and necessary laws of thought, the facts of reality, and the idea of the good and beautiful.

Metaphysics. — Metaphysics, which treats of the universal and necessary laws of thought, has the three parts Ontology (treating of being as such), Cosmology (treating of being in nature), and Phenomenology (treating of mind as such).

Ontology. — Ontology inquires (1) What is the absolute subject of being, the truly existent, the absolute supporter of properties? (2) How is the possibility of a variety of simultaneous and successive properties belonging to one and the same subject to be comprehended? (3) How can such a unity exist among a variety of things that the states of one become causes for alteration in the states of another? (1) Being appears at first blush as mere position, or affirmation of existence. But *pure* being is practically nothing. There must be properties in being, and simultaneously with it. Only logically is being primary, and its properties secondary. (It is, hence, an error to suppose a realm of pure, characterless being antecedent to the existent known world.) Properties united in being must be related. As being is not pure position, so it is not mere property, since property is property of something. Being is in reality the union of "position," on the one hand, with related properties, on the other. Being, that is to say, is concrete existence, a unity in multiplicity, and *vice versa*. From the side of its unity it is apprehended by us only in thought, and either as law (form), or as essence (matter), or, more properly, as the union of both, *viz.*, energy. Only as energy is it capable of producing effects or being affected, and hence real. As energy, being *is*: it is not subject to absolute becoming or decay; as energy (since energy is activity), it also *changes*, not losing its identity in change. (2) Being changes by passing into a "closed series" of forms, it being as a whole the totality, or sum, of the forms, each of which is but a state of the same abiding reality. Change is not antagonistic to being, but constitutes its life, prevents its collapsing into indistinguishable identity. (3) Every change has a cause or antecedent, which it has followed necessarily, or according to rule. It is incorrect to say that everything has but one cause. The effect which a causes never occurs without a relation, x, in which it stands to b, — *i. e.*, the effect depends upon b as well as a. The effect always has a twofold aspect, *viz.*, its content and its actuality. The content is explained by the content of the relation, x, between the conditions, a and b. The actuality must be explained from the fact of the relation. How can a and b be related, how act on one another? The ordinary explanation of such a case — *i. e.*, as a case of *causa transiens* — does not suffice: it is impossible to say what could pass from b to a, or how it could produce the effect in question. And even were these two things intelligible, we should be involved in the difficulty of the *regressus in infinitum*: b, to be able to act on a, must have been acted on by some other cause, and that by another, and so on indefinitely. The same is true of a considered as acting on b. To avoid this difficulty, and to provide for what is (wrongly) conceived as the action of absolutely independent beings upon one another, it is necessary to conceive all individuals as substantially one and the same; from the very beginning of things, as it were, they are only modifications of one individual Being (the Infinite, Absolute $= M$). Then a is only $M(x)$; $b = M(y)$. Every state α which takes place in a is likewise a state of M; and by means of this state M is necessitated, according to its own nature, to produce a succeeding state, β, which makes its appearance as a state of b, but which is in truth a state of M, by means of which its preceding modification, $M(y)$, is changed. Efficient causation, therefore, actually takes place, but takes place only *apparently* between the two finite beings as such. In truth, the absolute produces the effect upon itself, since by virtue of the unity and consistency of its own being it cannot be affected with the state with which it is affected as the being *a* without likewise being affected with the succeeding state, *b*, — a state which appears as an effect of *a* on *b*. "The manner in which it comes to pass that even within the one Infinite Being one state brings about another, remains wholly unexplained. How it is in general that causal action is produced in us, is as impossible as to tell how Being is made."

Cosmology. — Cosmology, as the theory of the external world in the abstract, treats of (1) space, (2) time, (3) motion, (4) matter and force, (5) the system of things. (1) Space is the (incomprehensible) possibility of the definite arrangement, relation, or form of things. It cannot be an external relation between things, since all relations are internal. It is a form of intuition rather than of things. But it is not a form set over against things and independent of them; the relations of space represent higher, non-spatial intellectual relations in or between things or their states. The reason for the apparent places of things is contained in their interior states as affecting the power of intuition. By means of the intuition of space things are arranged by us in thought according to the kind and magnitude of the effects they exercise upon us as percipient beings. Whether space be a merely human form of intuition is uncertain. (2) *Time*, like space, is an intuition, but, unlike space, it is not an *immediate* intuition. We obtain the intuition of time by the help of that of space, though at the same time in opposition to it; when we conceive of a line in space, the points of which exist together in like fashion, we gain from it a complete intuitive picture applicable to precisely the opposite case of time, whose line consists of points of which one exists only when the other does not exist. Time as objective would have no meaning, since it could in no way affect the causal activity of things. The objection advanced against the mere ideality of time, that "thought" itself occurs in time, is without weight if it be seen that we should never have a mental representation of that which is successive if our thought or representation were in itself *purely* successive. (3) *Motion* is not a "passing" through "objective" space; though it is a change of place which is merely a change of position in ideal space due to change of relations between non-spatial elements. In changing its place, a thing necessarily passes through all places intermediate between the two points from the one to the other of which it moves. The "law of inertia" is undoubtedly a true law, but it is not susceptible of metaphysical deduction. (4) *Matter* consists of a multiplicity " of real beings, each of which is of a supersensible nature and unextended, and all of which, by means of influences acting at a distance, prescribe to one another the reciprocal position that belongs to each as a spatial expression for all its intellectual relations to all the rest." It does not, therefore, continuously fill space, but consists of distinct elements between which there are intervals, — where nothing real is to be found. Nearness or remoteness of distance does not as such have anything to do with the magnitude of the reciprocal reaction of the parts of matter. By virtue of the reciprocal reactions of its (dynamical) elements or constituents, matter has extension, form, cohesiveness, and force of resistance. (5) All contents of the one Being must together form a coherent system. In this system are involved a plan, certain occurrences, and a law of occurrences. The plan of the whole can originate only with a single Being possessing a faculty for actions, the production of which depends on a regard for an end that does not yet exist, but is impending, — a Being able to accommodate itself to changing circumstances with a changing activity for definite ends. It is, then, necessary to suppose (1) that this Being experiences some influences in general from changing circumstances, and, besides, that the influences be changeable and proportional to the variety of the circumstances; (2) that this influence on the Being itself begets a reaction which is adjusted not merely with reference to it, but with reference to its relation to the final purpose. This Being must act unconsciously or consciously. In the former case it must respond to stimuli, — act mechanically merely. . But in either case there must be no arbitrariness whatever as to the actualization of the plan, since what accords with the purpose at any instant must be discovered by a comparison of the purposes with the circumstances of the instant. The Idea of the whole can be actualized only by means of mechanism. Determinism is just as truly the *result* of metaphysical cosmology as it is the *presupposition* of merely explanatory natural science.

Phenomenology. — Knowledge, as being the product of two factors, is not a copy or representation of either; it is merely formal. But though formal, it is in a sense true, since (1) it could not be otherwise than it is, and there is a general agreement in the knowledges of individuals, — knowledge forms a system; (2) our idea of all being is derived from what we know of conscious beings or beings whose characteristic it is to know; the highest, truest reality is spiritual or self-knowing being. Only such being is a true subject of properties and states, or unites the many truly into a unity; only such being is cause in the true sense, only such being being-for-self. The ordinary conception of cognition is a mere prejudice. "In science one act of representation serves in every case the purpose of ascertaining a matter of fact; but in the totality of the world it has another position. The mental representation is not designed to copy things, which, because they have no power of representation, are inferior to spirit; but things (in so far as this name has any meaning left at all) exist *besides*, in order to produce by their influence that course of mental representations belonging to the spiritual being, which accordingly has its value in itself considered, and its own peculiar content, and not in accord with an objective matter of fact." Genuine reality, the substance and end of all things, consists alone in the Highest Good Personal. The substantial ground of the world is a spirit whose essence our cognition is able to designate only as the living and existent God. "All that is finite is action of this Infinite: 'real beings' are those of his actions which the Infinite permanently maintains as centres of out-and-ingoing effects that are capable of acting and being affected; their reality consists, not in a being outside God (for such a being no definition could make clear), but only in this that they as spiritual elements have being-for-themselves. What we are accustomed to call things and 'events between things' is the sum of those other actions which the Highest Principle variously executes in all other spirits so uniformly and in such coherency according to law that these spirits must appear to be one world of substantial and efficient things existing in a space outside themselves. The meaning of the general law according to which the Infinite proceeds in the creation, preservation, and government of the apparent world of things, is to be found in their being consequences of the idea of the Good, which is its own nature."

Philosophy of Nature. — A general systematic treatment of the philosophy of nature (as distinguished from cosmology), the second grand division of theoretical philosophy, was not undertaken by Lotze. A few points may be noted. The underlying conceptions, space, time, motion, matter and force, etc., belong to cosmology. The idea of the Highest Good, though the "one real principle on which the validity of the metaphysical axioms in the world depends, cannot," according to Lotze, "profitably be converted into a major premise from which to deduce the sum of metaphysical truth;" and much less, therefore, can it be the sole guiding principle of a philosophy of nature as such, since nature is a mere mechanism. The fundamental distinction in nature, that between animate and inanimate existence, is one entirely dependent on the difference of mechanical arrangement of points of attack of forces which are the same for both kinds of existence. In animate existence, the organism, the points of attack, have such definiteness in themselves and their relations to one another that a previously arranged series of developments must follow from them. The organism, as compared with a machine constructed by art, is subject not only to purely mechanical laws, but also to chemical laws governing the transformation of the separate parts of the machine. As the result of its peculiar character as a machine merely, the organism has a power of self-preservation and self-determination which does not belong to inorganic being. A radical distinction of organisms into animals and plants is perhaps impossible. The conception of a graduated simple series of types has only a limited application in nature. It is certain, however, that man is the highest among living beings.

Philosophy of the Soul, or Psychology. — Psychology has two main problems, — (1) Under what conditions and by what forces do the processes of spiritual life originate? (2) How do they combine with and modify each other, and by such co-operation bring to pass the whole spiritual life? The former gives rise to descriptive or empirical, and explanatory, mechanical, or metaphysical, psychology; the latter to speculative psychology.

Empirical Psychology. — In the first branch of the subject Lotze treats of (1) sensations, (2) the course of ideas, (3) relative knowledge and attention, (4) intuitions of space, (5) the feelings, (6) will and bodily motions. We can only note a few of the principal points made in his very suggestive treatment of these topics: (1) Things are objects of perception, not by virtue of their mere existence, but because of effects they work in us. All efforts to demonstrate how it comes about that merely physical motion passes into sensation are wholly vain. No absolute laws can be laid down of the relations between motions and sensations. Sensations are wholly subjective: "they have only one place, one way how and where they can by any possibility exist, *viz.*, in the consciousness of a soul, and of course only at the moment when they are experienced by the soul." (2) The disappearance of ideas from, and their reappearance in, consciousness (in memory), cannot be satisfactorily explained by the mechanical notions of mere force and intensity of the ideas. Ideas disappear from and reappear in consciousness because there is a soul which, stimulated by them, reacts upon them in a manner according to its own inherent nature. It is impossible to frame a definite mechanical theory of why a definite idea which has been associated with numerous others returns into consciousness. (3) New ideas of a higher order, and general notions, are not mere mechanical resultants of the combination and reciprocal action of original, simple, sensible ideas alone, — as a force in mechanics may be a resultant of two or more combined forces, but are creations of the "entire peculiar and monadic structure of an ideating subject reacting to the stimulus of impressions upon it." Attention is not mere "intensity" of idea, but an act of a relating and comparing faculty. (4) Objects are localized in space through the idea of space and by means of different ideas of relation excited in us by different impressions produced upon us through sense. Every impression (say) of the color red produces in all places of the retina which it reaches, the same sensation, redness. In addition, it produces an accessory impression a, β, or γ, etc., dependent merely on the nature of the place excited. These accessory impressions become means, when associated with other impressions, of localizing those others, or '*local signs*' for such impressions. The two factors of this process of localization of impressions are a series of definite impressions and a definite relating activity of the soul. (5) The feelings, or states of pleasure and pain, as distinguished from sensations, or indefinite perceptions of a certain content, are the results of relations acting as stimuli on the entire nature of the soul. They probably are tokens of an agreement or disagreement between the excitation produced in us and the condition of our permanent well-being. Feelings of sense relate to our individual and personal well-being; the æsthetic feelings — including the ethical — relate to the universal spirit in us. The conditions of feeling are not well known. The feelings have the closest relation with individual self-consciousness, or that which distinguishes the psychological "mine" and "thine." "That which is my state announces itself in a manner wholly immediate, and admitting of no further deduction, — as something in itself altogether special; as something, that is to say, which is distinguished from that which is not my state, not merely as this state foreign to me is from a third, but in such manner that we have ample reason for separating this state of our own from all that occurs in the world, by an incomparable distinction. This is all done by feeling. A spirit that should penetrate everything, but have no interest of a pleasurable or painful sort in anything, would neither be capable of opposing itself as an ego to the rest of the world, nor would it have any inducement to do so." (6) Will is the source of motion only in case it harmonize with an "order of nature" independent of it through which the motion is actualized; otherwise it is merely a futile wish. We know nothing of the relation of will to the order of nature. Action is voluntary in case the interior state from which a motion would result is appropriated or adapted by the will, no matter how it be externalized.

Speculative Psychology. — Speculative psychology treats of (1) the soul in itself; (2) the interaction of body and soul; (3) the seat of the soul; (4) the time-relations of the soul; (5) the essence of the soul; (6) the changeable states of the soul; (7) the realm of souls. (1) The origin of a spiritual condition is never analytically comprehensible even from all possible combinations of physical conditions, or even so-called psycho-physical conditions.

Atoms, whether merely physical or endowed with psychical force, can at most be only stimuli calling forth the original and unique activity of the undivided and indivisible unity, which is the soul. (2) As has been demonstrated by the metaphysics, there is no direct interaction of any two independent elements in the universe; hence body and soul, as such, do not interact. But there is no *special* mystery here, — no more (nor less) mystery than hangs over the interaction of the parts of any visible machine. Body and soul are by and through the *general order* of nature in continual and complete reciprocity. (3) As shown by physiological experiment, the soul stands in *immediate* reciprocity only with the central organs of the nervous system. It is not to be located in any particular space on account of this reciprocity. Whatever the physical (nervous) processes microscopic analysis may succeed in showing it to be related to, these must be regarded as merely spatial forms under which present themselves to us certain immaterial forces that act upon the single immaterial agent as stimuli calling forth its spontaneous energy. (4) The *temporal* origin of each soul must be conceived as one with the germ of some organic being, the origination of the germ providing the incitement or moving reason, which induces the all-comprehending One Being to beget from himself a supplementing soul for the organism. Dogmatic opinions as to the immortality of the soul cannot properly be held. The soul can continue so long only as it is a necessary part of the universal system of things. Further than this nothing can certainly be known. (5) The soul can be conceived rightly neither as a "thing," nor as a bundle of perceptions, nor as a pure characterless simple activity producing faculties in reaction to stimuli. It is essentially a relating activity, determining its own content and character with the aid of stimuli from without. (6) While the soul is greatly affected in its states by the stimuli of bodily conditions, — such as sleep, disease, temperament, etc. — there are higher states of it answering to no bodily conditions whatever. (7) There is soul in all things; but only in the animal kingdom is there a regular gradation of soul-life. A distinctive attribute of the human soul is reason, or the "capacity for perceiving eternal verities immediately *per se*, as soon as external experiences have furnished consciousness with the matter of fact about which these verities have to express a judgment, — principally one of moral approbation or disapprobation." The principles of conscience have to be regarded as reactions of the original nature of the spirit, which are not explicable alone by the external stimuli calling them forth. Will also is a distinguishing attribute of man. "Choice, or the adoption of a decision that proceeds from the personal ego, is — however impossible it may be to comprehend it — a process in our inner life that is given us as a fact and is completely explicable by no mechanism of ideas. *Psychology*, however, does not *demonstrate* the *freedom of the will;* as, on the other hand, it cannot interpose any objection if there are reasons outside its own sphere for the freedom of the will.

Practical Philosophy. — Practical Philosophy, or the philosophy of the ideal, has, as we have seen (above, page 175), two branches, — Ethics and Æsthetics.

Ethics: Introduction. — *Problems and Divisions of Ethics.* — Ethics (or "Practical Philosophy" in the narrower sense) has the "task of investigating rules, according to which praiseworthiness or blameworthiness of disposition is estimated, and also the rules of that prudence of life which secures the acquisition of the different forms of outward good." Since satisfaction is found primarily in that inward good of self-approbation, moral problems, as such, here take the first rank. There are two main problems of Practical Philosophy in the narrower sense, *viz.*, (1) the investigation of the "maxims, by the observance of which our conduct acquires an approbation that is independent of all consequences;" (2) the "discovery of those forms of life, by means of which the greatest amount of external good can be realized in agreement with these laws, and at the same time with respect to the definite relations of the earthly life of man."

The Maxims of Conduct. — Here have to be discussed: (1) Ethical method and principles; (2) Simple ethical ideals; (3) The freedom of the will. (1) The method of ethics cannot be the *a priori* one of attempting to deduce practical rules from the nature of things in general, or of ourselves, for these we do not know. To be of practical value, the fundamental ethical rules must be immediately obvious and certain to the commonest individual, — there must be a voice of *conscience*, which gives direction in particular crises concerning the praiseworthiness or blameworthiness of actions. The law of conduct can be found neither in the principle of eudæmonism, or the doctrine of mere pleasure, nor in (Kantian) rigorism, which denies all validity to pain and pleasure as moral agencies. Pleasure is contingent and uncertain; the pure intellect is abstract and empty in an ethical regard. (2) In default of a discoverable abstract rule of conduct, we have to content ourselves with constructing a "series of occasions, on which we remind ourselves of the utterances of conscience." Such occasions are the moral ideals. These are (*a*) sensibility of mind to motives, — including intensity, many-sidedness, and proportionableness of feeling to the value of that which excites it;" (*b*) resignation, energy, conscientiousness, — which are conditions of soul relative to the realization of motives; (*c*) piety ("which considerately allows every natural product and every natural event, which occupies or appears to occupy a place in the plan of the whole to which it is entitled, to be undisturbed, and develop itself, and even assists the development of such product"), justice, retribution; (*d*) personality (including consistency), holiness (or moral habit, raising conduct above the level of momentary impulse), character ("it being positively *not* a moral command that one person shall be and act precisely as another," as rigorism implies).

The foregoing ideals possess different degrees of value: those of the first group are gifts of nature, not to be manufactured at will; those of the second correspond to the agreeable feeling without which moral conduct does not exist, but which does not constitute morality of conduct; those of the third group are ideals which excite unconditioned approbation, though the statement applies in a *strict* sense only to benevolence, since blind, unfeeling justice and retribution are not ethical. — "There is such a thing as moral conduct only on the assumption that this conduct leads to pleasure and pain. But to this, conscience joins the further truth that it is not the effort after our own, but only that for another's felicity, which is ethically meritorious, and that accordingly the idea of Benevolence must give us the sole principle of moral conduct."

Determinism. — In itself Determinism is consistent and irrefutable; it merely contradicts the inexpugnable dictum of consciousness that we are free, and the fact of regret and repentance. The real proof of freedom is the practical possession and exercise of it. Freedom can exist truly, however, only if there be a widely extended prevalence of law, since action could not be really free if the consequences of it could not be calculated beforehand. It is not, finally, freedom itself, but the action of which freedom is a *sine qua non* that is the object of moral judgment.

The Forms and Relations of the Realization of External Good. — It would be an idle attempt to undertake to deduce *a priori* the ethical forms, — individual, family, society, etc.; the relations, — duties, rights, and virtues; since the forms are changing historical products, and the relations depend on concrete circumstances. We have to consider in this Second Part (1) the individual person; (2) marriage and the family; (3) the intercourse of men; (4) society; (5) the State. (1) The individual exists in a moral capacity only in so far as he *acts* and is *benevolent.* All mere contemplation and all mere asceticism (which only conducts to the "impoverishing of life and hinders the origination of innumerable good things of beauty ") are anti-moral, permissible only as momentary forms of life, which endeavor to make what experiences are here had useful for subsequent life and for other persons." The individual, as such, has no rights; he has rights only as a member of society, and only to the extent to which the latter feels itself obligated to concede to him the exercise of his natural capacities. (2) The chief element in marriage, as a moral institution, is a relation of mutual respect between man and woman as personalities. Monogamy, as allowing freer scope for this respect than any other form of union, is the highest sort of marriage,— alone corresponds to the ethical ideal. How far society may recognize dissolution wished for by the partners in marriage is doubtful. (3) The family does not teach the conception of universal right. This has to be learned by general intercourse with persons. The original, self-evident right in this intercourse is freedom,— the free use of one's powers and free choice of ends to which they shall be directed. This right has its restrictions, but cannot be entirely destroyed. From it flow the rights of property and inheritance. The chief part of intercourse is in the communication of ideas. Here the fundamental demand is to speak the truth, — in case one has the right and duty to utter anything. Lying, even though there may be practical justification for it, always involves a certain shame to personality. On veracity all contracts are based. (4) Society is a "multiplicity of living individuals who are united for the common fulfilment of their aims in life." Though in reality society exists only under political conditions, the fact of commerce proves that a trustworthy union of men for comprehensive aims is possible without any political form. The first duty of society is not any positive regulation, but the removal of all hindrance to individual freedom. The State's right of punishment rests ultimately on the right of the individual to satisfy injured feelings or a sense of personal injustice suffered, by an act of vengeance, *i. e.*, on the nature of man as a subject of feeling. "The tempering of the natural impulse to vengeance seems to be the sole right under which a power of punishment belongs to society." No society has the right to inflict as punishment the penalty of death or life-imprisonment, — *i. e.*, to deprive the individual wholly of liberty. The positive task of society is the supplementing of the power of the individual by that of other individuals. Desirable as a form of society would appear to be a limited socialism. (5) Society becomes the State through the possession of a fixed territory as productive capital and historical home, of like endowments, common speech, common tradition, common feeling of historical continuity with past and future. Historical continuity is preserved through the (hereditary) magistracy. The form of State corresponds to the natural life of the people. A democracy approaches most nearly the conception of a mere society. The essence of the monarchy lies in the fact that authority is in it inherited. The best form of constitution is one alterable to suit circumstances of political life and growth. Three formal conditions, without which a constitution is scarcely conceivable, are: free communication of thought, right of assembly, right of petition. A precondition to the employment of these conditions is the existence of political parties. In a representative government two assemblies are necessary. The theory of universal citizenship is theoretically correct; practically it is dangerous. Except for the highest offices, there should be a legally prescribed preparation for office-holding. The phrase "right of revolution" is self-contradictory; revolution is outside the pale of right. Revolutions simply happen or are political accidents, and can be judged only according to their results.

Æsthetics. — Æsthetics treats of the ideal in art. It has the two parts, — (1) Beauty (and Fancy) as such; (2) The Actualization of the Beautiful and its Kinds.

Beauty and Fancy. — The beautiful is that, the impression of which harmonizes with our universal nature, — the agreeable being that which excites pleasure in our particular nature. The beautiful is apprehended neither as percept nor as concept, but as the union of the two, *viz.*, the Idea. Beauty is the "appearance to immediate intuition of a unity of substance and forces under law in a plan whereby a definite end is realized." Beauty belongs, strictly speaking, only to that which is moved; and primarily to the creative soul of the world. "Individual objects would either be beautiful through their bearing in themselves an active principle, such as the world-soul is to its totality, or else they are beautiful through their reminding us by the form of their combination of realities that are products of the world-soul in the same forms. It is due to the first reason that the living organism appears to us as the most direct exhibition of beauty, and to the second that we endeavor to apprehend every possible work of art as an organism, in order to be able to point out its beauty in like manner." Beauty is the manifestation in the finite of that harmony of the ideal and the real which the idea of Happiness as the world's end implies. As Happiness is possible only in beings with soul, the highest objective beauty will always be found in that form which has a soul. Beauty is not so much the outward form as every blissful self-enjoyment, such as presumably belongs to the totality of the world. The source of all beauty in the soul's creative world is the fancy, which not only combines given manifold materials, but feels their true value for the soul that enjoys them.

The Actualization of the Beautiful, and its Kinds. — We have to consider here (1) the domains and varieties of beauty and the individual arts; (2) music; (3) architecture; (4) plastic art; (5) painting; (6) the poetic art. (1) The domains of reality in which beauty manifests itself are (*a*) the universal forms of space, time, and motion; (*b*) the definite typical species of individual and actual beings; (*c*) the world of events. The harmony of the three elements of law, individual (substance or force), and plan in the relations of space, time, and motion, is free beauty; in those of type and actual beings (where beauty is not found in the abstract universal, but in what is characteristic rather), "characteristic beauty," which may include "free beauty;" in the world of events (where "beauty" lies in the concord between the free characteristic activity of the manifold living being and the universal laws of the environing world-plan) the "beauty of grace," including sublimity. "The supreme beauty of events will accordingly consist in the solemn sublimity in which the force that negates the individual as well as the other that is infinitely creative, appears as the peculiar life-likeness of a purpose valuable and sacred." Now, the reproduction of the forms of the beautiful apprehended by fancy constitutes art. This reproduction takes the form of a concentrating of elements which in actuality are separated by space and time, and so representing the totality of what is actual. Art has to fulfil the three conditions of pleasing the senses (physiological conditions), of satisfying all the general laws which control the course of our ideas, feelings, and acts of will (psychological conditions), of satisfying a well-considered view of the content, connection, and value of the world. (2) Music is peculiarly adapted to expressing the inner life of spirit. Mere law appears in music as measure; individuality and "life-likeness," as melody; end and plan, by the coincidence of melody with a harmonious accompaniment. Music expresses the universal force of things. (3) Architecture is defined by its aim in only a very general manner. Only a structure in which the lines of force, taken in relation to one another, secure the impression of an organic system of co-operating activities, falls within the domain of architecture. Law is manifested in architecture as gravity; individuality in "style," or the mode of transition from one element to another, or from support to load; plan in the "plan" of the building, in which is effected the concentrating of the most manifold number of vital elements into a single organism that is the summary of them all. Greek architecture is a perfect solution of a very limited architectural problem. Roman architecture (with its arch), combined with the Greek style, produced a powerful and impressive, though inorganic, whole. The Byzantine style is picturesque rather than truly architectural. In the Gothic style is secured the impression of a freely and actively aspiring force, yet scarcely a struggle of this force with a load foreign to itself. (4) The problem of sculpture is to represent spirituality interpenetrating its corporal organization, and this in such a way that the body does not simply obey a single impulse of the spirit in a merely passive way, but appears in its whole structure as a perfect expression for the totality of this individual spiritual life. Its highest aim is the delineation of ideal character. It finds its best scope in ancient mythology. (5) Painting represents actual life in its fulness, — not merely the scanty meaning of a single action, but also the echoes it awakens in the world, the way in which it is experienced by others, etc. Painting is either landscape-painting, genre-painting, historical painting, or historiographical painting (which treats of legends, stories, etc.). (6) The peculiar (though not the sole) province of poetry is the world of events in their inner connection: the "kernel of poetry lies in the representation of motion which ceaselessly combines with one another the parts of the world according to general laws and according to a sacred plan." Poetry has no didactic function; on the other hand, it does not by capricious representation violate the sacredness of the actual world. Poetry is narrative (including the epic and the romance), lyric, dramatic. Narrative poetry corresponds to an elevated and cheerful expansion of mind. Lyric poetry has for its end the opening a perspective from the mind's immediate mood out into a general view of the world. Dramatic poetry has the end of "showing that it is the general metaphysical weakness of every finite nature to come to harm as soon as it deems itself capable of playing the part of Providence and of laying hold on the coherent system of the world's course as a formative and guiding principle."

The Philosophy of Religion. — The concluding part of the entire system, and the union, in a sense, of the foregoing parts, is the philosophy of religion. Here have to be treated (1) the problem of the philosophy of religion; (2) the proofs of the existence of God; (3) the precise character of the absolute; (4) the metaphysical attributes of God; (5) the personality of God; (6) the conception of creation; (7) the preservation of the world; (8) the government of the world; (9) the conception of the world-aim; (10) religion and morality; (11) dogmas and confessions. (1) The *primary problem* of the philosophy of religion is the ascertainment of how much of the content of religion may be discovered, proved, or at least confirmed, agreeably to reason. The philosophical apprehension of religious truth, as distinguished from an act of mere "faith" (which is often asserted to be the organ of religious truth), and from the having of certain modes of subjective affection, or experience, or feeling, is an elaboration in thought of certain inner experiences taken as mere data of knowledge. Such inner experiences are: (*a*) the personal feelings of fear and absolute dependence on unknown powers; (*b*) æsthetic feelings, accompanied by the conviction that the beauty of the world cannot be a mere accidental product, but must be either the very principle of the world, or closely related to its creative principle; (*c*) ethical feelings which necessitate the attempt to conceive of a construction of the world in which the fact of the moral obligation of the will to a definite form of action finds an intelligible and rational place. (2) "Proofs" of the existence of God cannot demonstrate the existence of God as *necessary*, — *i. e.*, as depending on something else; they merely demonstrate our assumption of this existence as a logically necessary consequence of the given facts of the world. The ontological proof is chiefly important as expressing unconsciously the conviction that perfection cannot be homeless in the world or the realm of actuality, but has the best possible claim to be regarded by us as an imperishable reality.

This conviction, which has really no need of proof, has sought to formulate itself after a Scholastic fashion in this proof. Immanent conformity to end (the kernel of the "teleological proof" of God's existence) proves rather that the original nature of the elements and of their general laws of action include from the first *within themselves* the very ground capable of developing that which has "value," or which is an end in itself, than that things are the result of intelligent design. A "simpler datum" than the world's conformity to end, and a "more modest" conclusion than that of the existence of God, must form the starting-point of philosophizing on this point of the existence of God. The datum is that of universal reciprocity, whence it follows that an occurrence in one part of the All is (by virtue of the identity of the All) *eo ipso* a definite change in some other portion (see "Metaphysics," above, page 177). (3) Pure materialism, dualistic monism (*e. g.*, of Spinoza and Schelling), the doctrine of the "Unconscious," or of the Absolute, as blind force, have no real philosophical basis. The "theory of the Unconscious" wrongly appeals to the fact of the unconscious activity of genius. We really *know* of unconscious intelligence only as existing in that, the nature of which is to be self-conscious. The view (further) that conscious personal spirit originates by a process of development from unconscious impersonal spirit, that God *comes* to consciousness in himself or in finite spirit, has no religious bearing. (4) The religious nature demands an unchanging but living God. Metaphysics goes towards meeting the demand in so far as it conceives substance, not as a fixed, rigid self-identity, but as activity passing through a series of states that cohere according to one and the same formula. The "omnipresence" of God is metaphysically conceived as a being everywhere alike immediately and perfectly present, without difference of degree, his activity not being propagated by intermediate substance, nor diminishing with increase of distance. Omnipotence belongs to God as the immediate source and content of all being. The aphorisms, "God can do all things possible," "God can make impossible actual," are inadequate expressions of God's omnipotence in so far as they subject him to a sphere of conditions antecedent to himself, who is the reason of both the possible and impossible, as well as the actual. "Eternity" in God is perfect independence of temporal conditions. The religious nature seeks a personal God. To such a being the metaphysical doctrine of substance points, since the most perfect realization of the notion of substance is given in self-conscious spirit (which alone is the perfect unity of a manifold, — see above, page 180), although indeed it is somewhat more than substance. (5) If we conceive personality as, in essence, the feeling of self, which is rooted in the feelings of pleasure and pain (see above, "Psychology," page 184), we cannot think of it as having had a material origin, but as eternal, as not something which it were barely possible to *imagine*, but something which is necessarily imagined as eternally and unceasingly actual; the idea of perfect personality is, in short, reconcilable only with the conception of an infinite Being. (6) Religion assumes that the world is a product of a creative will. This will cannot be conceived as temporal in its action. The will to create is an absolutely eternal predicate of God. Creation is not so much a deed as a continued activity; it is the immediate realization of what is willed. The divine will is not, like the human, dependent on an external order of nature (since if it were, it would not be divine). The order of nature cannot be distinguished from God as it is from ourselves. The common religious notion of "a creation from nothing" is, of course, erroneous, since there is nothing antecedent to God's creative will. He is, indeed, subject to no external conditions whatever, — not even so-called eternal truths or laws. (7) Of the three views, that God created the world and left it to itself; that the world was not created and needs no support; that preservation is new creation (and *vice versa*), — only the latter (rightly understood) is religiously or metaphysically justifiable. The forces of nature act constantly and uniformly according to the same laws, not because these forces are in themselves eternal, and those laws in themselves efficient, but because it lies within the plan of the divine efficiency to employ at each instant of the course of the world this number of homogeneous actions as a means for the production of more composite results. By the "new creation" of the world it cannot, of course, be understood that the world at a given instant is as to its content entirely other than at the instant preceding. (8) We can speak of the "government of the world" by God only in so far as the world is independent of him; and "government" would then consist in the exercising of an influence not already included in the order of nature. The miracle (for such an influence would be a "miracle") involves no alteration whatever of the laws of nature, but only the change of one or more magnitudes to which these laws are applied; and such a change of the natures of single elements is just as thinkable as a change accomplished by a physical force. Divine intervention could not relate to the order of nature as such, but to spiritual individuals in nature, and would consist in supplying their activity with inducements or incentives which the external course of nature could not offer them. We may avoid the mere subjectivism of rationalism by including among these inducements such phenomena as religious visions. It is impossible to determine the limits of the application of the conception of miracle. (9) The conception of a world-end cannot be speculatively deduced. Admitting the conception, we find nothing answering to it except happiness,— the thing of supreme value. Happiness does not afford a direct explanation of the existence of the inanimate world, and does not harmonize with the existence of evil. But the existence of evil is not speculatively explicable; optimism and the pedagogical view of it fail to explain it. Happiness, notwithstanding the existence of evil, remains as an ideal, the gradual realization of which is the task of religion. Religion in this sense is, it is true, "never exactly a demonstrable theorem; but the conviction of its truth is a *deed* that may be accredited to character." (10) The religious view of the world receives a certain support from the ethical, although it is not identical with it, since a pure, unconditioned *ought*, or a law to which actuality in nowise corresponds, and which no person, or being subject to feelings of pleasure and pain, could obey, does not completely harmonize with the religious conception of worth or value. Religiously speaking, there is nothing commendable in Stoic ataraxy in and of itself. There are three convictions characteristic of religious apprehension: (*a*) Ethical laws are the will of God; (*b*) individual finite spirits are not products of nature, but children of God; (*c*) actuality is not a mere course of the world, but a kingdom of God. (11) These three convictions form the entire content of the Christian revelation. The Church represents our community with others in this religion; dogmas are mere symbols of it, — no more (and no less) symbols than "atoms" in physical science. The doctrines of the "Trinity," "satisfaction" through a sacrificial death, original sin, etc., are not speculatively justifiable, and possess, in themselves considered, no value for the religious life. On the subject of immortality and future retribution there is nothing concrete to offer. The visible Church is a human institution. It is an evil that the State exists without religious foundation and believes that it has no need of any. The religious life should be left by the State to unfold itself according to the maxim, *In necessariis unitas, in dubiis libertas, in omnibus caritas.*

Result. — The system of Lotze is, on the face of it, an ethical (not simply *moral*) ideal-realism. But the fact that in its metaphysics and its psychology it conceives activity too much as the consequence of mechanical stimulation, that in its psychology, practical philosophy, and philosophy of religion so much is made to depend on the mere *feeling or sensation* of self (as if personality were constituted by mere sensation), that in its practical philosophy it is so shy of logical principles,—make its ethicality wanting in positiveness and almost a mere æstheticality. But art is at least a second "remove" from, as Plato would say, the "king and truth." The system of Lotze probably unites a larger number of elements of philosophical truth than any other of the systems of the most recent sub-period of modern philosophy.

§ 149.

(4) *Italian Systems*.— Italian systems, mostly intuitionalistic, are largely eclectic in their make-up. They show in particular the marks of Scotch and German influence. We take up those of Melchiore Gioja, Domenico Romagnosi (empirical realists); Pasquale Galuppi, Antonio Rosmini-Serbati, Vincenzo Gioberti, Terenzio Mamiani (idealists); Giuseppe Ferrari, Ansonio Franchi (sceptics).

§ 150.

Melchiore Gioja (1767-1828). — Gioja, educated at the College of St. Lazare, in his native town of Piacenza, and at the University of Pavia, was at one time government historiographer and statistician. His life was largely devoted to the cause of republicanism in Italy. In his chief work, "Del Merito e delle Recompense," he sets forth a theory of social ethics. Besides this work may be mentioned "Filosofia della Statistica" (1828), and his "Nuovo della Scienze Economiche" (1815-1817), in which he appears as an opponent of Adam Smith. In ethics Gioja is a follower of Bentham; in psychology he follows Condillac; in logic or method, Bacon, the foundation of science being with him statistics.

§ 151.

Giovanni Domenico Romagnosi (1761-1835).— Romagnosi took the degree of doctor of civil and canon law in the University of Parma, was at different times prætor of Trent, general secretary of the minister of public justice, professor of public law in Parma, Milan, and Pavia, and professor in the University of Corfu. He is generally recognized as one of the great theoretical reformers of penal law in Europe in the present century. Among his numerous works occur the following: " Che cosa è la Mente Sana" ("What is the Sound Mind?"), (1827); "La Suprema Economia dell' Umano Sapere" (1828); " Vedute [Views] fundamentali sull' Arte Logica" (1842); " Della Genesi del Diritto [Law] Penale" (1791); " Introduzzione allo Studio del Diritto Publico Universale" (1805). With Romagnosi, knowledge depends on a harmony between the human facilities and nature. It has to do only with phenomena, and is a product of experience and reason. Rights are natural in their origin, and inalienable and immutable.

§ 152.

Pasquale Galuppi (1770-1846). — Galuppi took a course in jurisprudence in the University of Naples. Instead of practising law he entered into the employ of the financial department of the Government, following at the same time, to a certain extent, his bent towards scientific and philosophical pursuits. At the age of sixty he was appointed to the chair of logic and metaphysics in the University of Naples, which he occupied until his death.

Works. — Works of Galuppi are : " Sull' Analisa e sulla Sintesi" (1807); " Saggio [Essay] filosofico sulla Critica della Conoscenza [Knowledge]" (1819-1832); " Lettere filosofiche sulle Vicende della Filosofia relativamente ai Principii della Conoscenza Umana de Cartesio sino a Kant inclusivamente" (2d ed., 1838); " Elementi di Filosofia" (1832); " Introduzzione allo Studio della Filosofia per Uso dei Fanciulli [Beginners]" (1832); " Lezioni di Logica et di Metafisica" (1832-1833); " Filosofia della Volontà" (1832-1840); " Considerazione filosofiche sull' Idealismo transcendentale et sul Razionalismo assoluto" (1841).

Philosophy. — Repelled by the doctrines of Condillac, Galuppi found in those of Reid, and then those of Kant, the truth he sought. But he would have Reid supplemented by the making of knowledge a function of reason instead of mere "suggestion," or "instinct;" and Kant, by the making of consciousness both subjective and objective, since to feel, perceive, or will is to feel, perceive, or will something, — ego (as Fichte says) posits immediately the non-ego. We even possess a knowledge of the absolute, since the absolute is implied in the conditioned. Upon these and other psychological facts metaphysics has its basis. We find in our free will and our idea of anything beginning to exist a necessary relation to something exterior, — a relation of causality. The relation of finality or intelligent causality is, likewise, implied in the perception of an order among facts: the existence of God is demonstrated by the experimental method. Formally regarded, all knowledge is analytic; our general ideas all originate from comparison and abstraction conducted according to the law of identity, — the only law of thinking. Galuppi accepts substantially the Kantian view in ethics. Practical philosophy includes, besides ethics, natural theology, the problems of which are those of the nature of a divine creator, the moral law, and the immortality of the soul. Philosophy needs to be supplemented by revelation.

Result. — Galuppi appears to be the real initiator in Italy of the Third Period of Modern Philosophy as it has been characterized above (vol. i. p. 268). As appears immediately from our account, he holds a position in thought intermediate between the empirico-intuitionalism of Reid and the rationalism of Kant.

§ 153.

Antonio Rosmini-Serbati[1] (1797–1855). — Rosmini, of a wealthy and cultured family, had afforded him, it would

[1] See translation of "Sistema Filosophico," by Thomas Davidson, with Introduction, Notes, etc.

seem, every condition necessary to the gaining of learning and culture. Precocious and studious, he soon distinguished himself in his studies. On finishing his gymnasial course, he studied mathematics and philosophy two years at his home, and took a theological course at Padua; later he spent several years in philosophical reading and reflection, gaining a very extensive and thorough acquaintance with the great philosophical systems; and still later lived, as anchorite, in solititude and contemplation. In a practical regard, he appears as the founder of a new institution for training teachers and priests, — a new religious order, now known as the order of Rosminians; he labored for ecclesiastico-political reform in Italy, suffering persecution at the hands of political and ecclesiastical enemies; he was once member of the ministry at Rome, declining a nomination as president of the ministry. He is spoken of by a competent judge as a "saint (as well as a thinker) of the very first order."

Works. — Of his numerous (ninety-nine) works, the following are among the more important in philosophy: "Sistema Filosofico" ("Philosophical System"), (1850), (Introductory); "Nuovo Saggio sull' Origine delle Idee" ("New Essay on the Origin of Ideas"), (1830), (Ideological); "Il Rinnovamento della Filosofia in Italia" ("The Restoration of Philosophy in Italy"), (1843), (supplementary to the "Nuovo Saggio"); "Logica" (1854); "Psicologia" (1850); "Principi della Scienza Morale" (1831); "Antropologia in Servigio della Scienza Morale" ("Anthropology in Aid of Moral Science"), (1838); "Teosofia" (posthumous). The masterpiece is probably the "Nuovo Saggio."

Philosophy: Introduction. — Philosophy is the science of ultimate grounds. Ultimate grounds being absolute and relative, philosophy is general, and special (*e.g.*, philosophy of mathematics, history, physics, etc.). The beginning of philosophy is the recognition by the mind of its own cognitions and persuasions; then follows the endeavor to supplement and complete these in such a way as to satisfy scientific intelligence. In the beginning there must be absolute doubt; at the end there is complete intellectual satisfaction and repose. Cognition is either cognition by intuition, or by perception, or by reasoning; there are three corresponding grand divisions of (general) philosophy.

The General Science of Intuition — which has to do with ideas and knowledge as such — undertakes, (1) to investigate the nature of human knowledge; and (2) to "show that this nature is such as not to admit the possibility of error." In the former case it is Ideology; in the latter, Logic.

Ideology. — To know the nature of human knowledge, we must *observe* it as it is; internal *observation* is the instrument of ideology, as external observation is of the physical sciences. Observation merely fixes what is to be demonstrated. The cognition of real entities is merely an internal affirmation or judgment. The notion of real entity, or existence, is a prerequisite for such judgment. This notion is native to the mind; it is the *only* form native to the mind, and necessary to explain the origin of all others. Being is known by intuition. The object of pure intuition is ideal being; of sensuous intuition, real being, — the latter presupposing the former (though not reducible to it). Ideal being is nothing in itself; it is merely the light of the mind, the possibility of there being real being for the mind, — the form of cognition. Real being is the material of knowledge, and a second prerequisite for the judgment above-mentioned. This material is given in feeling. Every judgment, affirming a particular real being, contains, in indissoluble union, the three factors: feeling or sensation, idea of existence, and the union of the two. When a mind, first cognizant only of the essence of being, without knowing that a being exists, receives, experiences, observes a feeling, it immediately affirms that the being of which it previously knew only the essence also exists. Feeling constitutes the reality of beings, or, in other words, what is affirmed, in the perception of a real being, to be a being is always a *felt activity;* and to know the existence of a real being is to affirm a kind of identity between the essence of being and the activity manifested in feeling. The connection between ideal and real being is such that the two taken together form but one and the same being, with two modes, or two original and primitive forms. Their identity is not complete, since no activity, whether felt or feeling (sentient), ever exhausts the essence of being. The essence of being is in every kind of realization, — is in that in which beings differ, as well as in that in which they agree ; we require the whole of the essence of being in order to know even a small part. Quantity, therefore, belongs to realization, not to essence as such. All negative properties are known by means of the essence of being. The idea of the essence of being makes known numerous particular beings, and thus transforms into many concepts, becoming in this way the special concepts of all these beings. — The identity of essence of being and feeling is found only in real being as *known*, and it is in the finding of it that the *felt activity* is perceived and cognized. But though the mind supplies an element of its object of perceived being, this does not render its perception less true, since the mind clearly knows what it adds and what is given to it; and hence knows things as they are. The essence of being is cognizable in and through itself, and the cognition of it is prior to all other cognition, — prior to any act of our thought. There is in the cognition of it no reaction on the part of our spirits. The idea of being cannot come to us either from bodily sensations, from the feeling of our own existence, from reflection, or through the act of perception. That it does not come from our bodily sensations, is clear from its characteristics, all of which are opposed to those of sensation. The characteristics are objectivity, possibility or ideality, simplicity, unity or identity, universality and necessity, immortality and eternity, and indeterminateness. That it cannot come from the feeling of our existence is likewise manifest, partly on account of the same characteristics, and partly because, without first having the idea of being, we should never be able to distinguish the feeling of ourselves. That it cannot come from reflection is plain, inasmuch as reflection adds nothing to sensation, and sensation does not contain the notion of being. Finally, that it does not spring into existence in the act of perception and as a result of that act is obvious, for the simple reason that that act could never begin without it. The essence of being, simply by making itself cognizable to the mind, informs it and renders it intelligent. Ideal being (which, since it is not nothing, nor real being, is a distinct mode of being) is related to real being as *design, model, example*,— terms which in the last analysis imply *means of knowing*. Ideal being (ideas) is immutable and unalterable; real being may or may not be. The unity of feeling and essence of being in perceived being is to be understood as a consequence of the unity of man, the simplicity of human nature, which is attested by internal observation. The ego — that principle which knows what being is — is the same as that which feels in itself the action of it (feeling is only an action of being). So long as this action, or feeling, is kept apart from the knowledge of being, so long it remains unknown. But this principle, being entirely simple, though at once intelligent and sentient, is necessitated by reason of this very simplicity to bring together its feeling and the knowledge of being, and in this way it sees being operating, that is, producing feeling in itself. It is the same being that, on the one hand, manifests itself to us as *knowable*, and, on the other, as active, producing feeling. The unity of essence of being and feeling is a primitive judgment which, since only one of its terms (the predicate, essence of being) exists prior to the judgment, whereas the other arises in the act of judgment, is not a product of intelligence or intelligent will, but of our nature. Of all other judgments the terms are prior to the judgment itself. The faculty which produces the " primitive judgment," or, as we may term it, the " primitive synthesis," and which exercises reflection upon it when produced, is reason. The primitive judgment is an equation between feeling and essence of being, and either term is subject or predicate.

Logic. — Logic, or the Science of the Art of Reasoning, has two offices: (1) to defend the existence of truth in general and the validity of reason in particular; (2) to lead men to use their power of reasoning so as to arrive at complete possession and conviction of truth, — to arrive at certitude. Knowledge is true when that which is known *is :* the truth of a thing is its being; conversely, known being is the truth of knowledge. But the form of intelligence is being; hence the form of intelligence is truth. The first truth, therefore, is possessed by the human spirit through its very nature, — a fact which disposes of sceptics and agnostics. Having found that the result of observation is the intuition of being, we are able to convince ourselves of the truth of observation itself, inasmuch as we found by it intuited being, that clear light of truth which excludes from observation all possibility of deceit and error. What is true of the idea of being, holds of all other ideas as such (not necessarily the relations of ideas), since these are only specifications of the idea of being, — a truth which overthrows the sceptical objections of the transcendental idealist. The possibility of error enters with judgment and reflection, *i. e.*, with the establishing of relations among ideas. There is a class of judgments exempt from this possibility, *viz.*, those which express only what the mind intuits.(*e. g.*, The object of knowledge is being). Error is a product, not of the faculty of cognition, but of the will. In perception I am aware (not, as Fichte said, of ego and non-ego, but) only of the object ; I am aware neither of myself nor of the act of perception. This peculiarity of perception, that it is limited to a single being, explains how we know the corporeal world ; in perception there can be no confounding of object with anything else, and hence is it known as it is in itself. This occurs through the idea of universal being, in which we see only the objective. Every perception has its identity merely by the fact that it affirms its object; — it does not establish its own identity by *negating* other beings. Beings are discovered as different through being the objects of different perceptions (the principle of the discernibility of individuals). We know the *number* of contemporaneous perceptions when the individual beings are exactly the same, — a supposition logically possible. The reason of this is that we are able to see that the realization of two is more than that of one. Abstraction, later, gives us pure number. Difference in mode of realization constitutes the difference of species; the difference in quantity, or even of actuality, is the cause of accidental differences. When we refer the perception of bodies and of ourselves to universal being, and then compare the objects of the two perceptions, we find that the two limit each other, and our mind adds the negations and distinctions; then we know them as ego and non-ego. By a further reflection we reason from the finite to the infinite by considering what bodies and ourselves have in common, *i.e.*, their limitation: from either perception we may leap into the infinite. The principle of reflection is as follows: the human mind, knowing the essence of being, affirms being in feeling; then, drawing a comparison and referring the affirmed being to the essence of being, it knows its conditions, limits, and relations; afterwards, by means of new reflections, it refers in the same way the cognitions arrived at to the essence of being, and draws from it ever new cognitions. The perception of substance depends on the law that sensation cannot be perceived except as a modification of ourselves, since only being is perceivable, and that whenever a feeling is a reality which does not by itself constitute a being capable of forming an object of perception, intellective perception (or perception of pure being as distinguished from sense-perception) does not stop short of this reality, but affirms the being (substance) to which the reality (accident) belongs. Substance is simply the application of the idea of being to those felt realities which are not sufficient of themselves to form a perceivable being. The principle of substance does not admit of error, but is substantially true. The idea of cause arises when reflection compares perceived beings with the essence of being, and discovers their limitations and interdependence. The principle of causation is in itself infallible, inasmuch as the object of perception is free from error, and the essence of being, with which it is compared, is truth itself; all that remains is to recognize whether reality is or is not included in the essence of the being perceived. A being whose essence does not include subsistence is contingent. Reflection does not rest with the principle of cause until it has arrived at a first cause, in whose essence subsistence is included, and this cause is God. The principle of cause thus viewed is the *principle of integration*. All men use this principle with great rapidity; hence a universal belief in God among men. In the last analysis all operations of reflection reduce themselves to comparing a known object with ideal being, in order to see how far and in what mode it partakes of the essence of being, and how far it falls short of it. Hence all reflection is by itself an instrument of truth, having truth as its type and as the measure of things. Two precepts of reflection (reasoning) are : (1) Never affirm anything which you do not know, or in a mode different from that in which you know it. (The same applies to denying.) (2) Affirm with inner thought all that you know, but affirm it in the mode in which you know it, without addition or subtraction. (The same applies to denying.) According as the aim of reasoning is to demonstrate and defend truth, to discover truth, or to teach truth, its method is "apodictic" "heuristic," "didactic." The principle of the apodictic method is: Given a proposition which is certain, all that is implicitly contained in it is certain. That of the heuristic is, — The idea of being, which is the light of reason, when applied in the proper way to new feelings or to cognition already possessed produces new cognitions. That of the didactic, — Let the truths which it is desired to teach be arranged in such order that those which precede do not require those which follow in order to be understood.

Sciences of Perception. — The beings we perceive are either ourselves or the external world; the philosophical sciences of perception are *psychology* and *cosmology* (supernatural anthropology, the science treating of the feeling of God, transcends the limits of mere philosophy).

Psychology. — Psychology, as the doctrine of the human soul, treats of the soul's essence, its development, and its destinies. It is a primitive fact, the starting-point of all reasoning regarding the soul, that each individual feels and perceives his own soul. Body does not feel itself, but is felt by the soul. From the foregoing we derive a preliminary definition of the soul: "If the soul feels itself, it is in its essence feeling, since it is only feeling that is felt by itself (*per se*) : and if bodies are felt by the soul, and the soul is felt by itself, the soul is the principle of feeling. The soul, therefore, is a principle of feeling implanted in feeling." The soul not only feels, but also intellectively perceives (itself and bodies) ; is a principle at once sensitive and intellective. The complete definition of the soul is : The (human) soul is an intellective and sensitive subject or principle, having by nature the intuition of feeling, and a feeling whose term is extended besides certain activities consequent upon intelligence and sensitivity. From this definition follow the simplicity and immortality of the soul. The soul is simple because single and unconditioned by space : single, since it is the same principle which feels and understands ; unconditioned by space, for the act of feeling excludes extension through the opposition by which it distinguishes itself from the felt extended, as well as by the fact that it receives its form from the idea which is altogether free from space. The soul is immortal because, — (1) it is the principle which gives life to the body, is itself life, cannot die of itself, is immortal through itself;

(2) the form of the soul is the eternal and immutable idea. The soul, being in its nature contingent, might be annihilated, but only by God. God annihilates nothing he creates, annihilation being contrary to his attributes. All matter for the intellective operations of the mind is supplied by feeling, which has an extended *sensum* undergoing modifications. The extended term (object of feeling) is twofold, — space and body; the latter being a force which diffuses itself in a limited part of space. Space is immovable, simple, illimitable, indivisible; body is movable, limited, divisible, and hence composite. Whether we can explain the fact or not, it is a fact, not to be denied, that an *extended sensum* is presented to the soul, which is a *simple* principle. The soul feels the body through activity as well as passivity; moves the body as well as feels it. From this fact we may deduce an ontological principle: a sentient principle, besides its own spontaneous feeling, also feels and receives into itself, without losing any of its own simplicity, a foreign force opposed to its distinctive and spontaneous action, and even aids it. From this principle the secondary qualities may be deduced. The soul, as a simple principle, is the ground of continuity of the extended, since the existence of one part terminates with that part, and does not contain the ground of the other part adhering to it. Further, but for this principle the parts themselves of which we suppose the continuous to be made up, would vanish the instant we tried to look for them, for the extended being divisible *ad indefinitum*, the first parts could never be found, and indeed do not exist. The continuous as a whole exists by a single act in the simple principle which feels it. The soul acquires knowledge of the determinate figure of the body through the sensations produced in us by foreign objects; apart from these the soul has only an indefinite knowledge of the body. — The sensitive principle of the soul is, so far as the soul is active, instinct. The first act of instinct is that which produces feeling, and is called vital instinct. But every feeling roused in

the soul produces in it a new activity, and this second activity, which succeeds feeling, is called sensual instinct. From these three principles are explained the physiological, pathological, and therapeutical phenomena of the animal. "Principle" and "term" in the animal form a single being. Three things in the term of the animal give occasion to three kinds of feeling: (1) the corporeal continuous, — the term of the feeling of the corporeally extended; (2) internal movement of atoms or molecules, or of parts of the corporeally extended, — the feeling of excitation; (3) the harmonious continuation of said movement, — "term" of organic feeling. The sensitive "principle" may be destitute of the last two kinds of feeling, but not of the first. If it has only the first and second kinds of feeling, it may be said to be *animate*, but not animal. The distinctive characteristic of the animal is the organic feeling, which requires a suitable organization. The animal, but not the animate, dies. — The sensitive and intellective principles — which together form one principle with two activities — both have the body for their "term;" body is "felt term" and "understood term." Every "principle" being both active and passive with reference to its "term," there is communication or physical influence between body and soul. The intellective and sensitive principles are one by the fact that the former perceives what the latter feels, as the nature of the sensitive principle is due wholly to what it feels. If the sensitive activity be separated from the intellective, as happens when its term, the body, is disorganized and leaves its sensitive principle without the organized term which is proper to it, it vanishes, and the individual dies. — As the soul is one and rational, all the faculties which we call human, as well as the laws of their operation, must emanate from the rational principle in its relation to its two terms, being and the sensible world. There are three classes of laws, — psychological, ontological, cosmological. The supreme ontological law is the principle of cognition: the term of thought is being. Of cosmological laws, some have to do with the motion which the sensible term imparts to the soul; others determine the quality of this motion.— *The destiny of the soul* is not discoverable by mere use of natural reason or the mere examination of human nature. The soul is (1) intelligence, made for truth; (2) will, made for virtue; (3) feeling, tendency to enjoy. Will which adheres to truth, and is thereby virtuous, desires that all beings should be given to it to enjoy, since through enjoyment it completes its knowledge and its love of them; the soul naturally tends to and is destined for perfection, which consists in the full vision of truth, the full exercise of virtue, the full attainment of felicity (each of which implies the other two). Not a single condition in the present life fully corresponds to the end to which man aspires; this life must be viewed as part of a larger plan.

Cosmology. — Cosmology considers the world (1) as a whole; (2) in its parts as related to the whole; (3) in its order. Cosmology, as the *doctrine of the whole*, treats (1) of the nature of contingent real being; (2) of its cause. Contingent real being requires a creative cause outside itself: it is every moment drawn out of nothing. A second proof of the creation of the world is: everything that comes under feeling, *i. e.*, ourselves and the world, would necessarily remain unperceived, *i. e.*, would not be being, if the mind did not see it united to the essence of being. It is the essence, therefore, that imparts to all things the act of being, lends it to them as it were, creates them. A third proof is: we feel that we subsist, but we do not feel the force that causes us to subsist; therefore we feel that we do not subsist through ourselves. The *second part of cosmology* divides the universe into (1) pure spirit, (2) souls, (3) bodies. Cosmology cannot be treated fully except in connection with ontology, and, especially, theology.

The Sciences of Reasoning. — The sciences of reasoning draw their material from the sciences of intuition and perception, or the sciences of observation. There are two classes of the sciences of reasoning: (1) ontological, treating of beings as they are; (2) deontological, treating of beings as they ought to be.

Ontological Sciences. — The ontological sciences are *ontology* proper, and *natural theology*. 1. *Ontology* treats of essence and three forms which it assumes, — the ideal, the real, and the moral; the last-named being the relation that real being holds to itself through the ideal. Being, in so far as ideal, has the property of being a light and of being an object; in so far as it is real, it has the property of being force, an active individual feeling, and hence a subject; in so far as it is moral, it has the property of being an act which puts the subject in harmony with the object, of being a perfecting power, completing the subject by uniting it with, and rendering it adequate to, the object, — bliss of being. The law of the synthesis of being is that being cannot exist under one of its three forms without existing under the other two. 2. *Natural Theology.* — Our cognition of being in its totality and fulness is negative. The being that we perceive, and that constitutes the datum of our knowledge, is only a partial realization of being. Of the being of God there are four principal proofs: (1) The essence of being, which we intuit, is not nothing, but something eternal and necessary. It could not have these attributes if it did not subsist identically under the other two forms of reality and morality. But the essence of being is infinite, and, existing under all these forms, it is being in every way infinite and absolute, — it is God. (2) The ideal form of being is the life which creates intelligence; it is eternal light and eternal object; hence there must be an eternal mind, an eternal subject. This light is unlimited; hence this subject must have infinite wisdom, and its knowledge must not be a transient act; in it everything must be known through itself. A subject which at the same time exists as *infinite object* is the most perfect union of the two, and hence it is the *infinite act of goodness*, or moral perfection, that constitutes that primordial form of being. This being is, therefore, absolute, is God. (3) The contingency of real being requires a first cause and ground of all. (4) Infinite and irresistible is the authority of the moral law, infinite the excellence of virtue and the ignobleness of vice. The binding force, the dignity, of the moral law is not nothing, and must therefore be eternal, necessary, absolute. But it would be nothing if it did not exist in an absolute being. The essence of holiness belongs to the essence of being, and is its last complement; it belongs to the essence of being as much as the other forms do. There is, therefore, an absolute being, — God. — We know God only through reasoning.

Deontology. — Deontology, which treats of the perfection of being and the way in which this perfection may be acquired or lost, is general or special. The relations of perfection are relations proper to moral, intellectual, and real being. The perfections of moral being are perfections of personality; those of intelligent and real being are perfections of nature. There is in the case of real and intellectual beings only one exigence, or necessity: in order that they be perfect, they must be so or so. The perfection of moral beings brings with it two exigencies: the one springs from being considered in itself, and says, " Entity, truth, must be recognized by the will;" the other springs from the nature of the will, and says, " If the will does not recognize entity and truth, it has not perfection." The doctrine of perfection has three parts: the first describes the *archetype* of every being; the second, the *actions* whereby perfection is attained; third, the *means*. The archetype of being, or ideal perfection, is the example and guide of all the acts; the actions whereby the perfections of being are produced are arts, — mechanical, liberal, intellectual, moral; the *means* which lead to these arts constitute special education, or the school of these arts.

Special Deontology. — There is a "special deontology" for every kind of being, natural or artificial. Human Deontology has the three parts: (1) doctrine of the archetype, *Teletics;* (2) doctrine of actions, *Ethics;* (3) doctrine of means, which is, according as the means are applied to one's self, to others, to the family, to civil society, to the theocratic community of the human race, *Ascetics* or *Education, Pedagogics, Economics, Politics, Cosmopolitics.* Teletics is necessarily forever incomplete; Ethics is General Ethics, Special Ethics, Ethical Eudæmonology. General Ethics (which treats of will and liberty, law, conformity of liberty and will to law) contains among its principles the following law: Follow the light of reason, or, Recognize being; and since being has in itself an intrinsic order, this formula may be given the form, Recognize being as it is in its order. This recognition includes love proportionate to each order of being, and external actions flowing from that. God, as absolute becoming and end of all, is the final aim of the virtuous man's will and of its acts. Here enters religion, in which, as being morally perfected and raised to the highest degree of completeness, every duty becomes sacred and every virtue holiness. Among the special forms of moral good (treated in the second part of Ethics, Special Ethics) occurs that of respecting and honoring human nature in one's self and one's fellows, and in society as well as individuals. Eudæmonology, which treats of the excellence of moral good and evil, describes the dignity and joy of the virtuous soul, and shows that no truly virtuous man is unhappy, and no wicked one happy, and awakes the confidence that virtue will meet with an eternal reward, and vice with an eternal punishment. From Ethics flows the *Science of Rational Right.* It arises from the protection which Ethics, or the moral law, affords to the *useful good,* or more generally to all eudæmonologic goods which man can enjoy. All goods and rights which a man possesses in his relations with his fellow-men come under two forms, which constitute the basis of the fundamental classification of these rights, — freedom and property. Freedom is the power which a man has to use all his faculties and resources so long as he does not thereby encroach upon the rights of others, — *i. e.*, does not interfere with the good of his fellow-men. Property is the union of goods with man, — a union based upon a psychological law, in virtue of which a man may unite to himself things different from himself, in somewhat the same way as his body is united to his soul. To separate from a man that which he has united to himself by affection and intelligence is to cause him pain, to do him evil. But we may not do evil to others in order to do good to ourselves; therefore moral reason forbids us to injure the property of others. The Science of Right has two parts, — individual and social; the latter also having two parts, — universal and particular. Universal Social Right is internal or external. Three societies are necessary to the organization of the human race, — theocratic, domestic, and civil. The supreme problem of the Science of Right is to deduce laws from the principles of justice. *Doctrine of Means.* — *Education* is self-education, Domestic, Professional, Civil, Ecclesiastical, Providential; or it is, according to another principle of division, moral, intellectual, physical. The first law of education is unity: physical and intellectual education must contribute to the end moral perfection. *Politics.* — The end of civil society is public prosperity, which depends on justice and the concord of the citizens. The natural constitution of civil society is based upon five sorts of Equilibrium: (1) Equilibrium between population and wealth; (2) Equilibrium between wealth and the civil power; (3) Equilibrium between the civil power and material force; (4) Equilibrium between the civil and military forces and knowledge; (5) Equilibrium between knowledge and virtue. The political means which harmonize with the natural movement of civil society are good; the opposite, the reverse. The political means which with the smallest outlay of property and action produce the greatest amount of social good are the best. Religion, especially Catholicism, is the most valuable political means, — the one which tempers and harmonizes all the rest. The unity and organization of the human race attain completeness only in the theocratic society, the theory of which is Cosmopolitics.

Result.— The system of Rosmini appears to be essentially a system of Scotch (?) intuitionalism, rounded out by materials drawn from all portions of the history of philosophy. Intuition is its first material and formal principle; and its method is the scientifico-empirical method. It is ancient in type in so far as it begins with *being* rather than with *thought*, but modern in that it "criticises" the process of knowledge. It agrees with Kant as to the character of the process in itself of perception, but not as to the result of that process. Rosmini himself says, "If philosophy is to be restored to love and respect, I think it will be necessary in part to return to the teachings of the ancients, and in part to give those teachings the benefit of modern methods."[1] Rosmini is an inveterate opponent of what he calls the "sensism" of modern, even German, philosophy; his "intuition" is, as opposed to all this, an intellectual intuition.

§ 154.

Vincenzo Gioberti (1801-1852). — Gioberti prepared for the Church in the University of Turin. In 1825 he became professor of philosophy in that university, and some years later court chaplain at Piedmont. Owing to the liberality (republicanism) of his political opinions and the frankness of his speaking, the court party contrived to secure his banishment, in 1833. The next fifteen years of his life were spent in exile, mostly at Brussels. During the time he was engaged in study, private teaching, and writing. Political works of his, advocating a confederation of Italian States under a papal presidency, had made him favorably known in Italy, and on his return to Turin he was received with public demonstrations of favor. For a year he took an active part in the political agitations in his country. In 1849 political opposition practically exiled him again, by

[1] See art. Rosmini, "Encyclopædia Britannica."

causing him to be sent away as ambassador to Paris, where he died. He is one of the political and philosophical reformers of Italy.

Works. — Gioberti's principal philosophical work is entitled "Introduzzione allo Studio della Filosofia" (1839-1840). Other works are: "La Teoria de Sopranaturale" (1838); "Trattato del Bello" (1841); "Trattato del Buono" (1842); "Errori Filosofici de A. Rosmini" (1841-1844).

Philosophy. — Philosophy begins, not with the subject, but with the object, — the Idea. To begin with subject, — as did Descartes, and as does Rosmini, — is to pave the way for sensualism, materialism, scepticism, atheism, to do away with which is the very object of philosophy. To begin with a fact of consciousness is to base the universal and necessary upon the accidental, and to stick fast in mere phenomenism. The object is known through an act of intuition, — an act by which first we are rational beings, true subjects. The contents of this intuition become conscious to us only through reflection. This reflection constitutes philosophy; and it may, therefore, be said that all philosophy rests upon (religious) intuition, — is but the reproduction in reflection of the content of this. This content is expressed in the "ideal formula," *Ens creat existentias,* or, *Deus creat mundum.* This formula expresses a double process, — a descending (from being to existences) and an ascending. From the subject in the descending process we get the sciences of ontology; from the copula, that of mathematics; from the predicate, that of cosmology. From the predicate in the ascending process flows psychology; from the copula, logic; from the subject, theology. — The philosophy of Gioberti underwent an alteration, by which it renounced the position of being merely ancillary to Catholic theology.

§ 155.

Terenzio Mamiani (born in 1799). — Mamiani, a poet and statesman as well as philosopher, was, like Gioberti, for many years a political exile. During the period of the exile he devoted himself to philosophical and literary studies in Paris. After his return to Italy, in 1846, he held a number of important public offices, among them those of minister of the interior, deputy to parliament, senator, minister of public instruction, and professor of philosophy and history in the University of Turin.

Works. — Among his works are the following: " Rinnovamente [Reform] della Filosofia Antica Italiana " (1834); " Dialoghi di Scienza Prima " (1846); " Le Confessioni di un Metafisico " (1865); " Le Meditazioni Cartesianae " (1868); " D' un nuovo Diritto Europeo " (1859).

Philosophy. — Knowledge is direct relation through perception and intellection to the real and the ideal respectively. This relation is one of intuition; and its content is known only in reflection. In intellection are apprehended ideas, which are entities, and the basis of finite realities. The existence, but not the nature, of absolute reality is demonstrable from primitive intuition. Creation is a product of infinite goodness, power, and wisdom, and the subject of both efficient and final causes; the world is the best possible, evil being inherent in the finite as such. The cosmic system, or co-ordinated universe, has the three grand departments of nature, life, and mind. Nature is governed by mechanical cause only. Finality first appears in life. Life is a specific force. Its principal degrees are vegetation, animality, and spirituality. The Darwinian doctrine of organic evolution is contrary to fact, and is self-contradictory. Finality appears most fully in man. The human race, in common with all the rest of creation, obeys the law of indefinite progress.

§ 156.

Scholastic philosophy has been rehabilitated in Italy by Giovachino Vertrua, M. Liberatore, C. Sanseverino, and others.

§ 157.

Italian Positivism is represented by the two names of Giuseppe Ferrari and Ansonio Franchi; the former, professor of philosophy in the universities of Strasburg, Turin, Milan, Florence; the latter professor of the philosophy of history in the University of Pavia. Their doctrine was avowedly founded on the negative side of Kantian criticism. According to Ferrari, there prevails everywhere in nature contradiction; and the mind, with its logical principle of identity, is incommensurate with nature, — *i. e.*, cannot explicate it. It must be content to accept it as a mere fact; the law of knowledge is only the law of fact as such, and hence submission to nature. Politically speaking, the true philosophy is that of revolution. — Franchi maintains that there is in human consciousness an insurmountable antinomy between the instinctive belief in the reality of things and the reflective knowledge of them, in consequence of which we are shut up to the knowledge of mere phenomena. In religion the permanent element is feeling (corresponding to the spontaneous instinct of belief in sensible perception); the logical form of it varies with time and place.

§ 158.

(5) *English Systems.* — We take up here the systems of David Hartley, James Mill, Jeremy Bentham, John Stuart Mill, Herbert Spencer, George Henry Lewes, William Whewell, Thomas Hill Green. All of these but the last two are to be classed as sensationalists rather than otherwise, and are peculiarly British in their form of thought. The last two supplement and correct British by German thought.

§ 159.

David Hartley[1] (1705-1757). — Hartley, intended by his father for the Church, went to Cambridge to study the-

---

[1] See Bower's "Hartley and James Mill" (English Philosophical Series.")

ology in particular; he also studied mathematics, philosophy, and medicine. Instead of taking orders, he entered upon the practice of medicine. He is said to have been a man of varied scientific tastes and attainments, and of estimable character. His only philosophical work is entitled "Observations on Man, his Frame, his Duty, and his Expectation" (1749).

Philosophy. — According to Hartley, all the soul's functions originate from the association of ideas; this in turn depending on vibrations of the æther pervading the interstices of bodies. Moderate vibrations produce feelings of pleasure; violent, those of pain. The traces, "vibratiuncles," or miniature vibrations, remaining in the brain after stimulation, produce in their various combinations the phenomena of memory, imagination, reasoning. The law of association is: "If any sensation A, idea B, or muscular motion C be associated a sufficient number of times with any other sensation D, idea E, or muscular motion F, it will at last excite the simple idea belonging to the sensation D, the very idea E, or the very muscular motion F." Another important law, the "law of transference," is "that an idea associated with another through a third may after a time become directly associated with that other." It is according to this law that a thing (*e. g.*, money) desired as a means to an end (conveniences procured by money) may become an object of desire in itself. "Axioms" and "intuitive" principles "are merely results of early-formed and often-repeated associations;" belief, or assent, "inveterate associations," etc. The strength of associations depends upon vividness of associated ideas and frequency of association. There is no freedom of will: "will" is merely habitual and necessary association of sensations and ideas with motions. (Matter and motion, "however subtly divided, yield nothing," Hartley admits, more than matter and motion, it is true; but there is a necessary, though inexplicable, correspondence between vibrations and sensations and images). — From ultimate pains and pleasures of sensation follow, by different degrees of association, the pleasures and pains which constitute the moral sentiment,— pleasures and pains (1) of sensation, (2) of imagination, (3) of ambition (resulting from the association of pleasures and pains of imagination with those primary pleasures and pains), (4) of self-interest (combination of pleasures and pains of imagination with those of ambition), (5) of sympathy, (6) theopathy, (7) moral sense. The moral sense is the sum of all the rest. By the formula, W (love of the world) : F (fear of God) : : F : L (love of God), or $W = \frac{F^2}{L}$, we may express in their relations the factors of our moral nature. — The "sentiments of the beautiful and the sublime" are explicable by the principle of association. "The pleasures derived from the beautiful and the sublime objects of nature, for example, arise from the association of sensible pictures of rural scenes with mental pictures of the different comforts and advantages (such as pleasant tastes, sounds, temperature, sport etc.) originally repeatedly experienced in connection with them." The ultimate cause of all vibrations is God (matter being a merely "passive thing"). God is eternal, omnipresent, immutable, perfect. From God throughout all created being is a continuous chain of causes and effects; and the world shares his perfection. — Hartley's vibration-theory had its origin from a suggestion derived by him from a passage in the "Principia" of Newton; his association-theory from a work attributed to a certain Mr. Gay, entitled "Enquiry into the Origin of the Human Appetites and Affections" (1747).

Result. — Hartley is the "founder" of the association-school of psychology, which includes all the English philosophers in our list above given except the two last named.

§ 160.

James Mill (1773-1836). — James Mill was educated at a parish school, Montrose Academy, and the University of

Edinburgh. At Edinburgh he came under the influence of Dugald Stewart. After spending a number of years in special studies in history and philosophy, combined with preaching and tutoring, he went to London and engaged in literary work. He first merely contributed to periodicals, then founded and edited one journal, edited another, afterwards contributed heavily to leading reviews (among them the "Westminster"), the productions of his pen being largely in the field of political science, but also in those of education, history, social science and reform, ecclesiastical reform, etc. One of his literary productions at the time was a History of India. From 1819 until his death he was an official in the East India House. Among his friends were Bentham, Lord Brougham, and the political economist Ricardo. He deserves to be mentioned as the painstaking educator of his illustrious son, John Stuart Mill.

Works. — James Mill's chief philosophical works are : "Analysis of the Human Mind" (1829) and "Fragment on Mackintosh" (1835), containing his ethical opinions. We may also mention his Miscellaneous Essays (on Government, Education, Social Reforms, etc.).

Philosophy; Psychology. — All mental operations are either sensations and ideas, or originate from them. A sensation is a feeling. Sensations are sensations of the five senses, and of the muscular sense and sensations arising from the alimentary canal. Ideas are copies of sensations. The faculty of ideas is termed "ideation," as that of sensation is "sensation." Ideas combine according to certain laws of association. Synchronously combined, they form "complex notions;" successively or in a succession, trains of thought. Strength of association depends on the strength of ideas and the frequency of association. An "inseparable association" occurs when ideas, from frequency of association, "coalesce, as it were," and form a "single simple idea." The term "consciousness" is merely a generic term for feeling; consciousness itself contains nothing whatever not contained in the feelings as such: "to have a sensation and to be conscious of having a sensation are one and the same thing." The *general term*, instead of being, as the "Realists" supposed, the mark of a reality, or as the "Nominalists" thought, a word without a real content, is the mark of an "indefinite number of simple ideas associated together." Memory involves a notion of the thing remembered, and a notion of the self as remembering, which involves the notions of time and personal identity. Time we get from a succession of sensations which depends upon our perceiving the identity of ourselves in times past and present. The notion of identity is a result of inseparable association. Ratiocination also is a form of inseparable association. The same is true of belief, whether in real existence or in the object of human testimony or the truth of propositions. The relation of cause and effect is but that of invariable succession. An object is merely the sum of its separate qualities. Qualities are sensations with an "association of the object or the cause (or antecedent sensation)." Ideas of quantity are obtained from sensations of touch and muscular resistance. The idea (not the sensation) of a pleasure constitutes desire. By association the desire of mere sensations of pleasure becomes an impulse towards other things, as wealth, power, dignity, friendship, these things having been once associated with pleasure as means with end. The idea of a pleasure or pain associated with its cause is an affection. "The idea of a pleasure associated with that of an action of ours as the cause is a motive; that is, leads to action." Not *every* motive, but the *strongest* determines action. A readiness to obey motive is disposition.

Ethics.—The "moral sense" results from an association with the idea of our action, of the idea of the benefits derived from ourselves and others styled virtuous. "When this association is formed in due strength, which it is the business of a good education to effect, the motive of virtue becomes paramount in the human breast." The end of action is utility: so also is the criterion. Utility has to be determined by a calculation of probabilities when it has not already been determined by the experience of mankind. There are no such things as moral sentiments or moral intuitions determining directly, and independently of experience and calculation, the ends of action. The morality of an act in no way depends upon the motive, but altogether upon its consequences as contemplated by the agent. — The object of civil government is the "public good," which is synonymous with securing to every individual the greatest possible quantity of the produce of his labor, or greatest possible gratification of self-interest. Society requires (1) a power to "restrain instinctive rapacity and knavery; (2) a power to keep that power in check." The most secure form of government against rapacity and the abuse of power is, in modern times, the representative.

Education. — Education, which is but the process of forming right mental associations, has for its object to render, first, the mind, and then the body, "productive of the highest degree of happiness to the individual."

Æsthetics. — The sentiment of beauty depends entirely upon association.

Result. — Except as to the vibration-theory, Mill is a follower of Hartley. Mill's doctrine is one of the best possible illustrations of the meaning and tendency of the principles of sensationalism and associationism in psychology and ethics.

§ 161.

Jeremy Bentham (1748–1832). — Bentham, after courses in the Westminster Grammar-School and at Queen's College, Oxford, entered Lincoln's Inn to prepare for the bar. Instead, however, of practising law, he, the rather, theorized and wrote upon the principles of law, and devoted himself to the bringing about of legal reforms. He advocated life-tenure of office for judges, the abolition of the jury in civil cases, the abolition of monopolies, universal suffrage, vote by ballot, prison-reform, etc. It has been asserted that to "trace the results of his teachings in England alone would be to write a history of the legislation of half a century."

Works. — Bentham's writings on various lines are numerous. His philosophical works are: " Principles of Morals and Legislation " (1789), " Deontology, or the Science of Morality " (1834).

Philosophy. — The end of civil economy is the " maximation of well-being " and the " minimation of evil." The end of action is utility. " Useful " is whatever protects us from evil or procures us some good. " Good " and " evil " are synonymous with pleasure and pain, or the causes of these respectively. They are to be judged according to magnitude and extent (*i. e.*, their intensity, duration, certainty, fecundity, and purity), on the one hand, and the number of persons experiencing them, on the other. The principle of morality is the "greatest happiness of the greatest number." The pleasure or good of the individual is bound up with that of individuals ; egoism in morality is hardly a tenable position, since egoistic actions do not always result to the advantage of their authors. More tenable than egoism is personal prudence, which may have respect to others besides self and is not incompatible with sympathy. Prudence is either " self-regarding " or " extra-regarding." But there is room also for active well-wishing, or " effective benevolence," which, according as it is limited to refraining from the causing of evil to others, or as it extends to the increasing of the well-being of others, is negative or positive benevolence. There is no reason for sacrificing one's own well-being to that of others, since one's own well-being is as much a part of the general welfare as any other's. The notion of virtue is a product of experience : originally man has no moral sentiments whatever. There are four sanctions of morality : (1) the natural sanction (consisting of the natural, *i. e.*, physical consequences of our actions) (2) the moral sanction (consisting of pleasures and pains resulting from regard for public opinion) ; (3) legal sanction ; (4) religious sanction (consisting of pleasures and pains originating from the "immediate hand of a superior invisible being"). In judging the rightness or wrongness of an act we strike a balance between the "persuasive" and the "dissuasive" circumstances: we consider the entire intention of the act. — Bentham is reported as having been much influenced personally by the reading of the "De l'Esprit" of Helvétius. He has had some French and Italian followers, and is of course J. S. Mill's chief model in ethics.

§ 162.

John Stuart Mill [1] (1806-1873). — Stuart Mill, son of James Mill, and born in London, was, until his fourteenth year, in intellectual and moral regards entirely under his father's care, receiving from him instruction and discipline of a rigid sort and in unlimited quantity. He took up Greek at the age of three; Latin, algebra, and geometry, at eight; political economy and the Scholastico-Aristotelian logic, at twelve. He also read very extensively in history, as indeed he did in the classics. The father carefully inculcated in his mind the notions of individual intellectual independence, and of a self-consecration to a life of labor for the public good. Mill spent a year in France, not relinquishing study meanwhile, however. From France he took back with him to England political sentiments which colored his after-thought. In 1823, though he had intended entering the profession of law, and had given a year to the study of Roman law, Mill accepted a position in the East India House, where he remained until the year 1858, when the East India Company was dissolved. Excepting an interval of three years (1865-1868), when he sat in Parliament, — his moral independence and democratic free-thinking, it appears, lost him a re-election, — the remainder of his life was spent in literary occupation and lei-

---

[1] See Mill's Works (including analyses of the "Logic" by Stebbing and Kellick); also the "Metaphysics of Mill," by W. Courtney; the "Encyclopædia Britannica;" Morris's "British Thought and Thinkers;" etc.

sured retirement. Throughout most of his adult life, Mill's pen was occupied with writings — magazine articles and books — having their motive in earnestly-cherished schemes for the social and intellectual improvement of mankind; that is, in the profound conviction of the truth of the Utilitarian Ethics. In a very important intellectual and emotional crisis in his life, which, it would seem, was in part a reaction against the relatively ultra-intellectual effects of his early training, Mill formed the acquaintance of a highly gifted woman (a Mrs. Taylor), who (in 1851) became his wife, and who not only after, but also for many years before their marriage, was an intimate intellectual companion and adviser, influencing decidedly the composition of a number of his works.

Works. — Mill's principal philosophical works are perhaps the following : " A System of Logic, Ratiocinative and Inductive : Being a Connected View of the Principles of Evidence and the Methods of Scientific Investigation " (1843; 8th ed., 1873) ; "An Examination of Sir William Hamilton's Philosophy, and the Principal Philosophical Questions Discussed in his Writings " (1865) ; " Utilitarianism " (1861, in " Fraser's Magazine ") ; "Auguste Comte and Positivism " (1865) ; Essays on " Nature," " The Utility of Religion," " Theism," " Berkeley " (1874) ; and " Notes to James Mill's ' Analysis of the Human Mind.'"

Philosophy: Metaphysics. — Though professing to "abjure metaphysics," and to concern himself only with the physical sciences, Mill asserts that "the difficulties of metaphysics lie at the root of all sciences, and that until they are resolved, at least negatively, and positively whenever possible, there is no assurance that any human knowledge, even physical, stands on solid foundations." — All knowledge originates in sensation. The mind adds nothing to sensations. There is no such faculty as a consciousness distinct from sensations, by which we are cognizant of sensations; "sensation and the consciousness of sensation are one and the same thing." All so-called ultimate and primary truths are to be explained as products of a "mental chemistry," combining mere sensations. Some conceptions, which we know to be so constructed by the mind, have all the appearance of being what are regarded as intuitive notions, — *all* must be of like character with these. The primary law of this mental chemistry — a law which is to psychology what the law of gravitation is to astronomy — is the law of the association of ideas. This law has four exemplifications: (1) the principle of similarity; (2) the principle of contiguity; (3) the principle that "increased certainty is given by repetition to ideas associated by contiguity;" (4) the principle that the "inseparability of associated ideas is transferred to the facts answering to them." If to this be added the law of expectation and memory, or the law that the recurrence of an idea representing a fact leads us to expect the recurrence of another once connected in experience with it, we have all the mental conditions which in the occurrence of organic sensations give rise to connected experience, — including our ideas of body and mind, matter, cause, number, etc. As to real objects, corresponding to these, we can know nothing: the real in knowledge is sensation,— beyond this we can never get. We have, in this reference, merely to show how we come by the ideas which are thought to refer us to a world outside consciousness. Our idea of, and belief in, externality arises in the following way: On our having a sensation there arises the idea of the possibility of numerous others. These we conceive as so linked together that one involves all, and the idea of the possibility of sensations suggests that of a permanent source and substratum of sensations. The experiencing of an order in our sensations gives rise to the notion of the law of cause and effect. The perception of other individuals besides ourselves, as being governed by the idea of a permanent possibility of sensation, together with the belief that our actual sensations are our own, suggests the idea of a belief in a world external to ourselves. Matter, then, is merely a permanent possibility of sensation.

An argument analogous to the foregoing applies also to mind. Mind is really all given in consciousness, or our sensations; and the belief in mind is merely a belief in the "permanent possibility of sequent feelings." The "primary qualities" of "matter," from which matter itself is not distinguishable except as "permanent possibility," are the sensations of resistance, extension, and figure. The first of these we get primarily through the muscular sense, and secondarily (from inseparable association of this sense with touch) by touch also; the second through the sensation of continued muscular action combined with vision. The sensation of muscular action gives the idea of figure, length, surface, situation, velocity, etc. Our idea of nature, as uniform and subject to the law of causation, is merely a subjective product of experience,— merely a belief founded on inductions performed in past time. We have no warrant for applying the idea outside of consciousness or beyond experience. The notion of a cause as a productive power beyond mere phenomena is a pure delusion; it cannot be derived from that of the mind acting on the body, since the mind acts on the body through a series of intermediate terms of which we are not conscious. We have — experience can generate — no real conception of cause, except that of it as an invariable antecedent. The same mere subjectivity characterizes the objects of mathematics. "There does not exist in nature, or in the human mind, any object corresponding to the definitions of geometry;" "in all propositions concerning numbers, a condition is implied without which none of them would be true, and that condition is an assumption which may be false. The condition is that $1 = 1$; that all numbers are numbers of the same or equal units. Let this be doubtful, and not one of the propositions of arithmetic will hold true." Mathematical "axioms" are merely experimental truths, and beyond the range of experience we have no assurance of their application; two parallel straight lines might, for all we know, meet; two and two might make five, outside consciousness or experience. The inconceivability of the opposite of axioms is not a test of necessary truth in them: the inconceivable is neither necessarily nor always false. What people can conceive and what they cannot, are very much matters of accident, depending upon experience, habits of thought, etc. Inconceivableness is an affair merely of "inseparable association." Mill's subjective view of knowledge leads to the result in logic that the major premise, instead of being a universal objective truth, from which as from established reality a conclusion may be reached through a minor, is merely a convenient memorandum of what is contained in many experiences; and hence that inference is from particular to particular, and our conclusions are entirely conditioned by experience, and without absolutely demonstrative certainty.

Theory of Nature. — Mill directly treats of nature, not on its own account, but with reference to moral attributes in it, and its meaning in a theistic regard. Nature, instead of being a pattern which man may "follow" in his action, is just the opposite; instead of possessing moral attributes, it possesses attributes which in man would constitute extreme immorality. The forces of nature are absolutely reckless. Nature kills, impales, burns, starves, freezes, poisons, crushes with the most supercilious disregard of both mercy and justice, emptying her shafts upon the best and noblest indifferently with the meanest and worst,— upon those who are engaged in the highest and worthiest enterprises, and often as the direct consequence of the noblest acts. Her means for the perpetuation of animal life are clumsy. She takes away the means by which we live, on the largest scale and with the most callous indifference,— by a hurricane, a flight of locusts, an inundation. And there is no *part* of nature possessing the perfection that has erroneously been claimed for the whole. "Even the so-called natural instincts are not to be taken as a type of the good and perfect." Allowing everything to be an instinct which anybody has ever asserted to be one, it remains true that nearly every respectable attribute of humanity is the result, not of instinct, but of a victory over instinct, etc. Courage is from the first to last a victory achieved over one of the most powerful emotions of human nature, — fear; cleanliness — a quality which forms the most visible and one of the most radical of the moral distinctions between human beings and most of the lower animals — is entirely artificial instead of natural. Selfishness — to speak of the social attributes — is wholly natural. Sympathy and self-sacrificingness are mostly artificial; so too veracity, justice. "The only admissible moral theory of creation is that the Principle of Good cannot at once and altogether subdue the powers of evil, either physical or moral." On any other supposition nature, morally viewed, is the work of a demon.

Ethics: Freedom. — Human actions are subject to the same law of causation as other phenomena: "given the motives which are present to an individual mind, and given likewise the character and disposition of the individual, and the manner in which he will act might be unerringly inferred." This doctrine does not necessarily contradict that of freedom, — if by freedom be meant the fact of ourselves, *i. e.*, our desires being determining factors in action. This doctrine, in other words, though a doctrine of necessity, is not fatalism, or the doctrine that action is necessary in the sense of being constrained or compelled from without. It is true, however, that even our desires, as well as our motives, are subject to the law of causality; they are what certain antecedents have logically made them. Motives are not necessarily anticipations of pleasure and pain. When our purposes have become independent of pleasure and pain, we have character, or completely-fashioned will.

The Criterion of Right and Wrong: the Principle of Utilitarianism. — Our moral faculty, which is a branch of reason, and not of our sensitive faculty, supplies us only with general principles. There is required a test of right, which will be the means of ascertaining infallibly the right and the wrong,— provide us with really practical precepts. Such a test is to be found in the principle that actions are right in proportion as they tend to produce happiness or pleasure, and absence of pain; and wrong, as they tend to produce the reverse. This is the so-called "Greatest Happiness" principle. This principle depends on the truth, not to be demonstrated, that pleasure and freedom from pain are the only things desirable as ends, all other things being desirable merely as means. Now, some kinds of pleasure are more desirable, more valuable than others. It would be absurd that while, in estimating all other things, quality is considered as well as quantity, in estimating pleasure, quantity alone should be regarded. The Epicurean theory of pleasure must be supplemented by Stoic and Christian principles. Our criteria as to the most valuable and desirable kinds of pleasure are constituted by the feelings and judgments of the experienced. "Now, it is an unquestionable fact that those who are equally acquainted with, and equally capable of appreciating and enjoying, both, do give a most marked preference to the manner of existing which employs the higher faculties. Those who pursue sensual pleasure to the exclusion of others do not do so voluntarily, but because they have lost the faculty for the higher pleasures. Even if (as some object) men had no right to be happy, something might be said for the Utilitarian, or 'Greatest Happiness' principle, since utility includes not solely the pursuit of happiness, but also the prevention or mitigation of unhappiness." Happiness — a satisfied life — (the two main constituents of which are tranquillity and excitement) is not impossible. The causes making life unsatisfactory are selfishness and want of mental cultivation; and there is no real necessity for either of these. The objection that man can do without happiness is met by the assertion that doing without happiness is justified only on the ground of increasing the happiness of others; he who abnegates for himself the personal enjoyment of life, is no more deserving of admiration than the ascetic mounted on his pillar. In the present imperfect state of the world, however, the "readiness to sacrifice one's happiness for that of others is, no doubt, the highest virtue" that can be found in man. But what is required by the utilitarian principle is the happiness of all, — which education, laws, and social arrangements should aim to secure. It is not an objection to Utilitarianism that it does not allow a judgment respecting the rightness or wrongness of an action to be influenced by an opinion of the qualities of the person who does it. The objection that there is not time previous to action for calculating and weighing the effects of any line of conduct on the general happiness, may be met by the assertion that "there is no difficulty in proving any ethical standard whatever to work ill, if we suppose universal idiocy to be joined with it." Men must be guided by the established beliefs of mankind, in default of anything better.

The Ultimate Sanction of the Principle of Utility.— There is no reason why the external sanctions of love and sympathy, of hope of favor or fear of displeasure from our fellow-men or the Ruler of the Universe, should not be as applicable in Utilitarian morality as in any other. The same is true as regards the feeling of duty, or the voice of conscience. There is a natural association between this feeling and the idea of utility to our fellows, the social state being natural, necessary, and habitual to man. Here, in fact, lies the ultimate sanction of the morality of Utilitarianism.

The Proofs of the Principle of Utility. — The sufficient and only possible proof of the principle of Utilitarianism is that questions about ends are about things desirable, and happiness is an end because people actually desire it. Other things, it is true, than happiness, are desired, but only those things that are means to happiness, although they seem to be desired on their own account. It is a provision of nature that things originally indifferent, but conducive to or otherwise associated with our primitive pleasures, become in themselves sources of pleasure more valuable than the primitive pleasures both in permanency, in the space of human existence that they are capable of covering, and even in intensity. Virtue is of this description. But though virtue is of all things the most conducive to happiness, and, so, desirable in a certain sense, it may still be affirmed that nothing is *really* desired except happiness. Those who desire virtue " for its own sake " desire it because the consciousness of it is a pleasure, or because the consciousness of being without it is a pain, or for both reasons. Virtue which through habit has become independent of pleasure or pain is not desired, and is not an end, but a means merely.

The Connection between Justice and Utility. — The *idée mère*, or primitive element, in the formation of the notion of justice was, it would seem, conformity to law. Justice is correlative to a certain sort of duty. The basis of the idea of duty, or right and wrong, is the notion of not deserving or of deserving punishment. Moral duties are of two classes : duties in virtue of which a correlative right resides in some person or persons, — perfect duties ; and duties which do not give birth to any right, — imperfect duties. Now, justice is the right corresponding to perfect duty, or moral obligation. Hereby is justice distinguished from generosity or beneficence, for example, which is a duty that cannot be demanded as *right.* The sentiment of justice, or feeling accompanying the idea of justice, is merely (1) the animal desire to repel or retaliate a hurt or damage to one's self or to those with whom one sympathizes ; (2) widened so as to include all persons by the human capacity of enlarged sympathy, and the human conception of intelligent self-interest. To have a right, then, is to have something which society ought to defend one in the possession of, — ought, because utility demands it, security being a thing which no human being can possibly do without. The utility of moral rules which forbid mankind to hurt one another surpasses that of any maxims, however important, which only point to the best mode of managing some department of human affairs. These rules have the peculiarity that they are the main element in determining the social feelings of mankind and preserving peace. This doctrine does not identify justice with expediency, since the latter is not conditioned by the sentiment of retaliation necessary to the former; but it may be said that all cases of justice are also cases of expediency. Justice as utility, or the greatest happiness of the greatest number, implies impartiality; Bentham's principle, "Everybody to count for one, nobody for more than one," might be written under the principle of utility as an explanatory commentary. The equal claim to happiness, in the estimation of the moralist and the legislator, involves an equal claim to all means of happiness except so far as the inevitable consequences of human life and the general interest in which that of every individual is included, set limits to the maxim.

Natural Theology and Religion. — The *a priori* arguments for the existence of God are unscientific; the idea of God can only prove the *idea* of him. The "Argument of First Cause," which has an *a posteriori* element in it, has no application to the material universe, since, as physical science shows, there is in every object a permanent uncaused element, viz., the elementary substances and their properties. The highest generalization of science, the law of the conservation of force, leads to the conclusion that force is first cause. If force be not the cause of changes of phenomena, we can find no first cause, since each change has as its cause a prior change, and so on *ad infinitum*. If mind be the cause of force, what is the cause of mind? Force has all the attributes of a thing uncreated and eternal, — not so mind as far as known. The argument from the so-called general consent of mankind fails also. The religious belief of savages is not a belief in the God of natural theology, but a mere modification of the crude generalization which ascribes life, consciousness, and will to all natural powers of which they cannot perceive the source or control the operation. The strongest intuitionist will not maintain that a belief should be held for instinctive when evidence (real or apparent) sufficient to engender it is universally admitted to exist. The argument from consciousness, or the subjective notion of God, is likewise conclusive; the mere *idea* is not sufficient to prove the *existence* of God. The (Kantian) argument from duty excludes rather than compels the belief in a divine legislator merely as a source of obligation. Belief in the existence of God because the existence of a wise and just lawgiver is desirable, is not legitimate. The argument from the marks of design in nature possesses a really scientific character, — since it claims to be judged by the established canon of induction, *i. e.*, is wholly grounded in experience. But the evidence of design can never amount to more than that of the inferior kind of inductive argument called analogy. The circumstances in which it is alleged that the world resembles the works of man are not circumstances taken at random, but are merely particular instances of a circumstance which experience shows to have a real connection with an intelligent origin, the fact of conspiring to an end. To take one of the most impressive cases of the argument from design, — the structure of the eye. The parts of the eye have a common attribute, that of being related to vision. We are warranted by the canons of induction — the theory of chances in particular — in concluding that what brought all these parts together was some cause common to them all, between which and the fact of sight there must be some connection. The probabilities are in favor of the belief — even in spite of the doctrine of the survival of the fittest — that an intelligent principle operating to the end of producing sight is the cause of the eye; but the evidence amounts to no more than that of mere probability. As regards the attributes of the intelligent cause of the world, it is not too much to say that every indication of design in the Cosmos is so much evidence against the omnipotence of the designer. Design implies contrivance, adaptation of means to an end, and these imply a limitation of power. Such limitation is equally implied in the supposition that contrivance in nature is a means of the self-revelation of God to man. Further, we are not compelled to suppose that the contrivances in the world are always the best possible. No moral end can be attributed to nature. "The net results of Natural Theology on the question of the divine attributes are: a Being of great, but limited power, how or by what limited we cannot even conjecture; of great and perhaps unlimited intelligence, but perhaps also more narrowly limited than his power; who desires and pays some regard to the happiness of his creatures, but who seems to have other motives of action which he cares for, and who can hardly be supposed to have created the universe for that purpose alone." As regards immortality, the evidence we possess is of a negative character. The mere desire of immortality, upon which ordinary belief is founded, is not a guarantee of immortality. There are no *hindrances* to a *hope* of immortality. Whatever be the probabilities of a future life, all the probabilities *in case of* a future life are such that, such as we have been made or have made ourselves before death, such shall we enter into the life hereafter. The doctrine of revelation receives support from Natural Theology in so far as the latter relieves it of the necessity of proving the very existence of a Being from whom it professes to come. There is no *antecedent improbability* of a revelation. The internal evidences of revelation are only of negative value: there is no reason for believing that the human faculties were impotent to discover moral doctrines of which the human faculties can perceive and recognize the excellence. As regards external evidences, — *i. e.*, miracles, — Mill concludes, after an examination of the ordinary views and of Hume's argument (which he criticises in two important regards), that "no extraordinary powers which have ever been exercised by any human being over nature can be evidence of miraculous gifts to any one to whom the existence of a supernatural being and his interference in human affairs is not already a *vera causa;* that even assuming a God, the whole of our observation of nature proves to us by incontrovertible evidence that the rule of his government is by means of second causes; that the testimony we have received concerning miracles is very imperfect, and that they cannot be proved from the goodness of God." — The general result of Natural Theology is that the natural attitude towards the supernatural is scepticism, — the whole domain of the supernatural is an object, not of knowledge, nor even of belief, but of hope. But even this is, in a religious point of view, an advantage; human life stands greatly in need of any wider range and greater height of aspiration for itself and its destination which the imagination can yield to it without running counter to the evidence of fact. "It cannot be questioned that the undoubted belief of the real existence of a Being who realizes our best ideas of perfection and of our being in the hands of that Being as the ruler of the universe, gives an increase of force to these feelings beyond what they can receive from reference to a merely ideal conception." — The rational sceptic may derive advantage from the idea of the mere possibility of what the pure religionist believes, and in his scepticism possesses one advantage over those who believe in the omnipotence of the good principle of the universe, namely, in so far as he may cherish the feeling of helping God, — of requiting the good he has given by a voluntary co-operation, which he, not being really omnipotent, really needs, and by which a somewhat nearer approach may be made to the fulfilment of "his purposes." Religion is for us essentially a religion of humanity; every important end fulfilled by what is generally termed religion may be fulfilled by that sentiment which by proper cultivation "the sense of unity with mankind and a deep feeling for the general good" may easily become.

Result. — The doctrine of Mill falls, it is scarcely necessary to say, in the same category with that of Comte (see above, vol. i., p. 305), who was (confessedly) one of his masters, — Thomas Brown, James Mill, Hume, and Bentham being others. Mill's principal works have been translated into at least two foreign languages, — French and German, — and his ideas form a considerable part of the stock-in-trade of the popular philosophy of the cultivated world at the present time. In Mill's teaching appears, undisguised by any "evolutionistic" accessories, the inherent strength (or rather weakness) of the purely "psychological" metaphysics. Mill himself indeed admits the inexplicability, on the mere "psychological theory," of the "bond of some sort" constituting the "ego."[1]

§ 163.

Herbert Spencer[2] (born in 1820). — Spencer, whose education, for the most part privately conducted, was chiefly in scientific directions, began active practical life as a civil engineer. About the year 1845 he abandoned the profession of engineer for that of writer, having previously contributed articles to more than one journal. After about ten years of literary work in the more ordinary sort, he formed the design (1859) of a system of Synthetic Philosophy, involving the full development and illustration of the law of (physical) evolution in its application to the phenomena of life, mind, society, and ethics. The design is still in process of execution.

Works. — Spencer's chief philosophical works are: "The Principles of Psychology" (1st ed. 1855, 2d, revised and enlarged, 1872–1873, 3d, slightly enlarged, 1880); "First Principles" (1st ed., 1862, 2d ed., considerably altered, 1869); "The Principles of Biology" (1866–1867); "The Study of Sociology" (1872), — introductory to "The Principles of Sociology" (1876–   ); "Descriptive Sociology" (in nine volumes of tables and classified extracts by Spencer

---

[1] See Morris's "British Thought and Thinkers," chap. xi.

[2] See Spencer's works, and the "Epitome of the Synthetic Philosophy," by F. H. Collins.

and assistants); "The Data of Ethics" (1879); "Justice" ("Part IV. of Principles of Ethics," 1891). Other works of more popular character are: "Social Statics, or the Conditions Essential to Human Happiness" (1851); "Essays, Scientific, Political, and Speculative" (Æsthetic), (1857), reprinted from the "Westminster Review" and other periodicals; "Education, Intellectual, Moral, and Physical" (1861); "Progress, its Law and Cause" (1862); "Illustrations of Universal Progress" (1864); "Recent Discussions in Science, Philosophy, and Morals." (See the "Epitome of the Synthetic Philosophy," by F. H. Collins.)

Philosophy. — *First Principles: Introduction,* — *the Unknowable.* — All religious beliefs have a certain basis in reality, there is a common truth underlying all; and all science, though in a sense removed from common knowledge, has its basis in that knowledge, and therefore in reality. Between religion and science, having a basis, as they have, in reality, there must be a fundamental harmony; there cannot be two orders of truth in everlasting opposition. The truth in which they coalesce must be the most abstract truth of each. This truth must be the ultimate fact in our intelligence. The highest or ultimate truth of religion is the mystery of the universe, the unknowableness of ultimate reality. Our conceptions of it are symbolic merely, and have only an indirect value. No current hypothesis of it is tenable, and no tenable hypothesis can be framed. We cannot, without falling into contradiction, conceive it either as self-existent, self-created, or created by an external agency. We are sooner or later brought to the impossible task of conceiving unlimited past duration. The mystery of the universe is the ultimate truth of science. Our ultimate scientific ideas, — space, time, matter, motion, force, ego, — all become self-contradictory when the attempt is made to realize them in thought. Space must be conceived as infinitely extended and as infinitely divisible, and can be conceived as neither. The same is true of time. To conceive space and time as merely subjective is to multiply irrationalism. Matter cannot be conceived as infinitely divisible, or the opposite. Absolute motion and the communication of motion are inconceivable. Force also is incomprehensible; it cannot be like our sensation of it; and we have no terms that can apply to it as beyond consciousness. The substance of the ego is inconceivable. All explication presupposes certain highest general truths which are themselves inexplicable. Such are the notions First Cause, the Infinite, the Absolute. To attempt to explicate them is to limit them by the forms of thought or terms of consciousness, and so to fall into contradiction, since by implication they are outside consciousness. They are not conceivable in themselves, because they contain no plurality or relation in themselves, are unconditioned. All thought is conditioned, relative; what is not contained in relation is unthinkable. Of that which transcends consciousness we have, and can have, only a vague consciousness; of the unconditioned we have literally an unconditioned consciousness, — a consciousness which is but the raw material of thought, and to which we give definite form by thought. It is an ever-present sense of real existence, and the basis of all our intelligence. Its permanence is a warrant of validity. The existence of a non-relative is, further, implied in the fact that all our knowledge is relative, and that the relative is inconceivable except as related to a non-relative; that unless a non-relative, or absolute, be postulated, the relative itself becomes absolute; that, finally, the existence of a non-relative is involved in the process of thought. The highest truth of science and religion — of human intelligence — is therefore the conclusion that every phenomenon is a manifestation of an unlimited incomprehensible power.

The Knowable: The Conception of Philosophy. — Philosophy, in any positive sense, has to do only with the knowable, not with the incomprehensible and unknowable. As regards form, philosophy is completely unified knowledge, — knowledge possessing the highest degree of generality. The truths of philosophy bear the same relation to the highest scientific truths that each of these bears to lower scientific truths. Philosophy is General or Special. The problem of philosophy is the establishment of congruity between the intuitions that are essential to the process of thinking and the other dicta of consciousness.

The Data of Philosophy.— The primordial data of Philosophy are: the existence of an unknowable Power, of knowable likenesses and differences among the manifestations (which may be classed as vivid and faint manifestations, as perceptions and ideas) of that power, a resulting segregation of the manifestations into those of subject and object, ego and non-ego, or mind and matter. Derivative data are the notions of space, time, matter, motion, and force. The absolute character of space, time, matter, motion, and force we do not know; by virtue of their persistence they are realities, though relative ones, for us. Space is the sum of the relations of co-existence; time is irreversible sequence; matter is co-existent positions that offer resistance; motion is a correlation of space, time, and matter, and is derived from experiences of force. Force is the ultimate of ultimates, not definable by anything else. The sensation of force is correlative with an unknowable reality. Concerning matter, motion, force, there are to be enunciated certain truths of "highest generality," unifying concrete phenomena, or belonging to all divisions of nature. (Spencer does not stop to deal with general truths of space and time,— mathematical truth.) It is impossible by the laws of thought to conceive matter becoming non-existent, or to conceive it coming into existence. To attempt to do so would be to attempt to think a term of thought both within and outside consciousness at one and the same time. By the indestructibility of matter we mean the indestructibility of the force of the matter which affects us. Motion must be conceived as continuous. There can be no science if motion may proceed from and lapse into nothing. The cessation of motion, considered as translation,— which occurs at a certain part of the path of a swinging pendulum, for example, — is not the cessation of an existence, but of a certain sign of existence, the "translation" having passed into "strain." The principle of activity, shown now by translation, now by strain, and often by the two together, is alone that which in motion we can call continuous; it is ultimately conceived by us under the single form of its equivalent, muscular effort. All proofs of the continuity of motion involve the postulate that the quantity of force is constant; the persistence of force is *presupposed* by every experiment or observation by which it is proposed to prove it. The force of which we predicate persistence is the absolute force of which we are indefinitely conscious; it is the necessary correlative of the force which we know. A consequence of the truth that force persists is the truth that the relations among force persist also. What is called the uniformity of law is resolvable into persistence of relations among forces. A truth illustrated by innumerable instances in experimental science is that forces of one kind are transformed into those of another, — heat into motion, electricity, etc.; motion into heat, electricity, etc.; and that forces so transformed remain equivalent to themselves in those into which they have been transformed, — a truth applying to mental, social, and physical forces equally. This truth follows from the law of the persistence of force. Symbolically speaking, there are two universally co-existent forces of attraction and repulsion; whence result the laws that every motion takes place along the line of greatest traction or least resistance, or of their resultant; that motion along a certain line continues in that line, a change of relation to external forces rendering the line indirect, etc., — laws which apply to mental and social as well as to physical phenomena. A (final) law which, like the foregoing, is a corollary of the law of the persistence of force, is that motion is everywhere rhythmical, the probabilities being infinitely great against a truly rectilinear or perfectly circular motion, or a complete return to a previous state. This law also holds good of mental and social as well as physical motion. The law of rhythm is an inevitable corollary from the law of the persistence of force. — The foregoing truths of matter, force, motion, are philosophical conceptions in the proper sense by virtue of their generality. There is required still a synthesis of these. What must be the general character of the formula synthesizing them? It must be one that specifies the course of the changes undergone by both matter and motion. Every transformation implies rearrangement of component parts; and a definition of it, while saying what has happened to the insensible or sensible positions of substance concerned, must also say what has happened to the movements, sensible or insensible, which the rearrangement of parts implies. Further, unless the transformation always goes on at the same rate, the formula must specify the conditions under which it ceases and is reversed. The law sought must therefore be the " Law of the Continuous Redistribution of Matter and Motion," — a law that is exemplified in all concrete processes. Absolute rest and permanence do not exist. Every object, no less than the aggregate of all objects, undergoes from instant to instant some alteration of state, gradually or quickly; it is receiving motion or losing motion, while some or all of its parts are simultaneously changing their relations to one another.

Evolution (and Dissolution) : the Law of Evolution. — It is required to formulate the law of change, or the passage from the imperceptible to the perceptible, and *vice versa*. All possible changes are comprehended in the twofold process of "loss of motion," and consequent integration, eventually followed by gain of motion, and consequent disintegration. — Evolution is either simple or compound, the former being integrative only, the latter including secondary supplementary changes not integrative. Secondary changes are in proportion to quantity of motion and the time during which it is retained, and are readily wrought by incident forces when the contained motion is large in quantity. Secondary changes are characteristic of living aggregates and unstable compounds generally. Primary redistribution ends in forming aggregates which are simple where it is rapid, but which become compound in proportion as its slowness allows the effects of secondary distribution to accumulate. The complete formula of Evolution is: "Evolution is an integration of matter and concomitant dissipation of motion, during which the matter passes from an indefinite incoherent homogeneity to a definite coherent heterogeneity, and during which the retained motion undergoes a parallel transformation." This formula, deductively arrived at, is susceptible of endless illustration, or "inductive verification," in physics, in biology, in psychology, in sociology. (1) The solar system originally existed in a "widely diffused, incoherent state," and afterwards passed into a "consolidated, coherent state." Plants integrate elements diffused as gases. The parts of science integrate into wholes. Petty tenures integrate into feuds, feuds into provinces, provinces into kingdoms, etc. (We can, of course, cite only a few of Spencer's almost numberless instances.) (2) There has been a change from a condition of homogeneity to one of heterogeneity in climate, in the earth's fauna and flora, civilization, and the arts, etc. (3) Changes from the indefinite to the definite have occurred in the formation of the solar system as a whole (supposing it to have originated from diffused matter), in the seasons (which grew relatively decided as the heat of the sun became distinguished from the proper heat of the earth), in mammalian development, in the condition of originally migratory tribes (that found fixed locations), etc.

The Interpretation of Evolution. — The laws of evolution are correlated with those of the direction of motion and the rhythm of motion. The phenomena of evolution may be deduced from the law of the persistence of force. A preliminary distinction must be made here: the incident force affecting any aggregate is partly effective and partly non-effective; the temporarily effective and the permanently effective vary inversely; and the molar and molecular changes wrought by the permanently effective force vary inversely. The beginning of evolution must be found in the instability of the homogeneous, — a principle deducible from the law of the persistence of force. Inductive verifications of the law of the instability of the homogeneous are such facts as the following: The earth's surface underwent change in cooling; meteorologic phenomena constantly change; plants and animals adapt themselves to changing surroundings, etc. The incident force is differentiated by falling in different parts in unlike ways, and thus becomes a source of *multiplication* of *effects*, which must proceed in geometrical progression. The cooling of the earth's surface has had innumerable effects; an alarming sound may produce an excited action of the heart, a rush of blood to the brain, and if the system be feeble, an illness with a long train of complicated symptoms; a sensation does not expend itself in arousing some single state of consciousness, but the state of consciousness aroused is made up of various represented sensations connected by co-existence, or sequence with the presented sensation. The law of multiplication of effects is easily deducible from the law of the persistence of force. It remains to discover the cause of that local integration which accompanies local differentiation, — that gradually completed *segregation* of like units into a group distinctly separated from neighboring groups which are severally made up of other kinds of units. There is a twofold law here: the incident force impresses unlike motions on mixed units in proportion as they are unlike; and units of the same kind are differently moved by different forces. A complementary truth is that mixed forces are segregated by the action of uniform matters. Mixed fragments of matter differing in sizes and weights are, when exposed to the momentum and friction of water, joined with the attraction of the earth, separated from each other, and combined into groups of comparatively like fragments. Changing autumn leaves are picked out by the wind from among the green ones around them, etc. This principle of segregation is a corollary of the principle of the persistence of force. Evolution has an impassable limit; in all cases there is a progress towards *equilibration,* or the establishment of a moving equilibrium, or *equilibrium mobile.* Equilibrium is followed by *dissolution;* there are in the changes of things alternate eras of Evolution and Dissolution.

Conclusion. — The interpretation of all phenomena in terms of matter, motion, and force is merely the reduction of our *complex symbols* of thought to the *simplest symbols,* — nothing more than symbols. The reasonings we have pursued have given no support to either mere materialist or mere spiritualist as regards the *ultimate nature* of things; spirit and matter are equally only *signs of an unknown* reality underlying both alike.

Principles of Biology: The Data of Biology. — We find (in a surprising degree) in the substances of which organisms are composed, the conditions necessary for the redistribution of matter and motion which constitutes evolution. The differences of the four chief elementary constituents of organic matter — oxygen, hydrogen, nitrogen, and carbon, — are favorable in the highest degree to differentiation and integration under the same incident forces. The binary and ternary compounds of these elements possess great mobility, and divide into groups corresponding to living and non-living matter. In the colloidal and crystalloidal conditions of matter — which are, respectively, dynamical and statical — we have two necessary correlative factors of organic action. Organic matter is modifiable in an extreme degree by surrounding agencies. The law of the persistence of force is exemplified in the fact that whatever amount of power an organism expends in any shape is the correlate of a power that was taken into it from without. The definition of life harmonizes with the law of evolution: Life, whether considered as bodily assimilation or as intelligence, may be defined as the "definite combination of heterogeneous changes, both simultaneous and successive, in correspondence with external co-existences and sequences, the degree of life varying with the degree of correspondence."

Inductions of Biology. — Especially important points in Spencer's exposition under this head seem to be the following: Von Baer's law, that, in its earliest stage, every organism has the greatest number of characters in common with all other organisms in their earliest stages, and that at each subsequent stage traits are acquired which successively distinguish the developing embryo from groups of embryos which it still resembles, and that then the class of similar forms is finally narrowed to the species of which it is a member; differentiation of an organism from its environment occurs; structure and functions are formed by progressive differentiation, there being also a parallelism between the course of development of one and that of the other; waste and repair are constantly going on; there is a limit of adaptation of organism to environment; individuality is not absolutely fixed, the "individual being any centre, or axis, capable of carrying on that continuous adjustment of inner to outer relations which constitutes life;" that genesis in the highest order of organisms, *viz.*, gamogenesis, depends upon a condition approaching equilibrium between the antagonistic forces on which life depends, — a condition which must be overthrown by the uniting of slightly different physiological units; that each organism produces others of like kind with itself, — the law of heredity, — and variation occurs and is co-extensive with heredity; that a contrast of physiological units is necessary (in order to destroy equilibrium); that the natural groupings and the distribution of organisms points to an evolutional origin of them.

The Evolution of Life. — Of the hypothesis of Evolution as applied to the Conception of Life it may be said (as it cannot be said of the "Special-Creation hypothesis") that it is confirmed by advancing knowledge, is mentally representable at least in outline, if not in detail, — is a legitimate *symbolic conception.* It is supported by the facts of natural classification; by those of embryology, — that arrangement of classes, orders, genera, and species to which naturalists have been led, is just that which results from the divergence and re-divergence of embryos as they develop; by morphological similarity, or community of plan, which exists among allied organs when mature, and by the presence in all kinds of animals and plants of functionally useless parts corresponding to parts that are functionally useful; by the facts of the distribution of animals and plants, such as that in wider areas there are wider contrasts, in smaller, smaller, and that differences of distribution correspond to differences of media, etc. Organic evolution admits of being explained as a part of the general evolution (and only so), external and internal factors being duly considered. Everywhere there is equilibration, direct or indirect, refitting organisms to their ever-changing environment ("natural selection" playing a less, heredity a more, important part than Darwin assumes).

Morphological Development. — There is clear evidence that in Phanerogams all the appendages of the axis, whether bracts, sepals, petals, stamens, styles, or ovules, are homologues, all being modified leaves; that endogens and exogens were formed by differentiation from acrogens, etc.; that there is a definite relation between the forms or shapes of plants and their parts, and incident forces. The processes of morphological differentiation in the animal kingdom conform to the same general laws as those of the vegetable kingdom, — there being, however, one new and all-important factor, *viz.*, motion of the organism in relation to surrounding objects, or of parts of the organism in relation to one another or both; and there is the same adaptation of forms to forces in animals as in plants, — there is, *e. g.*, a habitual formation of denser tissues (and hence enlargements) at those parts of the organism which are exposed to the greatest strains.

Physiological Development. — The problems of physiology are problems to which answers must be given in terms of incident force. There is a strong distinction between the parts in contact with the environment and parts not in contact with the environment, or parts in contact with different parts of the environment, — *e. g.*, between the centre and the surface of a cell, or between the upper and lower sides of leaves. There is a direct relation between the demand for support and circulation, and the existence of vascular woody bundles which the higher plants habitually possess. The bending of a plant by the wind causes its growth in height by forcing the sap to elevations which it could not reach by capillary attraction. In animals the first contrast is that of inside and outside. A striking example of differentiation of tissue in animals appears in the fact that in little-developed and in lower types of animals respiration is performed by the entire surface of the body, while in the highest animals there is a special organ for respiration. The liver, pancreas, and various small glands all arise by differentiation from the coats of the alimentary canal, etc.

The Laws of Multiplication. — There are two forces preservative of race, — ability of the individual to preserve itself, and ability to produce other members. These are antagonistic. Every higher degree of individual evolution is followed by a lower degree of multiplication, and *vice versa*. Other things being equal, genesis is in proportion to nutrition. Human genesis is subject to the same general laws as other sorts. The relation between it and man's development is as follows : excess of fertility causes man's evolution in so far as it necessitates the exercise of his power in providing for offspring ; but such evolution, on the other hand, necessitates a decline in fertility. Hence population regulates itself. The evolution of man in the future is likely to be in the direction of higher intellectual and emotional development.

The Principles of Psychology: The Data of Psychology. — Psychological phenomena are incidents of the continued redistribution of matter and motion : are directly dependent upon the nervous system, varying in multiplicity and complexity with the size and complexity of that. The nervous system has two general functions in relation to psychical phenomena, — it is a receiver of disturbances, and distributor and apportioner of motion liberated. There are afferent or recipio-motor and efferent or dirigo-motor nerves, and libero-motor nerve centres. In its undifferentiated state (the gray and the white matter of the nervous system are primarily the same), nerve-matter unites in itself the passive and active functions. The spinal cord is the centre of relatively simple co-ordination, the medulla oblongata of compound co-ordination, and the cerebrum and cerebellum of doubly compound co-ordination (the former as regards space, the latter as regards time). In this progression is a striking illustration of the law of evolution. Every agent, whether mechanical, chemical, thermal, or electrical, is capable of altering the molecular state of a nerve, causing the nerve to produce a particular change, which it habitually produces. There is a rhythmical variation in nerve-activity; there are pulses of molecular action analogous to the pulses of blood. The centripetal wave is comparatively feeble; the centrifugal, strong. The subjective sides of nervous changes are feelings. Certain nervous changes which have subjective sides early in life cease to have them later. A subjective state becomes recognizable as such only when it has an appreciable duration. Each feeling produces a capacity for similar feeling, since each nerve-discharge makes easier a following one. A diminished ability to feel is a consequence of a waste of nerve-tissue. Feelings, according as they accompany direct and strong or indirect and weak excitations of the nerve centres, are vivid or faint, real or ideal feelings, sensations, or emotions. That feeling and nerve-action are respectively the inner and the outer face of the same thing is a necessary assumption, but not susceptible of direct proof. They are not the same thing; and psychology has to deal with an order of phenomena distinct from biological phenomena as such, — is in fact in its subjective aspect a totally unique science, independent and antithetically opposed to all other sciences whatever.

Inductions of Psychology. — Nothing is, or can be, known of mind as a substance or substrate : we know only states of mind. Individual sensations, though apparently simple, homogeneous, unanalyzable, inscrutable, are really not so, any more than a musical note is so : they are built up of a common unit repeated, a nervous shock of very slight intensity. From the modes of the integration of this ultimate unit result all unlikeness among our feelings. There are two general components of mind as known to introspection, *viz.*, feelings (proper) and relations, the latter being distinguished from the former by the fact of their occupying no appreciable part of consciousness. Feelings are peripherally or centrally initiated feelings, the former being sensations, the latter emotions. The former are epiperipheral or entoperipheral. The presence of relational elements among feelings causes them to cluster. Sensations cluster, while emotions do not. Feelings of different orders do not limit one another so clearly, nor do they cohere so strongly, as do those of the same order. An *idea*, or unit of knowledge, results when a vivid feeling is assimilated or coheres with one or more fainter feelings left as trace by such vivid feelings previously experienced. The method by which simple sensations and relations among them are compounded with definite states of consciousness is essentially analogous to the method by which primitive units of feeling are compounded into sensations : a similar holds of higher stages of consciousness. The evolution of mind corresponds to the laws of evolution in general : from a confused sentiency there is a transition to an ever-in-increasing integration of feelings with one another and feelings of other kinds to an ever-increasing distinctness of structure in such aggregates, — a change from indefinite, incoherent homogeneity to a definite, coherent heterogeneity. There is no similarity between internal feeling and the external agent in kind or degree : the feeling is only a symbol of objects. As such it has a certain correspondence with the object. The relations between feelings do not resemble relations between outer agents. Feelings are revivable in proportion as they are relational, the peripherally initiated feelings being the most revivable. The revivability of past feelings varies inversely as the vividness of present feelings. It depends on the strength of feeling and the relative number of times it has recurred. Relations are in general more revivable than feelings, the relation of co-existence being the most revivable of all. The associability of feelings is co-extensive with their revivability. The (only) law of association is that of contiguity. The feelings of pleasure and pain are, speaking generally, concomitants respectively of medium and excessive, beneficial and injurious, organic activities. In human nature there has occurred and must long continue a deep and involved derangement of the habitual connections between pleasures and beneficial actions and between pains and detrimental actions. The intrinsic nature of pleasure and pain is, psychologically viewed, apparently inexplicable.

General Synthesis (the Study of Mind as objectively manifested in its Ascending Gradations through the Various Types of Sentient Beings). — Mind can be understood only by observing how mind is evolved. The beginning of the evolution of mind, or psychical (as distinguished from physical) vital actions, occurs the moment we rise above correspondences between organism and the environment that are few, simple, and immediate. First, there is direct and homogeneous correspondence (as in the yeast-plant and in sponges); then correspondence direct but heterogeneous, or correspondence with the most general changes in the environment (as in vegetal life at large, while plant-animals exhibit in addition certain special changes corresponding with special changes in the environment). On ascending from the lowest types of life one marked manifestation of the heightening correspondence is the increasing distance at which co-existence and sequence in the environment produce adapted changes in the organism, — a process accompanying the development of the senses of smell, sight, hearing, etc. The next is the extension of the correspondence in time: after the ability to respond to the touches of surrounding bodies comes the ability to respond to those motions of them which precede touch; and since motion involves both time and space, the first extension of the correspondence in time is necessarily coeval with its extension in space. The correspondence between organism and environment also increases in speciality, and in generality and complexity. The advance of correspondence in generality appears in the recognition of constant co-existences and sequences, of attributes as well as objects. Increased correspondence in complexity appears in an increased power to apprehend a heterogeneity of stimuli, connected with increased power of displaying changes. The increase of correspondence depends more on the sense of touch than any other sense: the tactual impressions being those into which all other impressions have to be translated before they can have any meaning. The increase of correspondence means, according to the definition of life (see above, page 248), an increase of life in strength and fulness. Besides the advances in correspondence we have also to take into account the co-ordination and integration of correspondences. The performance of a compound action in response to a compound impression implies that the constituent sensations and contractions shall be combined after a particular manner. Compound impressions, as well as compound motions guided by them, continually approach in their apparent character to simple impressions and simple motions. The co-ordinated elements of any stimulus or of any act always tend towards union, and eventually become indistinguishable; and the connection between stimulus and act also becomes constantly closer, so that they seem but two sides of the same change. Perpetually repeated complex muscular actions eventually approximate in rapidity and ease to simple motions. From the foregoing in regard to correspondence it appears that psychical actions, separately and in their totality, in their broadest aspect obey the same law of evolution as physical actions.

Special Synthesis (the Presentation of Psychological Truths under their Differential Aspect). — The phenomena of the mind as occurring only in time present but a single series or succession. Co-existence, nevertheless, is representable by virtue of the fact that it is a form of sequence, *viz.*, reversible sequence. The law of intelligence is: The persistence of the connection between the states of consciousness is proportionate to the persistence of the connection between the agencies to which they answer. The strength of the tendency which a state of consciousness has to follow any other depends on the frequency with which the two have been connected in experience. The simplest purely psychical phenomenon is reflex action,— in which a simple impression produces a single contraction. A compound reflex action, — *i. e.*, a combination of impressions followed by a combination of contractions, — is Instinct. Instincts occur only in the nervo-muscular apparatus, which is the agent of psychical life. Through inheritance, instincts may be formed from simple reflex actions. They are formed in other ways also. Instincts may become so complex and incoherent as to pass into something higher. Instincts are automatic. Memory can exist only where psychical changes are not completely automatic. Of the impressions produced by adjacent objects during the movements of the organism, each is apt to make nascent, or render conscious, certain other impressions with which it has been connected in experience, and these arouse others, — so that memory pertains not to the class of unconscious automatic states, but to classes of states which are in process of being organized. When the automatic adjustment of states is uncertain, some one set — the strongest — prevails over others, and passes into action ; and as this sequence will usually be the one that has occurred oftenest in experience, the action will generally be the one best adapted to the circumstances. An action thus produced is a rational (not automatic) action. When instead of an action there occurs merely an act of passing in thought to attributes or relations not immediately present, we have another sort of reasoning, *viz.*, mere inference. Between instinct and reason (the two forms of which have just been described) there is no hiatus. Our ideas of time and space, considered as modes of activity, are formed according to the same law that instinct, memory, reason are formed according to, — *viz.*, that a cohesion of states results from, and is in proportion to, frequency and sequence in experience: being constant and infinitely repeated elements of thought, they must become automatic elements of thought. — Arising at the same time with memory and reason, *i. e.*, when psychical states become too complicated to be automatic, are the feelings. Every perception is made up of combined sensations, and hence necessarily contains feeling; feeling is present in, and cannot be disentangled from, the other forms of consciousness. Feelings are strong in proportion as they include many actual sensations or nascent sensations, or both. Will comes into existence through the increasing complexity and imperfect coherence of automatic actions: practices which are coherent and automatic are involuntary. There is no freedom of will. The term "will" is but the general name given to the special feeling that gains supremacy and determines action.

Physical Synthesis ("treating of the manner in which the succession of states of consciousness conforms to a certain fundamental law of nervous action that follows from first principles"). — How is mental evolution to be affiliated on evolution at large regarded as a process of physical transformation? The development of the nerve results from the passage of motion along the line of least resistance and the reduction of it to a line of less and less resistance. The formation of the simple nervous system capable of yielding a simple reaction is due to the fact that to some place of greatest and most frequent contraction lines of discharge will be formed from places habitually touched before contraction is set up. A compound nervous system capable of yielding reactions that are specially adapted, once arising, is by natural selection and heredity confirmed, continued, and developed. A combination of such compound systems or doubly-compound systems is formed by the intercalation of plexuses of connection between the separate compound systems. There occur simple, compound co-ordinations of systems. The higher the co-ordinations, the more cerebrum and cerebellum are involved. Corresponding to these various systems are certain classes of mental functions. For every different nervous plexus there is a different cluster of mental states, and *vice versa*. Ideas, or units of knowledge, arise when compound co-ordination passes into doubly-compound co-ordination. Emotions, like ideas, result from the co-ordinating actions of the cerebrum and cerebellum upon the medulla oblongata and the structures it presides over. There are special nervous plexuses for special feelings: localization of function is the law of all organization whatever. Now, physical activities have all to be interpreted in accordance with the law of the continuous redistribution of matter governing the nervous system. In early life, with its rapid waste and repair, the channels of the nervous system are filled to overflowing, and feelings are vivid. The opposite is the case late in life. The man whose nervous system works under high pressure has an abundance of ideas. Derangements of cerebral circulation cause temporary insanity, etc. All this, however, is no proof in favor of mere materialism, nor, on the other hand, of mere spiritualism.

Special Analysis (having for its Aim the Resolution of each Species of Cognition into its Components). — The emotions do not admit of further interpretation. We take up ideas. — An analysis must begin with the most complex phenomena of the series to be analyzed, — in the present instance with reasoning. *Reasoning* is, in general, the establishment of relations between terms. The establishing of relations between relations is compound reasoning.

In quantitative reasoning the relation established is one of equality of magnitudes. Quantitative reasoning is imperfect in the case of theorems asserting that a thing is greater or less than some other, or falls within or without another. Quantitative reasoning in general involves the three ideas of co-extension, co-existence, connature, — and only these, since there are no intuitions besides these that are perfectly definite. Perfect qualitative reasoning occurs where equality, or indistinguishableness, is asserted of two relations that are alike in the natures of their terms, and the co-existence of each antecedent with its consequent. Imperfect qualitative reasonings occur where conclusions can have their negatives conceived with greater or less difficulty: they are distinguished from perfect qualitative reasonings by the relative indefiniteness of their intuitions. The compared relations here are *like* and *unlike* (instead of *equal* and *unequal*). Under imperfect qualitative reasoning fall analogy, induction, and deduction. Analogy differs from so-called inductive reasoning only in degree. Induction and deduction have such relation that while in the latter the known relations grouped together as of the same character outnumber the unknown, in induction the reverse is the case. The two conflicting views concerning the value of the syllogism are reconciled by distinguishing between logic as the formulation of the most general laws of correspondence among existences considered as objective, and as an account of reasoning which formulates the most general laws of correlation among the ideas corresponding to those existences. — Closely allied to reasoning are *classification* and *naming*, the three presupposing one another and having the intuition of likeness of relations as their common basis. — In *perception* also there is involved the intuition of identity or similarity; a present object is ranged with objects of past experience kindred with it. The relation between subject and object in perception is threefold: (1) the subject may be passive, and a *dynamical property of the object* (sound, color, taste, etc.) is apprehended; (2) it may be both passive and active, *i. e.*, may act on the object, — whence result the apprehension of *dynamico-statical properties :* or (3) it may be merely active, apprehending *statical* **properties of objects** (bulk, figure, **position.**) Strictly speaking, the dynamico-statical properties are neither objective nor subjective, but products of subject, object, and environing activities. The process of combining the elements of a perception may be termed a process of "*organic classification.*" This semi-conscious process is necessarily preceded by an unconscious classification of its constituent attributes, of the relations in which they stand to one another, and of the conditions under which such attributes and relations become known. The several attributes, the relations in which they stand to one another and to the subject, as well as the conditions under which only such attributes and relations are perceived, have to be thought of as like before-known relations and before-known conditions. Between the statico-dynamical and the statical attributes there is an (inscrutable) relation of some sort. Of the statico-dynamical attributes (heavy and light, hard and soft, firm and fluid, viscid and friable, etc.), two classes have an objective origin, *viz.*, those referable to touch and pressure, and two of subjective origin, *viz.*, those referable to muscular tension and muscular motion. All perceptions of statico-dynamical attributes consist in the establishment of relations of simultaneity and sequence among our sensations of touch, pressure, tension, and motion : experienced as increasing, decreasing, or uniform, and combined in various modes and degrees. Our knowledge of the statical attributes is built up out of sensations of touch combined with those of vision. Largely instrumental in the acquisition of this knowledge is the knowledge of the position of our members towards one another derived from the " mutual exploration of members." The *idea of space* in the abstract is got by dissociation from numerous concrete experiences. The evolutional theory of space, which makes it a relation constantly experienced by the individual and the race, reconciles the ordinary experience-hypothesis and the hypothesis of the transcendentalists. To the Kantian hypothesis there are various objections: without insisting on the fact that our sensations of sound and odor do not carry with them the consciousness of space at all, — there is the fact that along with those sensations of taste, touch, light, which do carry this consciousness along with them, it exists in extremely different degrees, — a fact quite unaccountable if space is given before all experience as a form of intuition; that our consciousness of surrounding space is far more complete than our consciousness of remote space is at variance with this hypothesis, which, for aught that appears to the contrary, implies homogeneity; that in morbid states space should appear swollen is on the Kantian theory unaccountable, etc. — When it comes to be shown (below) that the ultimate element into which the consciousness of space is decomposable can itself be gained only by experience, the utter untenableness of the Kantian doctrine will become manifest. *Time* is known to us as the abstract of all relations of position among successive states of consciousness. The consciousness of time must vary with size, structure, and functional activity. The idea — or at least a nascent idea — of motion results when the two relations of co-existent and sequent positions are both presented to consciousness with a series of sensations of muscular tension. This (nascent) idea is developed by accumulation and comparison of experiences. The notions of time, space, and motion are evolved concurrently. The dissociation of these notions takes place through the instrumentality of sight. Our ideas of time, space, motion, and matter all finally resolve themselves into the perception of resistance, the primordial, the universal, the ever-present constituent consciousness. — Perception, we have seen, is allied to reasoning. It is, on the other hand, distinct from *sensation*: the distinction between them being the only valid distinction to be drawn in the whole series of mental phenomena. Perception and sensation cannot be said to vary inversely, but to exclude one another with degrees of stringency which vary inversely. Perception is an establishment of definite relations among the states of consciousness; sensation is known as an indecomposable state of consciousness. — Of the *relations* — simple and complex — *cognized in* **perception**, the most complex is that of simplicity, which when complete is the "co-intension" (likeness in degree between changes like in kind) of two connatural (like in kind) relations between states of consciousness like in kind but unlike in degree. Other relations are those of co-extension and non-co-extension, co-existence and non-co-existence, likeness and unlikeness, etc. Co-extension is equality in length of series of united sensations of touch and motion. Co-existence is a union of two relations of sequence which are such that while the terms of the one are exactly like those of the other in kind and degree, and exactly contrary to them in their order of succession, the two relations are exactly like each other in the feeling which accompanies the succession. By likeness and unlikeness we mean respectively *change* and *no-change* in consciousness. The two terms of a relation of likeness are the antecedent and consequent of what in one sense is *no-change*, seeing that it leaves consciousness in the same condition as before. Accurately speaking, a relation of likeness consists of two relations of unlikeness which neutralize each other. The relation of unlikeness is therefore the primordial one. The relation of sequence is but that of unlikeness in a changed aspect. The general result of the foregoing special analysis is that all mental operations are modifications of one and the same essential phenomenon: the highest reasoning is one with the lowest form of thought. Consciousness is forever changing: all mental action is the continuous differentiation and integration of states of consciousness.

General Analysis (an Inquiry as to the General Basis of our Intelligence). — We have arrived at the problem of knowledge as a relation between subject and object. Is the distinction between subject and object valid, and a real datum of philosophy? The metaphysicians (Berkeley, Hume, and Kant, in particular) have erred in their denial of object; and the source of their error has been their confidence in the indirect instead of the direct deliverance of consciousness. What Hume calls an "impression" must be an "impression" of something. Kant's assertion that time and space are subjective is untenable: the two ideas, *space* and *self*, will not combine, — their union is inconceivable. Further, to make space and time subjective is to deny that they are objective, which is absurd, since we cannot think away space and time from the objective world. Idealism as the denial of the objective world is false; it is false also as the denial of the direct consciousness of (the fact of) an objective world. It is a consequence of the confounding of two quite distinct things, *viz.*, the having a sensation and the being fully conscious of having a sensation. The having a sensation, or the simple consciousness of sensation, is primordial. Through immeasurably long and complex differentiations and integrations of such primordial sensations and ideas derived therefrom, develops a consciousness of self and a correlative not-self. In the history of the race, therefore, as in that of the individual mind, Realism, or the belief in the direct consciousness of reality, is the primary conception. Realism is simple, direct, apparently undecomposable; Idealism is long, involved, and indirect, not simply decomposable, but requires much ingenuity to decompose it. Realism involves but one mediate act; Idealism many. Realism has the advantage of distinctness as well as simplicity; the deliverances of consciousness composed of sensations are the more vivid, and are to be unhesitatingly preferred to those composed of ideas of sensations. Realism has a solid basis, then, in direct consciousness. But one proposition or idea does not make a science, and for the combination of ideas there is required a criterion, which must, of course, be some universal postulate. That theory is truest which requires the application of the postulate the fewest number of times.

(Spencer here enters into a discussion and classification of propositions which we are obliged to pass over). The universal postulate must be that the inconceivableness of the negative of a proposition shows, in every case, such proposition to possess the highest rank of truth and certainty. Inconceivableness is not (as Mill appears to think) synonymous with mere incredibleness or unbelievableness. It is unbelievable that a cannon-ball fired from England should reach America, but it is not inconceivable. Conversely, it is inconceivable that one side of a triangle is equal to the sum of the other two sides, — not simply unbelievable or incredible. Inconceivableness as corresponding to an inherited and stable condition of the nervous system is a better criterion than Mill's induction. Now, realism, as involving the application of the criterion the fewest number of times, has the highest validity. — But there is a positive justification of Realism, — a justification of it by consciousness working after its proper laws. The law of consciousness, that we are *obliged to think objective existence*, is the all-sufficient warrant for the assertion of it. Further, if we compare the states of consciousness which have been termed, respectively, vivid and faint states, we find that like effects are producible by antecedents existing respectively in these two great antithetical aggregates, — a fact which suggests that there must be something in common between the antecedents. In fact, we cannot by any possibility exclude the consciousness of a force in the vivid aggregate somehow allied to that which is distinguished as a force in the faint aggregate; the vivid aggregate, both as manifesting passive resistance (for our faint states are able to originate changes in it) and manifesting active energy (for it produces changes in the faint states), inevitably comes to have associated with it in consciousness the idea of power separate from but in some way akin to the power which the faint aggregate perpetually evolves within itself. — Subject and object, then, have a separate though correlative existence, — the one as the unknowable permanent nexus which, never itself a state of consciousness, holds together states of consciousness; the other an unknowable resisting somewhat underlying the aggregate of vivid states. The doctrine of Realism here advocated is Common Sense Realism purified, — Transfigured Realism; the error of ordinary Realism being its assumption that we not only know the *fact* of an objective existence, but also its nature. The history of metaphysical controversy, which is the history of conflict between Realism and Idealism, points to the truth of Transfigured Realism, since controversy always ends when ordinary Realism is purified of its errors, and subject and object are completely differentiated.

Congruities. — To complete the system of psychology it remains to co-ordinate and exhibit the congruities among the different aspects of psychological phenomena. (It is hardly necessary to follow out this after-thought of Spencer's.)

Corollaries ("consisting in part of a Number of Derivative Principles, which form a Necessary Introduction to Sociology"). — Mental phenomena, we have seen, are feelings and relations between feelings or cognitions. Cognitions are presentative, presentative-representative, representative, or *re*-representative. Feelings may be divided into corresponding classes of presentative feelings, presentative-representative feelings, etc. The degree of representativeness is the criterion of the degree of evolution of cognitions and feelings; the cognitions and feelings of primitive feelings are lacking in representativeness, etc. The feelings have an appropriate language, the origin of which is sufficiently explained by the law of the evolution of nervous structures and functions. Every feeling has for its primary concomitant a diffused nervous discharge which excites the muscles at large. There is also a restricted discharge, directed or undirected, controlling special muscles only. The external concomitants of non-pleasurable feeling, which constitute what we call its expression, result from incipient muscular contractions of like nature with those accompanying actual combat. (The expressions of pleasurable feelings are to be supposed natural to the organism in and of itself.) Sociality becomes naturally established when furthering the preservation of the species. Doubtless, also, gregarious creatures learn to take pleasure in one another's company, and to sympathize in general. The development of the sexual relations develops sympathy. So also does that of intelligence. Sympathy is hindered by the predatory instincts. Defining sentiments as the highest order of feelings, which are entirely re-representative, we may make these classes of sentiments, — egoistic, ego-altruistic, altruistic, and æsthetic. Egoistic are such as the sentiment of possession, of power, freedom, bodily and political. These all have at first particular characters and associations, and only gradually become general. The ego-altruistic sentiments have their origin in an unconscious imitation of the sentiments of others, and are not at first associated with the idea of the goodness or badness of their objects. They are, as a rule, variable among different societies; they have, however, important compounds that are constant, — a kind of sentiment which calls forth approval among all races, and in all times will be felt as right, irrespective of the people and the age (and *vice versa*). The variability of ego-altruistic sentiment is merely the concomitant of the transition from the aboriginal type of society, fitted for destructive activities, to the civilized type of society, fitted for peaceful activities. The sentiments must eventually prove permanent, for the reason that the conditions of complete social life are uniform and permanent. Altruistic feelings have been held in check by antagonism between societies and by the struggle for existence in society. Altruistic are generosity, pity, justice, mercy, — all products of evolution. Æsthetic sentiments have the peculiarity that they are associated with separateness from the life-serving function. That the æsthetic consciousness is essentially one, in which the actions themselves, apart from ends or from the object-matter, is shown by the conspicuous fact that many æsthetic feelings arise from the contemplation of attributes and deeds of other persons, real or ideal. Æsthetic feeling of the highest kind results from the full, but not excessive, exercise of the greatest number of powers without undue exercise of any. Æsthetic activities in general may be expected to play an increasing part in human life as Evolution advances.

The Principles of Sociology: The Data of Sociology. — Evolution is either Inorganic, Organic, or Superorganic. Superorganic evolution includes all those processes and products which imply the co-ordinated actions of many individuals. We shall confine our discussion to that form of superorganic evolution which societies exhibit, premising that superorganic evolution is found only among (some of) the higher vertebrata. The primary factors of social phenomena are climate, surface, flora, fauna (which may be classed as "extrinsic"), and the physical, emotional, and intellectual attributes of man (which are "intrinsic"). Secondary factors are: the changes of climate caused by the clearing of forests and by drainage; the effects wrought upon the flora and fauna of the surface occupied; the ever-accumulating, ever-complicating, superorganic products, material and mental. Social integration is slow and difficult in mountainous or desert regions; it is easy within a territory which, while equal to the support of a large population, affords facilities for coercing the population. Other things being equal, localities that are uniform in structure are unfavorable to social progress. The influences of geological and geographical heterogeneity are conspicuous. So also those of the character of fauna and flora, etc. The external factors of social evolution play a much more important part in the earlier than in the later stages of evolution. (We pass over, without venturing to summarize, numerous interesting discussions on the topic of "external factors.") Adequate knowledge of the original internal factors is impossible. Our conceptions of primitive man and his history have to be formed from those of existing races. Physically, the primitive man is inferior, — has inferior conditions of development, and matures too early. Emotionally also he is deficient; his feelings are not highly representative or re-representative; he is impulsive, uncertain, improvident; absorbed in the present, sluggish, egoistic, unsocial. Intellectually, he is without conceptions of general facts, has no prevision of distant events, no notions of definiteness and truth, no constructive imagination, no power of reflection, no grasp of thought, no curiosity. The ideas of the primitive man are crude. The course of their development is as follows: "Changes in the sky and on the earth foster the notion of duality, which is confirmed by shadows and echoes, dreams and somnambulism, and favored by such abnormal sensibilities as swoon and apoplexy, which temporary forms of unconsciousness become linked with lasting kind of unconsciousness, from which the double [second self] cannot be brought back at all, — with death. The belief that these doubles of dead men are the cause of all strange and mysterious things leads primitive men to guard themselves from them by the aid of exorcists and sorcerers, or to propitiate them by prayers and praise, — from which latter observances every other kind of worship has arisen. Besides the aberrant developments of ancestor-worship which result from the identification of ancestors with idols, animals, plants, and natural powers, there are the direct developments of it. Within the tribe, the chief, the magician, or some one otherwise skilled, held in awe during his life, as showing power of unknown origin and extent, is feared in a higher degree when, after his death, he gains the further powers possessed by all ghosts. Still more, the stranger, bringing new arts, as well as the conqueror of superior race, is treated as a superhuman being during life, and afterwards worshipped as a yet greater superhuman being. Thus setting out with the wandering double, which the dream suggests; advancing from the ghost, at first supposed to have but a transitory second life, to ghosts which exist permanently, and therefore accumulate, — the primitive man is led gradually to people surrounding space with supernatural beings, small and great, which become in his mind causal agents for everything unfamiliar. And in carrying out the mode of interpretation, initiated on the way, he is committed to the ever-multiplying superstitions we have traced out. How orderly is the genesis of these beliefs will be seen on now observing that the general formula of evolution is conformed to by the changes gone through."

The Inductions of Sociology (the Empirical Generalizations that are arrived at by comparing Different Societies and Successive Phases of the Same Society). — Society is analogous to the living body, — it is an organism : it undergoes continuous growth; its parts become unlike; it exhibits increase of structure; the progressive differentiation of its structure is accompanied by progressive differentiation of its functions; in it there is mutual dependence of parts, "physiological division of labor," etc. The social organism is unlike the physical in certain important regards : while the parts of an animal form a concrete whole, those of a society form a whole which is discrete; while in the one, consciousness is concentrated in a small part of the aggregate, in the other it is diffused throughout the aggregate, all the units possessing the capacity for happiness and misery in approximately equal degrees. On account of this cardinal difference, while in the physical organism the end is the welfare of the aggregate rather than the united, in the social organism the end is that of the units, instead of the aggregate as such. The beginning of societies, like that of living bodies, is in germs. Increase is by multiplication of units, — by union of groups, and groups of groups. Social growth shows the fundamental trait of evolution under a twofold aspect : integration being displayed in the formation of a larger mass and in the progress of such mass towards that coherence due to closeness of parts, — "increase of structure," with "increase of mass." As in the lowest types of animals no organ strictly so-called exists, so in the most primitive stages of society there is a condition in which each worker carries on his occupation alone, and himself disposes of the product to consumers. Again, the compact cluster of cells has its analogue in the related families which formerly monopolized industry. Other structural analogies exist (which we have not space to specify). As regards functions, as evolution advances the consensus of these in the individual and in the organism becomes closer, etc. The social organism has its systems of organs corresponding to outer and inner, and distributing in the physical organism; it has its sustaining, regulative, and distributing systems, which are, respectively, its governmental-military organization, its productive industries, trades. Primarily societies may be arranged according to their degrees of composition as simple, compound, doubly-compound, trebly-compound; secondarily into the predominantly military and the predominantly industrial. The trait characterizing the militant structure throughout is that its units are coerced into their various combined actions, — co-operation in it is compulsory. With social organisms, as with individual, the structure becomes adapted to the activity. The most important transformations are those of the militant into the industrial, and of the industrial into the militant forms of society, — social evolution forms a part of evolution at large.

Domestic Institutions (the Maintenance of the Human Race). — For the maintenance of the human race reproduction must be proportioned to mortality. The highest constitution of the family is reached when there is such a conciliation between the needs of the society and those of its members, old and young, that the mortality between birth and reproduction falls to a minimum, while the lives of adults have their subordination to the rearing of children reduced to the smallest possible. Primitive domestic relations are unregulated: marriage is informal, wives are exchanged, marriage is exogamous, endogamy being a concomitant of the higher stages of the family, promiscuity is not uncommon. An advance is made by the passage from promiscuity to polyandry, thence to polygamy, which possessed a superiority over earlier forms of marriage, — and hence superseded them, — in that it provided a greater chance for social survival. Polygamy naturally passed into monogamy by the elevation of one wife and the depression relatively of others into a condition relatively servile and unauthorized. Enduring monogamic relations were established by slow stages only, — the chief aids tending to establish it being a more developed conception of property and progress towards the equalization of the sexes. Monogamy is doubtless the highest form of sexual relation for the human race. Disintegration occurs in the family by the substitution for domestic groups of groups formed of mingled individuals belonging to many stocks. In modern nations this disintegration has partially dissolved the relations of domestic life and replaced them by those of social life; the State has to a considerable degree usurped the parental function in respect to children, and, assuming their claims upon it, exercises coercion over them. We must assume, however, that this degree of family disintegration is in excess, and will hereafter be followed by partial reintegration. The status of woman has undergone a marked evolution. In savage life the treatment of woman is cruel in the extreme. An improvement in the condition of woman occurs with an increase of likeness between the occupations of the sexes. A probable further cause was the obtaining of a wife by service rendered. Improvement in condition of woman, and increase of industrialism, have gone along together. The series of changes in the status of children corresponds with that in the status of women. In the future there will be a nearer approach to the equality of the sexes.

Ceremonial Institutions: (*the Natural History of the Third Kind of Government, etc.*). — The earliest kind of government (or control of conduct involving relation to other persons), the most general kind of government, the government which is ever spontaneously recommencing, and which most influences men's lives, is the government of ceremonial observance. Ceremonies originate by modification of acts performed for personal ends, and by natural sequence rather than by intentional symbolization. Ceremonial organization disappears only as far as political and ecclesiastical organizations usurp its functions. Ceremonies comprise trophies, mutilations, presents, visits, obeisance, forms of address, titles, badges, costumes. The trophy was primarily a proof of victory won and a token of prowess; secondarily it was a supposed means of coercing the ghost of an enemy by the (supposed) fact that possession of a part of the body gave power over the spirit of the enemy. Trophy-taking relates to a predominantly militant society, and decreases with the increase of industrialism. A sequence of trophy-taking is (partial) mutilation of the body of the conquered person. The being mutilated was a badge of slavery. Allied to mutilation is the giving of presents as a sign of homage. Present-giving naturally evolves into the paying of tribute or tax. Offering presents to the dead, *e.g.*, by placing supplies of food on their graves, becomes in the course of time sacrificing to a god. Visits are first made as a sign of allegiance. Propitiation of a more powerful being declines into that of an equal, thence to ordinary civility. Obeisance ranges in its manifestations through precise degrees, from prostrating the form on the earth to merely slightly bending the body. All obeisance originates in militancy, and declines with its decline. Having a common origin with obeisance is the form of address. Titles have been formed by differentiation from proper names. Badges originated in trophies; dress was originally a sort of badge merely. Ceremony has its antithetic counterpart in fashion, which is a form of voluntary, instead of involuntary, co-operation. The conclusion to be gathered from the study of ceremony is that the rules of behavior are natural products of social life which have been evolved; their advance in integration, heterogeneity, definiteness, and coherence proves their agreement with the laws of evolution at large.

Political Institutions. — The complexity and confusion of the evidence bearing upon political institutions is such that only certain general conclusions can be positively established. Political organization has for its end the removing of antagonism and the aiding of co-operation by creating a demand for commodities. It has its disadvantages, — which may outweigh its advantages; the maintenance of controlling structure is expensive, imposes restraints, indirectly entails evils on those who exercise it; an established organization is an obstacle to reorganization, impedes further growth. Political integration has the following traits: the incorporation of materials for growth, which is in small aggregates carried on at one another's expense in feeble ways, — by taking one another's game, robbing one another of women, etc.; in larger aggregates, by the enslaving of members of conquered tribes and the annexation of tribes and territory. Furthering or hindering conditions of social growth are: fitness or unfitness of habitat for supporting a large population, great or small facilities for intercourse within its area, presence or absence of natural barrier, the joint reaction or not of the units against external action, etc. Co-operation in wars is the chief cause of social integration. As political integration advances it obliterates the original divisions among the united parts. The state of homogeneity in the social aggregate is unstable. The primary political differentiation originates from the primary family differentiation of man and woman, who early form the two political classes of ruler and ruled. The slave class, at first indistinctly separated, acquires separateness only as fast as there arise restrictions in the powers of the owners. Conquered peoples become serfs, the militant class land-owners or possessors of wealth. The succeeding distinction is one of wealth (owing to differences in inherited wealth), with certain concomitant physical and mental distinctions, and distinctions of rank. A competing non-inherited wealth tends to the equalization of the position of citizens before the law, etc. Political forms and forces originate in the following ways: an organized horde, in the effort to decide some question of public interest, differentiates first into two parts, one composed of the elder, wiser, and stronger members of the assembled horde, and another younger, weaker, and less wise; there occurs also a differentiation of the first of these, whereby some aged hunter, some distinguished warrior, some cunning medicine-man, becomes leader, or chief. The ratios among the powers of the components will vary. Political power originates in the feeling of the horde or community. This feeling is *mostly the accumulated and organized sentiment of the past.* Political supremacy in rude groups depends exclusively on personal attributes, as skill in war or in divination, sorcery, etc. Such supremacy is but transitory. A permanent headship becomes established by the principle of inheritance, and particularly inheritance in the male line, since this fosters ancestor-worship and the consequent reinforcing of natural by supernatural authority. Compound headship, or oligarchic rule, arises where there is a league of independent communities: it is first elective, becoming hereditary only later. It becomes, in course of time, narrower or wider. By a natural differentiation from the council of war there comes into existence a consultative body, which in time may develop into a body of mere advisers of the king or chief. Representative bodies come into existence in large communities in times of peace or when a subsidy has to be asked for by a king going to war. Ministers, or men chosen by the ruler to assist him, are met with in early stages of social evolution. At first chosen from among immediate companions of the ruler, — friends, relatives, attendant priests, — they afterwards are selected from beyond these narrow limits. Local governing agencies come into existence when after war the victor finds it necessary or the best policy to respect the substantial autonomies of the vanquished societies. The autonomies disappear or become entirely subordinate in a struggle with the central government. Family organizations do not disappear when separated from and subordinated to political organization and rule. There may exist under political rule the governing agency of a guild or union of family or clan in some occupation. The supplementary governing agencies proper to the military type dissolve as the industrial begins to predominate. As war declines, political and military systems in government differentiate: a standing army comes into existence. The judicial and executive systems are at the outset closely united in a state of militancy; the judicial function may be in the hands of the military or the sacerdotal class, or in the hands partly of one and partly of the other. With the rise of industrialism it comes to be administered by persons of the industrial class, etc. Laws are mainly embodiments of ancestral injunctions, the living ruler being able to legislate independently only in respect to matters unprovided for, unless he chance to be regarded as divine. As the number of independent regulations grows, there comes to be a differentiation of human from divine laws, etc. Laws were at first primarily concerned with the maintenance of the military status: current theories are adapted to a compromise between militarism and industrialism. Property, at first private only in respect to movables and game killed, becomes, on the transition from a nomadic state to a settled state of society, private to a larger extent, — the ownership of land by the community being somewhat qualified by individual ownership. In the military *régime* there is a graduated ownership of land. Only in industrial society is equal private ownership of land a possibility. The growth of revenue has been directly or indirectly a result chiefly of war. The militant and industrial types of society have each their special traits, which may be known *a priori* or by the inspection of existing societies, or by a consideration of the characters of the kinds of individuals composing them respectively. In the militant type there is corporate action of all; in the industrial this is not a primary requirement. In the militant type actions and possessions are held at the service of society; in the industrial, the life of society is incidental to that of its units. In the militant type co-operation is compulsory; in the industrial, voluntary. In the militant type the agency of government is despotic; in the industrial it is representative, etc. The political organization of the future will be of the industrial type. "The conclusion of the profoundest moment, to which all lines of argument converge, is that the possibility of a high social state, political as well as general, fundamentally depends on the cessation of war, — the decay of militancy."

Ecclesiastical Institutions. — Religious ideas are a product of evolution; they do not exist in the minds of primitive peoples. The chief factors in the genesis of religious belief are: the belief in the return of the other self after death; ministrations to the "double" of the deceased; conception of the other life as like the present, praise and prayer accompanying the development of grave-heaps into altars, and of grave-sheds into religious edifices; belief that the effigy of the dead man was the habitation of his ghost; the identification of the doubles of the dead with animals; star-worship. All gods originate by apotheosis; originally the god was the superior living man, whose power was conceived as superhuman. The proofs of the natural genesis of religion are abundant. Priestly functions were originally performed by members of the family: every man must have a male descendant (the eldest) to serve as a family priest, the devolution of the sacrificial office accompanying that of property. The priestly function is differentiated from the patriarchal with the growth of the family into the cluster of families. The function of priest is differentiated from that of ruler also, when the duties of the ruler became pressing; it is deputed to a brother or other member of the family. If the tribe be joined by an immigrant stranger who in virtue of superior knowledge excites awe, an additional cult may arise from his teachings or apotheosis. Polytheistic priesthoods arise as concomitants of the division and spreading of tribes, or as a concomitant of conquest, in which the conquerors do not destroy the worship of the conquered. Many facts make it clear that both the genesis of polytheism and its long survival are sequences of primitive ancestor-worship. Inequalities arise among gods in consequence of conquest. By gradual change, owing to favoring conditions, monotheism arises, and with it a unification of priesthood. Ecclesiastical organization develops *pari passu* with political organization. The functions of the priesthood have undergone evolution. With them were at first united military and civil functions. By his military functions the priest represented, not the higher, but the lower traits of human nature, contrarily to what — according to modern ideas — he should represent. In his civil office the priest was first ruler, then judge, and then minister or adviser. One phase of the differentiation of the priestly office appears in the modern separation of Church and State. (The main cause of this differentiation is the rise of industrialism.) The general influence of ecclesiastical institutions has been (and is) conservative, in a double sense: it has maintained and strengthened social bonds, and conserved the social aggregate. In the future of religion there will be a decay of the anthropomorphism of the past. "The conception, which has been enlarging from the beginning, must go on enlarging until by the disappearance of its limits it becomes a consciousness which transcends the forms of distinct thought, though it remains forever a form of consciousness. The germ of truth in primitive consciousness is that the power which manifests itself in consciousness is but a differently conditioned form of the power which manifests itself beyond consciousness."

The Principles of Ethics: the Data of Ethics. — To understand human conduct as a whole, we must study it as a part of that larger whole, constituted by the conduct of animate beings in general; and we must look upon the conduct now displayed by creatures of all orders as an outcome which has brought life to its present height. We have to frame a conception of conduct as correlated with the evolution of structure and function. Conduct is purposeful action. Advance in conduct is the more numerous and better adjustment of acts to ends. The evolution of conduct is threefold: it is an evolution tending to the preservation and larger life of the individual, as such, and of the species, and to the mutual help of the individuals in the advancement of ends. Conduct tending to the increase of life in self, the species, or fellow-men, is good; the opposite bad. There is one postulate upon which all moralists — optimists and pessimists alike — agree: that life is good or bad according as it does or does not bring a surplus of agreeable feeling. To define good conduct in terms of perfection is indirectly to define it in terms of itself, since the notion of perfection, like that of goodness, can be framed only in relation to ends. The only possible end is happiness. The intuitionist confides in conscience because he believes that conformity to it furthers the welfare of himself and others, and that disregard of it does the opposite. The religionist who inflicts pain upon himself or refrains from pleasures does so because he believes he will thereby escape greater future pain and secure greater future pleasure. All the current methods of ethics have the fault that they neglect ultimate causal connections, setting up in their stead the will of God, law, the voice of Conscience, etc. — Moral phenomena forming a part of the total aggregate of phenomena which evolution has wrought out, we have to consider them as phenomena of evolution. Conduct has to be viewed in a physical, a psychological, and a sociological aspect. In a *physical* regard, we have to view it as a set of combined motions, and inquire whether it displays in increasing degree the traits of evolution. Man even in his lowest stages displays in his conduct far more coherent, definite, and heterogeneous combinations of motion than the lower animals display; and the civilized man more than the savage. And what is called moral conduct is more coherent, definite, and heterogeneous than non-moral and immoral. *Biologically*, the moral man is one whose functions are all discharged in degrees duly adjusted to the conditions of existence. If there is not always a perfect correspondence between beneficial acts and pleasures and injurious acts and pains, that is because the human race as such is (as we have already seen) in a transitional condition, and there is a consequent temporary derangement of the normal relation of feeling to function. Ideally it is impossible to frame ethical conceptions from which pleasure is absent. The *psychological* aspect of ethics is that aspect under which the adjustment of two related phenomena in the "environment" to two related phenomena in the "organism," subjectively regarded, appears not as an intellectual co-ordination simply, but as a co-ordination in which pleasures and pains are alike factors and results. The study of evolving conduct, human and subhuman, discloses the truth that for the better preservation of life the primitive, simple, presentative feelings must be controlled by the later-evolved, compound, and representative feelings. It is an error, however, to suppose that the rule of the lower must be resisted even when it does not conflict with the rule of the higher, or that a gratification which forms a proper aim if it is remote, necessarily forms an improper aim if it is proximate. There are four forms of relinquishment of immediate and special good to gain distant and general good: *viz.*, relinquishment from fear (1) of legal punishment, (2) of divine vengeance, (3) of public reprobation, or (4) all together. These are at first practically co-extensive and undistinguished: they differentiate in the course of social evolution, and moral control, with its accompanying conceptions and sentiments, emerges as independent. The moral motive differs from the motives it is associated with in this, that instead of being constituted by representations of incidental, collateral, non-necessary consequences of acts, it is constituted by representations of consequences which the acts naturally produce. Moral sentiment is evolved later than all others, and is conditioned by them: it is an abstract sentiment generated in a manner analogous to that in which abstract ideas are generated. Emerging as the moral motive does but slowly amidst the political, religious, and social motives, it long participates in that consciousness of subordination to some external agency which is joined with them, and only as it becomes distinct and predominant does it lose this associated consciousness, — only then does the feeling of obligation fade. Hence the startling conclusion that the sense of duty, or moral obligation, is transitory, and will diminish as fast as moralization increases. The pleasures and pains which the moral sentiments originate will, like bodily pleasures and pains, become incentives and deterrents so adjusted in their strengths to the needs that the moral conduct will be the natural conduct. From the *sociological* point of view ethics is merely a definite account of the forms of conduct that are fitted to the associated state in such wise that the lives of each and all may be the greatest possible, alike in length and breadth. Different sociological principles rule in peace and war: in war the welfare of social groups takes precedence of individual welfare; in peace there is room for voluntary co-operation. For harmonious co-existence in a society, there is, beyond the primary requirement that its units shall not aggress on one another, the secondary requirement that they shall not indirectly aggress by breaking agreements; and there is also the requirement that there be spontaneous efforts to further the welfare of others. — In reply to Professor Sidgwick's criticism of the hedonistic method, that guidance by mere balancing of pain and pleasure is impracticable, it has to be said that it is quite consistent to assert that happiness is the ultimate aim of action, and yet to deny that it can be reached by making it the immediate aim. The proximate end is to use effectively each more complex set of means, the accompanying feeling becoming the immediate gratification sought; though there may be and habitually is an associated consciousness of the remoter ends and remoter gratifications to be obtained. The Benthamian doctrine that the supreme legislative body ought to make the greatest happiness of the greatest number its immediate aim seems to imply that there are no conditions to be fulfilled in order to secure the aforesaid happiness. But there *are* such conditions, and the immediate end is not happiness itself, but the fulfilment of conditions to the attainment of happiness. In general, the condition to be fulfilled is the maintenance of equitable relations between men. Recognizing in due degrees all the various ethical theories, conduct in its highest form will take as guides innate perceptions of higher, only enlightened by and made precise by analytic intelligence; while conscious that these guides are approximately supreme solely because they lead to the ultimately supreme end, happiness special and general. — There must be taken into account here a truth of cardinal importance as a datum of ethics, *viz.*, that pleasures and pains are relative; *e. g.*, they depend on the existence of a structure called into play, on the condition of that structure, on the character of the species in which it occurs. Recognizing this fact, we the better appreciate that only when human nature is perfectly adapted to its environment — but certainly then — will pleasure and pain be precise criteria of moral conduct. — As regards the relative importance in moral conduct of egoism, or action benefiting self merely, and altruism, or action benefiting others instead of self, it holds that egoism precedes altruism, since the acts which make continued life possible must on the average be more peremptory than all those other acts which life makes possible, including the acts which benefit others. But it is also true that altruism is no less essential than egoism, — defect of it causes death or inadequate development of offspring, and involves disappearance from future generations of the nature that is not altruistic enough. Pure egoism and pure altruism are both illegitimate. On the one hand, the ends of self are often promoted by a regard for those of others; on the other, there can be no real sympathy with others where egoistic feelings have no real strength. An important psychological objection to altruism is that it assumes that the representative feelings are stronger than the **presentative, which is** an impossibility. A **fatal** objection **to altruism as a** theory is that while the right principle **of action must be** more and more practised as men improve, **the altruistic** principle becomes less and less practicable as men **approach an ideal form, because the** sphere for practising it continually decreases. **Altruism** is inconsistent in implying both a readiness to sacrifice self for others and to accept sacrifice made by others for **ourselves.** A conciliation of egoistic and altruistic principles is **required ; and** our conclusion must be that general **happiness is to be achieved** mainly through the adequate pursuit **of their own** happi**ness by individuals ;** while reciprocally **the happinesses of individuals are to be achieved in part by the pursuit of the general happiness.** — It is necessary to make a distinction between *Absolute Ethics*, as ethics which deals with **perfect conduct, or conduct in the abstract, and** *Relative Ethics*, **dealing with imperfect conduct, or conduct in the concrete. Absolute Ethics serves as a standard that has to be adapted to concrete cases by taking into account** incidental factors. To make **the ideal man serve as a standard** he has to be defined in **terms of the conditions which his** nature **fulfils; we must consider him as existing in the** ideal social state. — It remains **merely to delare the** *scope of Ethics*. **Ethics has for its subject-matter conduct, not merely that conduct commonly approved or reprobated as right or wrong, but all conduct that furthers or hinders in either direct or indirect ways the welfare of self and others. It includes the two great divisions of** *Personal* **and** *Social Ethics.* *Personal Ethics* **has to do with the principles of private conduct which follow from the conditions of complete** individual **life : or what is the same thing — their modes** of private **action which must result from the eventual equilibrium of internal desires and external ends. Whether it will ever be practicable to lay down rules for private conduct is doubtful.** *Social Ethics* **has to do with acts that** affect others and are judged good or bad mainly by their results to others. It has the two subdivisions of Justice and Beneficence: the former being concerned with action as achieving ends that do or do not interfere with the pursuit of ends by others; the latter with actions influencing the states of others without interfering directly with the relations between their labors and the results, in one way or the other.

Justice (Part IV. of the Principles of Ethics). — There is an Animal Ethics, — a conduct that stands towards each species of animals as the conduct which we morally approve stands towards the human species. The two cardinal — and opposed — principles of animal ethics are: (1) During immaturity benefits received must be inversely proportionate to capacities possessed; (2) After maturity is reached, benefit must vary directly as worth, which is measured by fitness to the conditions of existence. Animal, or *sub-human, justice* involves only the second of these, — the law that each individual ought to be subject to the effects of its own nature and resulting conduct. Owing to various natural causes (as inclemency of weather, scarcity of food, invasion by parasites or enemies) sub-human justice is very imperfect, — far from actually realizing this law: is more perfect as organization is higher. Among gregarious creatures a second law — the negative element of sub-human justice — obtains also: each individual receiving benefits and injuries due to its own nature and consequent conduct has to carry on that conduct subject to the restriction that it shall not in any large measure injure the conduct by which each other individual achieves benefits or brings on itself injuries. A second qualification of the general law of sub-human justice is found in the responsibilities growing out of parenthood, which require that females with their offspring be protected by males, instead of protecting themselves. — Sub-human justice is the foundation of *human justice,* which is merely a further development of it, as human life is merely a further development of sub-human life. But in human justice the two qualifications, or rather (since the species takes precedence of the individual) corollaries, of the general principle of justice are more imperative than in sub-human justice: mutual self restraint and a sacrifice of the individual for the species as a whole are more requisite. The self-subordination of the individual to the species is, however, limited to such as is required for defensive (never for offensive) warfare. The *sentiment* of justice in man is a consequence of the law of organic evolution that when the circumstances of a species make certain relations between conduct and consequence habitual, the appropriately linked feelings may, through inheritance and survival, come to characterize the species. The egoistic sentiment of justice is easily accounted for; the altruistic may be accounted for by means of what may be termed a pro-altruistic sentiment of justice, having as components the dread of retaliation, of social dislike, of legal punishment, of divine vengeance, and gradually leading through these to the pure sentiment of justice. The *sentiment* of justice corresponds always to the social type, militancy being less favorable to its existence than industrialism. Intimately connected with this sentiment, but to be clearly distinguished from it, is the *idea* of justice, or the clear conception of that limit of each kind of activity up to which there is freedom to act. The differences that have existed in ideas of justice have been differences as to the relative importance attached to the two — positive and negative — elements of it, *viz.*, liberty, or inequality, and equality. Militancy emphasizes inequality; socialism equality; industrialism co-ordinates the two. Pure justice, which is the complete co-ordination of the two antagonistic elements, is an ultimate conception, not applicable to a transitional age such as the present. Formulated, the idea of justice is as follows: Every man is free to do that which he wills, provided he infringes not the equal freedom of any other man. This formula, it must be noted, does not countenance a superfluous interference with another's life, committed on the ground that an equal interference may balance it, — does not countenance aggression and counter-aggression. The practical advance that man has made in his conception of justice has been one away from this misapprehension towards the notion of non-interference. The authority of the formula of justice is twofold, *a priori* and *a posteriori*, deductive and inductive : justice is a natural and immediate dictum of human consciousness, and is deducible from conditions to be fulfilled by man., *viz.* (1) for the maintenance of life at large, and (2) for the maintenance of social life. — The *corollaries* of this formula, the forms which it assumes when applied to various classes of circumstances, express the individual liberties or *rights* of men. These corollaries coincide with ordinary conceptions and with legal enactments. From them law derives its warrants, but not *vice versa*. The rights flowing from the formula of justice are : the right to physical integrity, the rights to free motion and locomotion, the rights to the uses of natural media (air, light, surface of the earth), the right of (corporeal) property, the right of incorporeal property, the rights of gift and bequest, the rights of free exchange and free contract, the right of free industry, the rights of free belief and worship, the rights of free speech and publication, together with certain special rights of women and children. These corollaries, true unqualifiedly in absolute ethics, are, in a system of relative ethics, subject to qualification by the necessities of social self-preservation. Besides being self-evident consequences of the formula of justice, the law of equal freedom, they have as foundation the course of social evolution and the accompanying evolution of man's mental nature : they are both deductively and inductively demonstrable. The right to physical integrity had, apart from the deliberate destruction of incapable members of the tribe, which very generally had the excuse that it was needful for the preservation of the capable, no habitual existence in primitive social groups. Murder was regarded as an injury not so much to the man slain as to his family or clan. Whether the murderer or some other member of his class were killed in return was indifferent. The slave had no *wergeld* or *bot*. A slight step in advance occurred when part of the money paid in compensation for the life of the slain went to the king, — the destruction of the subject of a king being viewed as the destruction of a portion of the king's power over his subjects. Class distinctions arose, — a murderer who knew how to read escaped — up to the time of the Plantagenets — from nearly all punishment. Murder was, at first, a private, then a family or clan affair, then a social one, finally a moral one. By evolution the principle contained in the law of equal freedom practically established itself as respects the right to physical integrity. Murder, manslaughter, mutilation, assault, and all trespasses against physical integrity down to the most trivial have become transgressions, not in virtue of laws forbidding them, nor in virtue of interdicts having a supposed supernatural origin, but as breaches of certain naturally originated restraints. As with the right to physical integrity, so (Mr. Spencer undertakes to show at length) with the other rights, — they have an evolutionary origin and basis. The right of bequest presents what is in some sense an exception, in that an *a priori* derivation of the right to prescribe *uses* of bequeathed property where the testator is without children is impracticable, and we are in such a case left to an empirical compromise. Woman's participation in the rights above enumerated is affected by her domestic and maternal duties. Since she cannot be held equally responsible with man for the family maintenance, she can hardly have an equally unqualified ownership of property. though the discharge of her peculiar duties may ordinarily be held a fair equivalent for the earning of an income by the husband. As man is the more judicially-minded, he, rather than woman, should possess the balance of authority in the control of the household. As regards the possession and management of the children, the power of the mother may fitly predominate during the earlier part of the child's life, and that of the father during the latter part. As regards the political position of women, unless women furnish contingents to the army and navy such as men furnish, the question of equal political rights so-called cannot be entertained until there is reached a permanent state of peace. Children have "rightful claims" rather than "rights," — claims to the materials and aids needful for life and growth, *gratis*, and to such parts of the spheres of adult activity as they can advantageously use, since they must learn the conditions of self-preservation. The child is bound, in return for the satisfaction of its rightful claims, to submit to the direction of the parent. As the child approaches maturity it of course acquires rights in the proper sense. Of so-called "political rights" there are none. The supposition of their existence is an illusion resulting in part from the confounding of means and ends, of the governmental arrangements which conduce to the maintenance of rights proper with rights as such, and in part from overlooking too much the positive element of justice. Rights are original and antecedent to such arrangements; and further, the acquirement of political rights (*e. g.*, the right of suffrage) is not at all equivalent to the acquirement of rights properly so-called. — *The State* is not a fixed, unchanging thing, but a subject and product of evolution. Originally of a militant type, it is gradually becoming industrial. And the constitution of the individual state must depend on its relation to these two types. In a state of the militant type, a type that subordinates the individual to the community, centralization is necessary, government is autocratic, or, at least, oligarchic. The coercive consitution has therefore a relative justification. In the industrial type of state, which seeks the welfare of the individual as such, the administration is diffused rather than concentrated. It does not follow, however, that all citizens in an industrial government should have an equal share of power; representation should be a representation of interests rather than of individuals. Female suffrage appears unwise, owing to the comparative impulsiveness of women, their greater absorption in the proximate and personal to the exclusion of the remote and impersonal, their tendency to give most where capacity is least, their worship of authority, and consequent conservatism. But experience does not countenance the plea that without enfranchisement women cannot obtain legal recognition of their equitable claims. The distribution of public burdens can, while militancy continues, be nothing more than a rude approximation to justice. Taxes should be direct and tangible, instead of the opposite. As regards the *duties* of the State, induction demonstrates that government is initiated and developed by the defensive and offensive actions of society: the *first* duty of the ruling agency is national defence, not the maintenance of justice among individuals. The secondary function, possessed by government, of defending its components against one another, arises by differentiation from the primary one. Once established, the secondary function increases in importance while the primary diminishes: but its importance is still far from being fully recognized. Subordinate functions are the authorizing of the employments of the surface of the earth other than those already established and recognized by the community, and the preventing of interferences with individual action beyond such as the social state itself necessitates. The authority of the State is limited to the promotion of justice, or the equal freedom of all. Human rights do not exist by the authority of the State, but precede it; hence if, instead of preserving them, it trenches upon them, it commits wrongs instead of preventing them. — In the course of evolution there is a differentiation and relinquishment of functions of the State rather than the opposite: all-embracing State-functions characterize a low type of social organization. Experience shows that private corporations may advantageously assume functions gradually relinquished by the State. The strongest reason for limiting the functions of the State is to be found in considerations touching the formation of individual character. State control of education must result in the production of (1) uniformity of character among men, which retards advancement; (2) passive reception of whatever the State decides to impress; (3) a condition antagonistic to the natural processes by which human beings tend to become adapted to their social environments.

Results. — In so far as Spencer's doctrine maintains the existence of reality outside consciousness, it is a species of "realism;" but it is for the same reason a species of idealism, *i. e.*, *subjective* idealism. As a matter of fact it is identical (or nearly so) with the psychological or sensational idealism of Mill, Comte, and Hume. There is an *apparent* difference between it and that in the advantage which it seems to derive from the "evolutional" doctrine of inherited experience as explaining "innate notions," or intuitions which are acknowledged conditions of present experience. But if the mind has no really constitutive activity of its own, if, therefore, mere "sensation" is the origin and criterion of knowledge (conscious or unconscious), it is difficult to see how there can be any experience to be inherited, or any inheriting of experience gained. In a word, it seems entirely correct to say that, from a really philosophical point of view, the doctrine of Spencer is on the same level with that doctrine of Hume which Kant is almost universally acknowledged to have done away with. In saying this we do not entirely deny "evolution." — Spencer is, of course, the corypheus of (physical) "Evolutionists."

§ 164.

George Henry Lewes[1] (1817-1878). — Lewes studied medicine, and, afterwards, for two years, in Germany, philosophy and psychology. About the year 1840 he entered upon a literary career in London, working at first in the more purely literary fields, but afterwards in those of

---

[1] Lewes's Works.

science and philosophy. He was at one time editor of the "Fortnightly Review." **As** the husband, he was also the literary adviser of "George Eliot." Two works of his in æsthetic criticism, and a biography of Goethe by him, are **regarded as** works of high excellence.

Works. — His chief philosophical works are : "A **Biographical History of Philosophy**" (1st ed. 1845–1846 ; **4th** ed., enlarged and revised, **1871**) ; "Comte's Philosophy of the Sciences" (1853) ; "**Aristotle** : a Chapter from the History of Science" (1864) ; "Problems of Life and Mind: " First Series, — "The Foundation of a Creed" (2 vols. 1874–1875) ; Second Series, — "Physical Basis of Mind" (1877) ; Third Series, — "Psychology" (1879–1880).

Philosophy: *The Problem, Scope, and Method of **Metaphysics**.* — The problems of metaphysics formerly regarded (by himself as well as others) as insoluble cannot be lightly dismissed. "Few researches can be conducted in any one line of inquiry without sooner or later abutting on some metaphysical problem, were it only those of matter, force, cause, laws." A distinction must, at the outset, be made between the metaphysical and what may be termed the metempirical. By the term "metempirical" we may designate that which lies outside the positively known or the knowable. The term "metaphysical" may then be reserved for that which is (speculatively) knowable, the term "positive" designating the known. The "metempirical" begins where the speculative "quits the ground of sense and verification." By means of this distinction between the metaphysical and the metempirical we eliminate all insoluble questions from the problem of knowledge, and prepare the way for the application to metaphysics of the only method of knowledge, — *viz.*, the method of science. In pursuance of this distinction we have in dealing with any metaphysical problem to disengage the metempirical elements and then to treat the empirical elements with the view of deducing from them the unknown elements, if that be practicable, or, if the deduction be impracticable, of registering the unknown elements as transcendental. Such transcendental elements may be illustrated by reference to unexplored remainders in mathematics (*e. g.*, $\pi = 3.1416$ ETC.). A proper understanding of the nature of metaphysics obviates the objections made against it, that it moves in a world of mere abstractions, and seeks to penetrate causes and essences. All science is abstract; metaphysics differs from physical science only in degree of generality. Metaphysics deals, not with unknowable causes and essences, but laws, — the laws of laws. Metaphysics has an independent position among the sciences, — a position comparable to that of logic. Logic is the codification of the rules of proof; metaphysics is the codification of the laws of cause, — it is the logic of the Cosmos. It has a clearly defined object, *viz.*, the disengagement of certain most general principles, such as cause, force, life, mind, from the sciences which imply these principles, and the exposition of their constituent elements; it has a clearly defined and independent place in the region of research, *viz.*, that of an objective Logic; it has a clearly defined method of applying the results of experience, — that of dealing exclusively with the known functions of unknown quantities, and every stage of inquiry separating the empirical from the metempirical data. The conception of applying to metaphysics the procedures of science, first put forth by Comte, is " now for the first time definitely expressed in its principles and bearings."

Methodological and Psychological Principles. — The separation of the insoluble from the soluble in experience introduces us to the problems of the Limitations of Knowledge and the Principles of Certitude. Certain methodological and psychological principles have to be laid down by way of introduction to the discussion of these problems. Lewes here gives fifteen " rules for philosophizing," which contain the essence of the empirico-scientific method, and a brief outline of what may be termed biological psychology. Among the " rules " occur the following : No problem is to be mooted unless presented in terms of experience (i.) ; No agent to be admitted unless it have a sensible basis, nor any agency unless it be verifiable or calculable (iv.) ; No proof can be valid beyond the range of its data ; no conclusion is exact which shuts in what is not included in its premises (vii.) ; Philosophy, being the harmony between concrete and abstract, the synthetic and its explanatory analytic, demands that everywhere the abstract be subordinate to the concrete in respect to its validity, though it is superior in point of dignity (xiii.) : Newton's first, third, and fourth rules, and Comte's first law of Primary Philosophy. Among the psychological principles occur the following. There are two sorts of *conditions* of mind, and two corresponding aspects of mind, biological and sociological. Biologically regarded, the mind is a group of processes of feeling depending upon corresponding neural processes in such manner that neural and sentient processes are respectively the objective and subjective aspects of one and the same thing. Feeling as such, or when felt, is the real ; when thought, the ideal ; the latter having no value except as an abstract representative of the former. All thinking is seriation, and the thinking principle, therefore, does not possess ultimate unity and simplicity ; it is not an antecedent, but a resultant. Sociologically regarded, the mind is an intellectual and moral activity, without metempirically innate ideas, but with inherited tendencies or congenital aptitudes which are the products of racial experience ; owing to sociological conditions, it employs language, reasons, exercises sympathy, and performs all its higher functions. But all mental activity, whether cognitional, emotional, or volitional, has its beginning and its end in feeling, which alone is the real. There is no distinction to be made of phenomenon and noumenon : an object is what we feel it to be.

Theory of Knowledge : I. *Limitations of Knowledge.* — Psychology settles the question whether there are, over and above the recognized avenues of sensibility, other avenues in no respect allied to them, through which consciousness may be affected in the negative. So-called innate ideas or mental forms are, it says, "organized tendencies" acquired through successive experiences: the existence of such forms does not indicate *metempirical* sources of knowledge. The mental forms are, it is true, innate as regards the individual, but not the race. They are intuitions, but acquired or inherited intuitions. There is no metempirical factor in either the biological or the sociological data of experience. This true doctrine reconciles the antagonistic position of the sensationalist and the intuitionist. The sphere of knowledge is limited by (1) sensible impressions, *i. e.*, definite sensations, and (2) inferences which are the reproduction and combinations of such impressions. Sensation is certain, indisputable, true as far as it goes; we feel what we feel: it is the test and measure of certitude. Error begins with inference. We are liable to err even in a simple case of direct perception, where unapparent sensibles are rendered apparent; we are still more liable to error in ratiocination, *i. e.*, that process of mental vision in which ideas are reinstated in their sensible series, and the *relations* of things are substituted for things themselves. To avoid error in ratiocination we require to be able at every step to translate our ideas into sensations. It is not strictly true to say that our primary knowledge is limited by sensibility,— if we mean actual sensibility; that there is a knowledge of the world of the *possibly* sensible, which we may term the extra-sensible, is certain from various indications, *e. g.*, the existence of the chemical rays of light, which are not directly an object of sensibility. Only one condition is affixed to the inclusion of the sensibly invisible, the object of *possible* intuition, within the circle of science, *viz.*, that the objects be in such rigorous agreement with sensibles as to be presentable to intuition with a certainty equal to that of sensation; whenever the invisible is only an extension of the visible, we pronounce it rationally certain. Of the suprasensible, which is beyond all that is actually or possibly sensible, we certainly can know nothing, can neither affirm nor deny its existence. — As sensation is the measure and test of reality, so abstraction is merely ideal, and all science, as being abstract, is merely ideal construction. Point, line, circle, are elements of ideal, not of sensible space; motion in a straight line is purely ideal motion; real motion always pursues the line of least resistance. And the first law of motion therefore is an ideal law. The "type" of the botanist or zoologist is an ideal: the moral type is of like nature. In general the abstraction is not real, it is merely a symbol or direction for an operation or an act to be performed, and even as such it cannot be realized, — if it could, it would lose its dignity and degenerate into a concrete sensible. The fallacy of realizing abstractions appears in speaking of the laws of nature as controlling nature; speaking of phenomena as being governed by what are their resultants. The law is merely an ideal construction. Of laws, we may distinguish two sorts, in accordance with two distinguishable degrees of ideal construction, — the law proper and the hypothesis; the latter being more a construction than the former. The hypothesis as a construction removed from immediate fact has certain peculiar limitations as regards its use. The danger of abusing it has to be obviated by verification. It has, properly used, been of eminent service in scientific research. Hypotheses are real, auxiliary, and illusory. Examples of auxiliary hypotheses are the corpuscular doctrine of light and the Cartesian vortex-theory; of illusory hypotheses are electricity, ozone, vital force. The question arises here, How can science, as ideal construction, avail in our search after the external order, and explain the relations of things? How are we to pass from the abstract to the concrete? The passage from the abstract to the concrete is merely the inverse of the passage from the concrete to the abstract. What was dropped out of sight in establishing the ideal — namely, all the details which particularized the particular phenomena — must be restored in each particular case as we return towards the concrete.—The object of philosophy as the generalization of research is the discovery of causes. The quest for causes, if all metempirical elements be eliminated, is not only justifiable, but may be successful. The "Why" of the old metaphysics must be resolved into the "How." The cause of water, for example, is simply the conditions under which certain two gases unite. There is no other "why" in the operation,—no "power" over and above the sensible conditions, as the metaphysicians maintain. No one asks for a "why" in mathematics. Demonstration is the *showing* to sense or intuition, understanding by intuition, mental vision, or the perception of relations. Demonstration rests on the intuition of equivalence: it is the exhibition of the equivalence of propositions, the presentation of some object, which is not apparent, through its equivalence with some object or property which is apparent. Axioms are no more *certain* than other truths. They are not distinguished from other truths by the mark of self-evidence,—they are not necessarily self-evident, except in the sense that no doubt is suggested of them by contradictory instances. They have a wider application but not a higher validity than particular truths. If demonstration be the exhibition of intuited equivalence, it is easier to demonstrate axioms than to demonstrate particular propositions. The distinction between necessity and contingency applies to propositions, not to truths; there is no more contingency in a *true* biological proposition than in a true mathematical one. Contingency in a proposition is due to an indefiniteness of its terms. Fix the terms and specify all the relations formulated, and a biological truth stands on the same level of certainty and universality as a mathematical truth.—Mathematical truth, like other truth, is a resultant of experience: mathematics has a similar origin, method, validity, and similar limitations with other sciences. A single body, seen and touched, presents extension and form; several bodies present plurality, number. In bodies thus perceived are groups of sensibles from which we abstract the qualities of extension, form, number. The bodies are also perceived in motion, *i. e.*, changing their places without at the same time undergoing any change in their qualities; place thus becomes detached from the bodies, to be considered by itself: and the abstract of all places is space, etc. The majority of mathematical truths are founded on intuition. The superior certainty of mathematics arises from the superior facility with which certainty is reached and revealed to others. — The purpose of philosophy being to regulate conduct, and the nature of knowledge being that of virtual feeling, the importance of sentiment both as regulative and as representative is indisputable. Moral science is founded on sentiment. II. *The Principles of Certitude.* — Our world arises in consciousness: cosmos and consciousness are correlatives: existence is objective experience, and experience subjective existence. It is a fallacy to separate the two, and then seek for a bond between them. The ideal and the real cannot contradict one another. — The famous distinction between being and phenomena is a logical artifice or else a speculative illusion arising from our tendency to dissociate abstractions from their concretes, and endow the former with a permanent reality denied to the latter. The real distinction between the two is coincident with that between the ideal and the real, the general and the particular. The idea of unchanging being or substance behind phenomena is not sustained by experimental fact; hydrogen and oxygen, when they unite to form water, lose all their specific qualities and acquire new qualities. To arrive at truth we have merely to discover the equivalences among phenomena, truth being the equivalence of terms, of sign and thing signified. Truth takes the form of the equation, or identical proposition. The safeguard in equating our perceptions and conceptions is reflection, which discerns the values of symbols. To this test of truth the logical principles of identity, contradiction, and sufficient reason may be reduced, by substituting for *identity, identity of equivalence,* for *reason, equivalent value,* and treating the principle of contradiction as merely a correlative form of the principle of equivalence. On this principle of equivalence all the manifold and complex phenomena of nature are regarded as modifications of one another or different combinations of *invariant values.* Phenomena are what they are in virtue of their determinants, and the same determinants always have the same result (the "law of invariants"); effect and cause are co-related as product and factors. The popular explanation which ascribes the same effect to different causes is fallacious. The true expression of the relation of cause and effect is a mathematical one. The knowledge of causes tends more and more towards a quantitative expression, and is in each case final when to the discovery of a function there has been added the exhibition of the form of the function. Feeling of itself possesses certitude, thought possesses certitude when our symbols can be re-translated into feelings and an equivalence of signs and their significates can be shown. The certitude of ideal constructions is only another aspect of the certitude of feeling. III. *The Passage from the Known to the Unknown.* The attempt has been made — with disastrous consequences — to pass from the known to the unknown by a theory of the processes of judgment and reasoning which held these processes to be synthetic, attaining in the predicate or in the conclusion to knowledge not already existing. But the truth is that both judgment and reasoning are merely processes of analysis and inclusion. In the judgment is contained merely the statement of the equivalence of two things which are really but correlative aspects of the same thing, as are cause and effect. In the conclusion of the syllogism we have merely a re-statement in a new form of what is already contained in the premises. In neither case do we get beyond the "given;" the truth is *reached* by the process of reasoning: truth is there only *inferred*, to be reached only, if at all, by a process of verification. The mind passes from the known to the unknown by the triple procedure of induction, deduction, and reduction (verification). (The unknown that is rendered known by verification does, of course, not belong to the metempirical realm.)

Matter and Force. — Matter is an abstraction which can be known only in and through its concretes. "If we are speaking of the abstraction, it is equivocal to say that matter cannot be known, since every abstraction as such is known; and if we are speaking of the concretes expressed by abstraction, these are known or knowable only when they are sensibles and extra-sensibles. Matter and force are two aspects (passive and active, static and dynamic) of the same thing; either is unthinkable without the other. Matter as a substratum is a pure fiction. It is the personification of logical artifice. We logically separate the subject from its predicates, and then commit the mistake of supposing this logical separation to be real. We logically separate the symbol of the group of qualities from the qualities severally considered, and then suppose the group to be a different real from the particulars grouped. . . . Only logically may we view a substance as distinct from its qualities." — The properties of matter are not something inherent in matter *per se*, but relations of parts of matter, or modes of its existence. The complex of relations of a thing is the thing itself. The properties of matter are as many as the ultimate sensible experiences. The several peculiar ranges of the senses are the ultimate and irreducible aspects of existence, — each specific sensation being irreducible to any other. The several provinces are connected by links of mutual dependence, the whole organism being a connexus of activities; these links are so close that one sense cannot be called into action without another. Only in mental analysis are they separable. The traditional distinction between primary and secondary qualities is without meaning, except in so far as the one class stands for relations among things or feelings which are invariable, and the other for relations which are variable, conditional aspects. Both classes of qualities are feelings on their subjective side, and attributes on their objective; the primary qualities no more tell us what matter is, apart from sensibility, than do the secondary qualities. Extension is a necessary property of matter; we know nothing of it apart from sensibility. Time and motion are involved with space as properties of matter. Impenetrability, or resistance to *unlimited* compression, is a necessary property of matter: all facts which seem to prove penetrability prove merely that the particles are movable and separable. As impenetrable matter is not infinitely divisible, " the indestructibility of matter " is a scientific axiom, matter being understood as the correlative of force. If matter were merely the manifestation of an unknown force, the axiom would be questionable. The axiom of the indestructibility of matter is an induction that is not verifiable; since if matter is destructible, it must be in such small quantities as cannot be reached by balance or spectrum. Gravity is merely a theoretic assumption; the law of gravitation is an ideal construction, not the transcript of observed fact. Inertia is the constancy of force, — not absolute inertness or passivity. As we do not know what matter is apart from its relation to sensibility, and as the atom (whether static or dynamic) has no sensible properties, the hypothesis of the atom has truth and value only as an aid to calculation; " it is of the last importance to bear in mind that atomism is an artifice of analytical expression analogous to that of the differential calculus, which expresses sensible facts in terms of extra-sensibles, and is wholly indifferent to the objective existence of atoms." The atom objectively considered as an isolated element, is a fiction; it is without properties, since it is without relations. It has no extension, solidity, color, etc., since these are reactions of sensibility. How can we conceive masses to be constituted by groups of such nonentities? Only by such mathematical fiction as reduces surfaces to lines, lines to points having neither length nor breadth, or reduces continually varying movements to movements that are uniform for an infinitesimal time! Getting rid of the atom, we have to conceive existence as a continuity and a plenum. This enables us to avoid the untenable supposition of action at a distance. The continuity of existence is maintained by an imponderable medium, æther, which we know to exist by the pressure exerted by it. It is, however, extra-sensible. Matter is the passive side of experience. As experience is continually extending the particular questions respecting the properties of matter, and their mutual dependence can be answered only by confining them to properties known at the time, we must always be prepared for fresh extensions of knowledge as more and more of the illimitable unknown is brought within the range of experience.

Force and Cause. — Force may be defined as the "measure of the tendency of energy, or power, to overcome resistance, to transform itself from the negative condition of motion, *i. e.* rest, to the positive condition of motion." The quantity of force in the universe remains the same in all changes of form (law of "conservation of force"). The origin of the conception of force is indubitably in the experience of pressure, active and passive, obtained through movements of our bodies and the resistance of other bodies. Force, considered as a cause, is not distinct from the factor entering into the effect. Causation is not an operation of a metempirical "power," but the action of agents. Truly viewed, power is merely an abstract term symbolizing the action of agents. Every effect is merely the algebraic sum of the pressure of its agents; there is no power or causal link over and above the action of agents. Cause is not to be distinguished from condition, except artificially for mere logical purposes. "According to the purpose of the moment, we may say that the cause of the apple's fall is gravitation, or the wind, or the gardener's scissors. While the apple hung upon the tree the pull of gravity operated, but was counteracted by the pull of cohesion; and so long as these forces were balanced, gravitation could not cause the fall. Some new and additional force was needed, and it is this addition, — wind or scissors, — which, being conspicuous, we name the cause." The cause is not an antecedent, except in a logical sense. Punch does not follow from the combination of whiskey, sugar, lemon, and abstract possibilities of various kinds, but *is* their combined action. Cause and effect are identical, as the concave and convex aspects of one and the same curve are. From the "effect" (pure and simple) we may distinguish the "emergent" as the effect the process of whose production is unknown; it is precisely because effects are mostly emergents that deduction is insecure. It is a very mischievous error to conceive the effect as unlike its cause, and then, on the ground of the supposed unlikeness, to regard our perceptions in the light of signs of unknowable objects. A sensation may be the *sign of other sensations;* but as regards the object "causing" it, it is the relation of that object to feeling, — it is the object as known or knowable.

The Absolute in the Correlations of Feeling and Motion. — The absolute is the universe, or living whole of things. It is, in a sense, perfectly true (but perhaps idle) to say that we cannot know all existence or modes of existence. But we certainly know concrete existences, and also the abstraction ("existence") by which we condense these in a symbol; and beyond these there can be in kind nothing for us to know. It is contended by those who declare the absolute to be unknowable that beyond the sphere of knowable phenomena there is an existent which *partially* appears in the phenomena, but *is* something wholly removed from them, and in no way cognizable by us. This may be so, but we can never know that it is so. In any case, it is supremely indifferent to us, and nothing but the very wantonness of speculation could lead men to occupy themselves with it. If existence, or reality, is altogether unknowable, by what right can any one affirm that it is different from, and separated from, manifested existence in things? The transformation of motion into feeling is cited as a thing inexplicable. But there is no evidence of a real transformation. All evidence points to the very different fact that the neural process and the feeling are one and the same process viewed under different aspects. The assumption that motion is transformed into feeling contravenes the law of the conservation of energy, since in such case motion would terminate in what is neither motion nor any mode of motion. There is no evidence, either, of the existence of a spiritual agent producing feeling. The assumption of a spiritual agent would contravene the law of continuity. There is overwhelming evidence that the mental state is a function of the physical. So far as knowledge now reaches, it appears that the forces at work in consciousness are the forces at work in the organism, and that these latter are the same in kind with those in the cosmos. The assumption that motion or the bodily state *produces* sensation, or the mental state, is a baseless assumption, which can be sustained only upon the erroneous notion of causation as mere antecedence. The neural process and the sentient process are the same process differently viewed; both are modes of feeling, which is ultimate, the much-sought thing-in-itself.

Result. — Lewes styles his theory "Reasoned Realism." It appears rather to be pure sensational idealism, since it practically denies that there is any reality except for mind, and mind as sensation. It is, like the theory of Spencer, essentially Humian, and for a like reason (see above, page 289). It should be noted that the theories of both Lewes and Spencer are, or contain as an essential factor, an attempt to "reconcile" empiricism and intuitionism, — an attempt which, if successful, would certainly have had to be taken into account in the characterizing of the two theories. But for an accidental reason these two "systems" and their predecessors would fall into line before instead of after Kant's in the history of philosophy.

§ 165.

William Whewell (1794-1866). — Educated at the Lancaster and Heversham grammar-schools and at Trinity

College, Cambridge, Whewell was afterwards successively fellow, mathematical lecturer, tutor, professor, and master of Trinity College at Cambridge. Between the years 1838 and 1855 he was professor of moral philosophy. He was distinguished as the most widely learned Englishman of his day, besides being especially eminent as a mathematician, a physicist, and an historian of science. He was also prominent in the affairs of the college and university with which, from the time of his entrance there until his death (1812-1866), he was connected.

Works. — Whewell's principal works are: "History of the Inductive Sciences from the Earliest to the Present Time" (1837); "The Philosophy of the Inductive Sciences" (1840), — which was published later in three parts: "History of Scientific Ideas," "Novum Organum Renovatum," "Philosophy of Discovery;" "Elements of Morality, including Polity" (1845). Besides these we may mention "Lectures on Systematic Morality" (1846), — a defence against criticism of the "Elements;" "Lectures on the History of Moral Philosophy in England" (1852); "Platonic Dialogues for English Readers" (1859-1861); not to speak of numerous scientific and other works on a great variety of subjects.

Philosophy of Science and of Morality. — As indicated by the foregoing list of works, the philosophical theories of Whewell are theories in the philosophy of science and in that of morality in the broadest sense of the term.

Philosophy of Science. — Knowledge has the two aspects of matter and form, is a combination of impressions, or perceptions, and ideas. The philosophy of science is, on the one hand, a theory of ideas, and on the other a theory of their combination, — *i. e.*, the methods and results of their union, with perceptions, — a theory of knowledge. Ideas — to take the former theory first — are, as distinguished from perceptions, *a priori* forms of mental apprehension; they are universal and necessary, independent, in origin, of experience. They are such notions as space, time, number, cause, medium, polarity, affinity, symmetry, likeness, life, etc. They are either "fundamental ideas," or "ideal conceptions;" the line of distinction between the two classes being, however, an indefinite one. The "ideal conception" is a modification or a limitation of the fundamental idea, and an idea less remote than a "fundamental idea" from perceptions, a form more closely fitting the matter of knowledge. The idea of space is a "fundamental idea;" that of an ellipse is an "ideal conception." A fundamental idea and certain ideal conceptions lie at the basis of each science; the idea of space underlies geometry, time the science of number, cause the primary mechanical sciences, polarity the mechanico-chemical sciences, symmetry the morphological sciences, likeness the classificatory sciences, life the biological sciences. Whewell makes the idea of cause depend upon the muscular sense. Final causes, he thinks, may be pushed farther back by the discovery of new secondary (mechanical) causes, but cannot be dispensed with. The process by which *knowledge* arises, a process in which fundamental ideas or ideal conceptions are superinduced upon impressions or perceptions, is termed induction; it is the process of interpretation of the ideal in terms of the real, and *vice versa*. Ideas superinduced upon mere perceptions result in facts; upon facts, in theories. The process of constructing knowledge or science is twofold: it is a process of "explicating conceptions" and of "colligating facts." In the constructing of given facts into an ordered body of knowledge, or in the practical inductive process, three steps are necessary, — the "selection of the idea" appropriate to the facts to be ordered, the "construction of the conception" by which they are to be ordered, and the "determination of magnitudes" or quantitative relations. There is no mechanical method of selecting the idea, as Bacon supposed; such selection depends upon intellectual sagacity and felicity of inventiveness, as well as on labor and circumstances. In the colligation of facts the framing of hypotheses is of first importance. Methods of grouping and combining observed facts are the "method of curves," the "method of means," the "method of least squares," the "method of residues." Methods of determining magnitudes are the method of resemblance, the method of gradation, the method of natural classification.

Philosophy of Morality. — The moral theory of Whewell professes to be rather a basis for moral philosophy proper than such philosophy itself, — as the science of geometry might be a basis for a philosophy of the subject. Morality exists of necessity, is a consequence of the nature of man, his powers of observation, reflection, reasoning, conscious free agency, — just as the body of geometrical truths is a necessary consequence of certain definitions, axioms, etc. The moral rules springing from the common rational nature of man are adjusted to certain springs of action, *viz.*, bodily appetites, affections, desires, moral sentiments, reflex sentiments (*self*-love, self-admiration). Moral rules depend upon actually existing conditions of society; for man is born into society, and is dependent upon it; morality is based in part upon legality; moral sentiments have their germs in jural. The legal rule is by an inherent idea or disposition in us transformed into a moral one; the existing legal family relation, for example, is by "filial affection" elevated into a moral rule for us. "The supreme law of human action requires us to consider moral good as the object to which all other objects are subordinate, and from which they derive their only moral value." The supreme rule of action supplies a reason for which it commands merely by being the supreme rule. Of subordinate rules of action there are five: Be kind! Be just! Be true! Be pure! Be orderly! These correspond to five essential legal rights, *viz.*, the rights of personal security, property, contract, marriage, government. The virtues contemplated by these rules are: benevolence, justice, truth, purity, order. These are supplemented by earnestness and moral purpose. Conscience, or the faculty by which we determine the moral quality of our dispositions or actions, is not infallible, but represents our individual degree of moral culture and stage of moral progress. The supreme desire of man is for happiness. Happiness can be identified with duty by means of the idea of a benevolent creator. Morality requires to be supplemented by religion. But religion not merely "sanctions the obligations of natural morality, but prescribes new duties, — reverence, worship, praise, prayer, — and makes God the object of all other duties." The State exists necessarily and prior to the individual: it derives not its rights from social contract. Its rights are the right to national territory, the right of war and peace, the right of capital punishment, the right of imposing oaths. The obligations resting upon it are self-preservation, national defence, the upholding of the law, the repressing of sedition. Its duties are those of truth, justice, humanity, purity, order.

Remark.— The philosophy of Whewell may be described as a compound of Scotch intuitionalism and Kantism; it is one of the earliest of English attempts to correct British metaphysics by added German ingredients. His philosophy of science, it should be noted, anticipates by a few years J. S. Mill's work ("Logic") in the same general field, to which it is superior, at least in so far as it makes science a function of real spirit rather than of sensation. Whewell's obligations to Butler in moral philosophy appear on the surface.

§ 166.

Thomas Hill Green[1] (1836–1882). — Green entered Rugby at the age of fourteen, and Balliol College, Oxford, five years later. Of a reflective rather than of an acquisitive turn of mind, Green did not shine particularly as a scholar, in the more usual sense of the term, and indeed seemed lacking in scholarly ambition both at Rugby and at Oxford. Through the stimulating influence of some of his

---

[1] Green's Works.

teachers at Oxford, particularly Professor Jowett, he exerted himself to win honors — and was successful in his effort — in *litteræ humaniores*, and law and modern history. In 1860 he was appointed lecturer in ancient and modern history, and also fellow of his Alma Mater. Largely through Jowett's influence, for the next few years Green's mind was turned to the study of philosophy. He was at one time fellow and tutor of Oriel College, Oxford, and at the time of his death professor of moral philosophy. He took an earnest practical interest in political, social, and educational reforms in England.

Works. — Green's chief philosophical works are: Introductions (two in number) to Hume's "Treatise of Human Nature" (1874-1875); "Lectures on Kant's Philosophy;" "Lectures on Logic," — with special reference to Mill and Mansel; "Mr. Herbert Spencer and Mr. G. H. Lewes: Their Application of the Doctrine of Evolution to Thought" (1877-1878, in "Contemporary Review"); "Prolegomena to Ethics" (1883); "Lectures on the Principles of Political Obligation." Minor works are: "The Philosophy of Aristotle;" "Popular Philosophy in Relation to its Time."

Philosophy : [1] *Introduction.* — Philosophy is, in the present age, in the position of having to prove its right to exist. Particularly is this true of moral philosophy. The moral philosopher has at the very outset of his task to make clear " why and in what sense he holds that there is a subject-matter of inquiry which does not consist of matters of fact attainable by experiment and observation," and what place he assigns to morals in this subject-matter. To a being who were simply the result of natural forces, moral law must be unmeaning. There arises the question, Is man merely a part of nature? Can the *knowledge* of nature be a part of nature? Can the principle by which man determines himself be a part of nature?

[1] In the following account we depend chiefly on the "Prolegomena to Ethics."

Metaphysics of Knowledge. — Nature as known involves a system of relations. Of these, mere matter and motion cannot be the source; there must be a being who "can know nature, — a principle which is not merely natural and which cannot without a ὕστερον πρότερον be explained as we explain the facts of nature as known." The existence of such a principle is presupposed by experience, both subjectively and objectively viewed. We make a distinction between the "real" and the "not-real." The term "real" (and its equivalent "objective") can have no meaning except for a consciousness which presents its experiences as determined by relations, and also conceives a single and unalterable order of relations determining them, *i. e.*, for a consciousness which employs conception, and possesses a faculty of understanding corresponding thereto. Such a consciousness is quite distinct from a consciousness of a series of independent or even related objects or events: "No one and no number of a series of related events can be the consciousness of the series as related." The understanding cannot be an event in nature in the same sense that known facts and occurrences are such. The consciousness of related events is something that must be equally present to all of those events of which it *is* the consciousness. Nor can it be explained as the product of any series of previous events, since the question would have to be answered, What is the origin of the consciousness of that previous series, and so *ad infinitum*. Knowledge then on its subjective side is not a part of nature. But known nature, or objectified knowledge, presupposes an understanding like that which knows it. There is implied by the system of relations constituting nature, the existence of unity outside or beside the mere manifold of things which holds them in relation, — a combining agency such as that with which we are familiar in our own intelligence. The exact character of this agency we cannot know. We know the agency as a principle making possible nature as a system of related things, and presumably of ourselves as aware of this system. We may fitly designate it as a "world-consciousness of which ours is a limited mode," or as the divine self-consciousness.

The Relation of Man as Intelligence to the Spiritual Principle in Nature. — From the foregoing it appears that consciousness in general has a double character, — it is a unity and a manifold. As manifold, it is subject to change, to development, and has a history; is conditioned; is a vehicle, or means to an end; as a unity, it is eternal, ungenerable, without a history, all-conditioning, an end realizing itself in and through consciousness as a manifold. In the individual mind the eternal consciousness manifests itself as a "forecasting idea," an ideal, or end of being, and a principle of knowing.

The Freedom of Man as Intelligence. — As the vehicle of, and as determined by, universal consciousness, which, instead of being a part of nature, is the condition of there being such a thing as nature, man is a free cause in relation to nature, partaking of the self-subsistence and self-activity of the universal consciousness itself. What is natural in man, namely, his animal portion, does not take away his freedom, since, as a product of that intelligence of which his higher nature is a manifestation, his animal portion is organic to his spiritual, instead of mechanically dominating it.

The Will. — "As the presentation of sensible things, on occasion of sensation, implies the action of a principle which is not, like sensation, in time, or an event, or a series of events, but must equally be present to and distinguish itself from the several stages to which a sensation is given, as well as the several sensations attended to and referred to a single object, — so the transition from mere want to consciousness of a wanted object, from the impulse to satisfy want to an effort for realization of the idea of the wanted object, implies the presence of the want to a subject which distinguishes itself from it, and is constant throughout successive stages of the want." By virtue of its presence to, or its being organic to such a subject, the mere want becomes a *motive* which cannot, like the mere want, be a link in a chain of purely natural occurrences. Whether a given want really has become organic to self-consciousness or not, self-reflection must determine. To be free from error, self-reflection must be conducted with constant reference to the expressions of moral consciousness in use among men and to the institutions in which men have embodied their ideas or ideals of permanent good; but in the interpretation of such expressions self-reflection again must be our ultimate guide, without which they would have nothing to tell. Since the "motive" is not a mere want, it is of course misleading to speak of a "strongest motive," as always being the determinant of choice. Action is determined by self-consciousness as embodied in character in relation to the circumstances of the moment.

Desire, Intellect, and Will. — From the foregoing view of the character of moral action (as a product of self-consciousness) it follows that what for mere analysis' sake may in moral action be distinguished as an element of mere impulse (*i. e.*, desire), a calculating element (reason or intellect), and an arbitrary element (will) must be viewed as but three aspects of one and the same thing, — desire, implying intelligence and will; intelligence, desire and will; and will, desire and intelligence. There are no *mere* desires: in all exercise of the understanding desire is at work, — the result of any process of the understanding being desired throughout the process; desire does not cease to be desire when it has become an act of will, although it has acquired a new character; a thoughtless will would be no will, — without the thought of a self and a world as mutually conditioned, of an object present to the self in a desire felt by it, but awaiting realization in the world, there would be no will, but only blind impulse. Desire, thought, and will are in different degrees and ways the expression of the entire *self-conscious*, not merely *natural*, being, want.

The Moral Ideal and Moral Progress: The Good and Moral Good. — All wills agree in that they aim at the self-satisfaction of the (self-conscious) subject: the differences lie in the differences in the character of that in which self-satisfaction is sought; or of the object of "desire." The criterion of the good or the bad can never, as the hedonist holds, be the degree of mere pleasure action affords or promises to afford; for mere pleasure cannot be desired by a self-conscious being. Defining the good in general as the object of desire, moral good is that which satisfies the moral capability. What that capability is, is not fully known to us, since it has not fully realized itself. It has, however, shown to certain extent by actual achievement what it has in it to become; and by reflection on the so far developed capacity we can form at least some negative conclusion as to its complete realization, — a conclusion which may serve for the continual progression towards the absolute good. In general, the moral capability is a capability of self-realization or objectification on man's part: man's reason is a capacity to conceive the higher true self; his will is an effort, or capacity for the effort, to satisfy reason's conception of man's or its own nature.

Characteristics of the Moral Ideal. — From the immediately foregoing it follows that our ultimate standard of worth is an ideal of *personal* worth: all values are relative to value for, of, or in a person. This is true, whether as regards the life of the individual, of the nation, or of historical development. (In this notion of the good there is implied the permanent continuance of existence, a non-extinction of all those agencies, namely, persons, by and in which the idea of the self-end is realized). As personal the good presupposes society; only in and through society is any one enabled to give objectivity and reality to the idea of himself as the object of his action. Some practical recognition of an "I" by a "Thou" and a "Thou" by an "I" is necessary to any such consciousness of the idea as can express itself in act. It is society that supplies all the higher content to the conception of personality, all those objects of a man's personal interest, in living for which he lives for his own satisfaction, except such as are derived from the merely animal nature. In society is given the sanction and the means for the realization of the idea of "something that must be done merely for the sake of its being done," or of the self-realizing end. — On this view (and only on this view) the moral law (Kant's "Categorical Imperative") receives a full content and meaning.

The Origin and Development of the Moral Ideal: (a) Reason as the Source of the Idea of a Common Good. — The self of which a man forecasts the fulfilment is not an abstract or empty self, but a self affected, already in the the most primitive forms of human life, by manifold interests, among which are interests in other persons. The moral self is not a mere product of physical evolution. The idea of an absolute good is the beginning and source, not a result, of development. The idea of a possible well-being of himself that shall not pass away with this state or that pleasure; and relation to some group of persons whose well-being he takes to be as his own, and in whom he is interested, as being interested in himself, — these two things must condition the life of any one who is to be a creator or sustainer either of law or of that prior authoritative custom out of which law arises. Reason fulfilled intrinsically the same function in primitive associations of man with man as it does at present. (*b*) *The Extension of the Area of Common Good.* — The first of the movements into which the development of morality may be analyzed consists in a gradual extension for the mental eye of the moral subject of the range of persons to whom the common good is conceived as common, towards and between whom accordingly obligations are understood to exist. With growing means of intercourse and the progress of reflection the natural outcome of the idea of a common good is the theory of a universal human fellowship. The Greek lacked the explicit notion of a universal human fellowship;

the modern, in consequence of the teachings of Christianity, possesses the conception (realizes the absolute value) of humanity as such. (*c*) *Determination of the Idea of the Common Good.* — The question arises whether the absolute good — an object capable of yielding satisfaction to the desiring man, or self as such — can or must be the greatest sum of pleasures that he can imagine. Pleasures as such, *i. e.*, states of *mere feeling*, are incapable of being *summed*, they *are* only as *felt*. A *sum* of pleasures is *not* a pleasure. A *sum* of pleasures can exist only for the *thought* of a person considering pleasures as addible quantities, but neither enjoying them nor even imagining their enjoyment. The idea of satisfying one's self with *mere pleasures* cannot be the idea of the highest good for man. The idea of the highest good must be the idea of that which man as such vitally or inherently desires, not of the succession of enjoyments which will be experienced in the realization of the idea. Foremost among our vital interests is our interest in the family, — an interest which the mere feeling of pleasure does not at all answer to. The satisfying of this interest presupposes the projecting of one's self into the future as a permanent subject of possible well-being or ill-being, associating one's self with one's kindred, and *vice versa*. Thus we conclude that even in the earliest stages of human consciousness in which the idea of a true or permanent good could lead any one to call in question the good of an immediately attractive pleasure, it was already an idea of a social good, of a good not private to the man himself, but good for him as a member of a community. (Hence the popular distinction between considerate benevolence and reasonable self-love is a mere philosophical fiction.) (*d*) *The Greek and Roman Conceptions of Virtue.* — " Once for all, the Greek philosophers conceived and expressed the conceptions of a free or pure morality as resting on what we may venture to call a disinterested interest in the good ; of the several virtues as so many applications of that interest to the main relations of social life ; of the good itself not as anything external to the capacities virtuously exercised in its pursuit, but as their full realization." The differences between our standards of virtue and those recognized by the Greek philosophers are merely such as have arisen from the greater fulness of conditions which we include in our conception of the perfecting of human life. The modern conception of fortitude, for example, instead of being that of proud self-sufficing strength, includes the qualities of self-adjustment, sympathy with inferiors, tolerance for the weak and foolish, — the willingness to endure even unto complete self-renunciation, even to the point of forsaking all possibility of pleasure. Instead of restricting temperance to control over the mere animal appetites (as Aristotle does), the modern philosopher includes under "temperance" self-denial of a far wider range, and even within the same range of a stricter nature, particularly in the matter of sexual enjoyment. (*e*) *Conclusion.* — From the history of the moral ideal we derive a certain conception as to what the idea of the common good requires for its present and future fulfilment, *viz.*, the perfecting of *man* as a whole. We are justified in affirming that that idea could not be realized in a life of mere scientific activity, or, on the other hand, in a life of practical exertion in which such activity were wanting; and in affirming that the life in which it is realized must be a social life, in which all men freely and consciously co-operate, a life determined by one harmonious will having for its object perfection.

The Application of Moral Philosophy to the Guidance of Conduct: The Practical Value of the Moral Ideal. — Except in judging *our own past* or *present* actions, our criterion for estimating the value of actions must be the tendency or absence of tendency to promote "good will," or will aiming at the perfection of mankind, — that is to say, must be the *effect* of action. We cannot know enough of the motives of the actions of others or the motives of possible future actions of ourselves to be com-

petent to judge such actions by their motives. The value
of the habit of scrutinizing one's own motives with a view
to determining the value of action contemplated or performed, *i. e.*, of conscientiousness, is a doubtful one; the
habit certainly has its limitations. In a general way it may
be admitted that the comparison of our own practice as we
know it on the inner side in relation to the motives and
character which it expresses with an ideal of virtue is the
spring from which morality perpetually renews its life.

The Practical Value of a Theory of the Moral Ideal. —
The value of a theory of the moral ideal must in any case
be negative rather than positive; rather in the way of deliverance from moral anarchy which an apparent conflict
between duties equally imperative may bring, or of providing a safeguard against the pretext which in a speculative
age some inadequate and misapplied theory may afford to
our selfishness than in the way of pointing out duties previously ignored.

The Practical Value of a Hedonistic Moral Philosophy.
— The doctrine known as "Universalistic Hedonism," or
"Hedonistic Utilitarianism," the principle of which is that
the *summum bonum* is the greatest happiness of the greatest number, has unquestionably tended to improve human
conduct and character; but this has been merely because
of its insisting that it is "the greatest number" whose good
is to be taken into account, not of its identifying that
highest good with the greatest net quantity of pleasure.
Logically the tendency of the doctrine must be to paralyze
action, inasmuch as if the impulse to seek pleasure is the
only criterion of reality, no action *ought* to be or *can* be
other than what the strongest *mere* impulse of the moment
makes it; or, in other words, all action is fatalistic.

*The Practical Value of Utilitarianism compared with
that of the theory of the Good as Human Perfection.* —
That form of Hedonism which makes universal pleasure the
ultimate good, but also places the aim of action in something other than mere pleasure, seems to afford no solution
when conventional morality, — as representing accumulated

experience, cannot be appealed to; and the field is left to the doctrine of ideal perfection, since, as regarding pleasure and pain as morally indifferent, it (and it alone) can consistently depart from custom. And the doctrine of ideal perfection is more available since it is easier to say whether a given course of action will promote human excellence than to say whether it will increase universal pleasure.

The Principles of Political Obligation.[1] — Political society is a product of self-consciousness. The essence of it, as distinguished from other products of self-consciousness, is that it is the identity of units *reciprocally recognized as the like and the equal of each other.* This reciprocal recognition constitutes right, which therefore belongs to every being capable of yielding or acknowledging such recognition, or to every person. From this it follows, on the one hand, that there are no " natural rights," or rights belonging to individuals not in reciprocal relation with other individuals, *i. e.*, not members of a social organization, and, on the other hand, that no rights belong to society apart from the individuals composing it. All rights have reference to man as a moral being, or being who, by virtue of self-consciousness, lives for himself and others at one and the same time in one and the same way. The underlying principle of authority and also of obedience to authority in society is the idea of a common well-being. The State is founded on (intelligent) will, not on mere force. Resistance to authority becomes a right when the repeal of a law operating counter to the common good is not by law provided for; nay, it is even then a duty. In general, however, resistance to authority has no ground in right, since the common good must suffer more from the resistance to the ordinance of a legal authority than from the individual's conformity to a particular law that is bad, until its repeal can be obtained; the individual, in

[1] See Green's Works, vol. ii.; also Nettleship's Memoir, vol. iii.

other words, has no rights founded on any right to do as he likes. The first of all rights is the right to life and liberty, to "free life," since, if a man be prevented from using his body to express a will, the will itself does not become a reality; the man is not really a person. No distinction can be made between the right to life and the right to liberty, for there can be no right to *mere* life, no right to life on the part of a being that has not also a right to use the life according to the motions of its own will. Justly is slavery universally condemned. On account of this right, war, in which men are deliberately deprived of it, is never an unmixed good, is always a reason for general self-reproach; and this is true, because war is never entirely unavoidable. Property, as a means or instrument of free life or of realizing a will, is a thing of right. The limit of the employment of the right of property is, like that of every other right, the common good; that is to say, when by reason of inequality among men in the power to acquire property, the common well-being is interfered with by the exclusion, from the possession of the amount of property required for the moralization of man, of any class of men in society. Such a state of affairs seems not necessarily inherent in the right of property as such, but results merely from the abuse of it. The conception of right involves that of the punishment of every violation of right, which punishment should be retributive, preventive, reformatory, one or all. Punishment by death or by perpetual imprisonment is justifiable only on either of two grounds; namely, that the association of extreme terror with certain actions is under certain conditions necessary to preserve the possibility of social life based on the observance of rights, or that the crime punished offers a presumption of a permanent incapacity for right on the part of the individual. Wherever the death penalty is unjustifiable there must also be that of really permanent imprisonment; one as much as the other is the absolute privation of free social life and of the possibilities which that life affords. The right of the State to promote morality is limited by the fact that morality is dependent on the spontaneous action of social interest; it seems confined to the removal of obstacles to moral improvement, — though under this head there may and should be included much that most States have hitherto neglected, and much that at first sight may have the appearance of an enforcement of moral duties; *e. g.*, the requirement that parents have their children taught the elementary arts. The rights of marriage and all that is implied in it are rights to a large extent prior to legal right; they are not of a kind which can in their essence be protected by associating penal terror with their violation, as the rights of life and property can be: they are claims which cannot be met without a certain disposition on the part of the person upon whom the claim rests, and that disposition cannot be enforced. That, however, "marriage should be only with one wife, that it should be for life, that it should be terminable by the infidelity of either husband or wife, are rules of (legal) right as distinguished from morality." The disposition to exercise in some way contributory to the public good the powers which constitute one's rights constitutes virtue; and there are, accordingly, virtues corresponding respectively to each of the rights of "free life," "property," etc.

Religion. — The eternal self-consciousness in man attains its fullest manifestation in understanding and love, knowledge and self-sacrifice, — a fact which suggests that God, though only partially comprehensible by us, is best conceived by us as ideal humanity. This conception of the identity of the divine nature with the human is, even though anthropomorphism, anthropomorphism of a rational sort, since it is necessary to true subjective self-consciousness and to the understanding of the fact of a world experienced by us. If God is the ideal human'self, he is present in that consciousness which the human self has of its unfulfilled capabilities, or its faith in itself, and makes that faith faith in him also. In this faith we have an apprehension of something not, it is true, sensibly verifiable, but the reality of which follows, as we have seen, from the fact of that self-consciousness by which alone experience and an experienced world have existence for us.

Result. — Green obviously occupies the "standpoint" of Kantio-Hegelian rationalism or idealism. His importance as a thinker (which, it is not rash to say, is very considerable) is due largely (much more than we have been able to make appear in the foregoing account) to the masterliness of his interpretation of empiricism, — the empiricism of Hume, Mill, Spencer, Lewes, in particular, — in the light of the rationalism named. Green's thinking may almost be said to mark the beginning of a new epoch in English philosophy, though it may be too much to expect that sensationalism will henceforth have no real standing in English philosophy, as for a long time past pure materialism has had no standing in the history of philosophy in general. — In connection with Green we may barely mention the names of a number of men, still living, who with him are chief representatives of a sort of neo-Hegelian school that has grown up in England during the past twenty-five years: James Hutchison Stirling, earliest, and perhaps foremost in ability, Profs. Edward and John Caird of Glasgow, Prof. Adamson of Manchester, Prof. William Wallace of Oxford, Mr. F. H. Bradley of Oxford.

§ 167.

(6) *American Philosophy.*[1] — There have been not a few opponents of the "Edwardsian" doctrine of the will (see Vol. I., page 267), of whom we may mention Henry P. Tappan (b. 1805), professor in the University of New York and chancellor of the University of Michigan; Albert F. Bledsoe (b. 1809), professor in the University of Virginia;

---

[1] Porter's "Account of American Philosophy;" article in "Mind," vol. iv. (by G. S. Hall), etc.

and Rowland G. Hazard (b. 1801), of Rhode Island, Daniel D. Whedon (b. 1808), a professor in Michigan University. — The theological school of Edwards has been succeeded by "schools" which, if less purely American, have been more truly philosophical. The Scottish school has had in this country a large number of adherents. Of these we may mention as perhaps the most important: John Witherspoon (1722–1794), who was a Scotchman who emigrated to America and became professor in and president of the College of New Jersey (at Princeton), and there introduced Scotch thinking into the country (at the same time driving out Berkeleyanism from Princeton); Thomas C. Upham (1799–1867), professor in Bowdoin College; Asa Mahan (b. 1798), president of and professor at Oberlin College; Francis Bowen (1811–1889), professor at Harvard University; Joseph Haven (1816–1874), professor at Amherst College and Chicago Theological Seminary; Henry N. Day (b. 1808), professor at Western Reserve College, etc.; James McCosh (b. 1811), a Scotchman who was elected president of Princeton College (in 1868); Noah Porter (b. 1811), professor at and president of Yale College; B. F. Cocker (d. 1883), professor at Michigan University; etc. Some of these men — notably Porter, McCosh, Bowen, and Cocker — have been open to other influences (*e. g.*, Kantian and scientific) than the purely Scottish. — Kantian (rather than Scottish) are Laurens P. Hickok (b. 1798), professor at Western Reserve and at Union College; Julius H. Seelye (b. 1825), professor at and president of Amherst, — a close follower of Hickok; John Bascom (b. 1827), professor at Williams College, and president of the University of Wisconsin, said to be "in some sense a follower of Hickok." — The Kantian philosophy, pure and simple, seems to have been introduced into the country by James Marsh (1794–1842), professor at and president of Vermont University; George Ripley (b. 1802); Frederic H. Hedge (b. 1805–1890) of Harvard. — Hegelianism, with William T. Harris, editor of the "Journal of Speculative Philosophy," as its chief representative, has had, as more or less close adherents, C. C. Everett, professor at Harvard University; Elisha Mulford; George S. Morris (1840–1889), professor at Johns Hopkins and Michigan Universities, and editor of "Griggs's Philosophical Classics;" G. H. Howison, professor at the Massachusetts Institute of Technology and at the University of California; G. Stanley Hall, professor at Johns Hopkins University, and president of and professor of psychology at Clark University; J. H. Kedney, Seabury Divinity School; D. J. Snider, author of a philosophical commentary on Shakespeare; John Watson, professor at Kingston (Canada); G. P. Young, professor at Toronto; and others, particularly at St. Louis, Mo. — Spencerianism has had numerous followers, the chief of them being John Fiske, of Harvard, and Washington University, St. Louis, and E. L. Youmans, editor of the "Popular Science Monthly." — Other philosophical writers are Mark Hopkins (b. 1802), professor and president at Williams College, whose teaching has been described as a "combination of those of Edwards and Jouffroy;" William Dexter Wilson, professor at Geneva College and at Cornell University; Francis Wayland (1796–1866), president of Brown University; C. S. Henry, professor in University of New York (French-eclectic?); C. S. Peirce, professor at Johns Hopkins University (Sceptical?); Chauncey Wright; F. E. Abbot; O. A. Brownson; and last, but not least in philosophical insight, the poet and essayist R. W. Emerson. — Within the past fifteen years the study of philosophy for its own sake and independently of theological influences has been more seriously undertaken than ever before in the higher institutions of the country. It seems safe to predict a vigorous future for philosophy in America.

MASTERPIECES OF FOREIGN AUTHORS.

This series comprises translations of single masterpieces by some of the best known European writers. The volumes are well printed on good paper, and very prettily bound.

16mo, cloth, 75 cents a vol.; half vellum, gilt top, $1.25 a vol.

The Morals and Manners of the XVIIth Century. Being the Characters of La Bruyère. Translated by Helen Stott. Portrait. 1 vol.

La Bruyère is in prose what Racine is in verse, — the quintessence of the classical style of the French seventeenth century. — *The Athenæum, London.*

Doctor Antonio. By GIOVANNI D. RUFFINI. 1 vol.

"The true and touching interest of the story would carry a reader through a much heavier medium. . . . The outline of the story is simple; it derives its charms from the grace and delicacy with which the details are filled in, and the strong individuality impressed upon every point of character, scenery, or incident."

Wilhelm Meister's Apprenticeship and Travels. By JOHANN WOLFGANG GOETHE. Translated by Thomas Carlyle. With Critical Introduction by Edward Dowden, LL.D. Portrait. 2 vols.

"To this day," says Matthew Arnold, "such is the force of youthful associations, I read the 'Wilhelm Meister' with more pleasure in Carlyle's translation than in the original."

Portraits of Men, by C. A. Sainte-Beuve. Translated by Forsyth Edeveain. With Critical Memoir by William Sharp. Portrait. 1 vol.

Mr. William Sharp says of this sovereign critic: "It is conceivable that the future historian of our age will allot to Sainte-Beuve a place higher even than that claimed for him by one or two of our ablest critics, Matthew Arnold in particular, and Mr. John Morley."

Portraits of Women, by C. A. Sainte-Beuve. Translated by Helen Stott. Portrait. 1 vol.

The essays on Mesdames de Maintenon, de Sévigné, de Staël, and de la Fayette, with those on Marie Antoinette and Joan of Arc, can never be read in any form without delight and profit. — *The Athenæum, London.*

Novalis (Frederich von Hardenberg): His Life, Thoughts, and Works. Edited and translated by M. J. Hope. 1 vol.

"Novalis," says Carlyle, "is a figure of such importance in German literature that no student can pass him by. . . . A man of the most indisputable talent, poetical and philosophical."

The Comedies of Carlo Goldoni. Edited, with Introduction, by Helen Zimmern. 1 vol.

It is Goldoni's supreme merit, and one of his chief titles to fame and glory, that he released the Italian theatre from the bondage of the artificial and pantomime performances that had passed for plays, and that, together with Molière, he laid the foundations of the drama as it is understood in our days. This volume comprises some of his best known and most successful plays.

Sold by all booksellers, or mailed, on receipt of price, by

A. C. McCLURG & CO., Publishers, CHICAGO.

HOME LIFE OF GREAT AUTHORS.

By HATTIE TYNG GRISWOLD.

12mo, 385 pages.
Price, $1.50; in half calf or half morocco, $3.50.

A COLLECTION of upward of thirty descriptive sketches, having for their subjects Byron, Burns, the Brownings, Bryant, Bulwer, Brontë (Charlotte), Carlyle, Dickens, De Staël, De Quincey, Eliot (George), Emerson, Fuller (Margaret), Irving, Goethe, Hawthorne, Holmes, Hugo, Kingsley, Lowell, Lamb, Longfellow, Macaulay, North (Kit), Poe, Ruskin, Shelley, Scott, Sand (George), Thackeray, Tennyson, Wordsworth, and Whittier.

No such excellent collection of brief biographies of literary favorites has ever before appeared in this country. Mrs. Griswold's taste and discretion are as much to be admired as her industry in the composition of these delightful sketches. — *The Bulletin, Philadelphia.*

Most often we have a condensed biography, with special attention given to the personal element in the way of description, anecdote, reminiscences, and other such matters as a skilful collector could gather from the plentiful sources of such information. There is a noticeable good taste shown in dealing with those more intimate portions of the lives of the heroes and heroines, — the *affaires de cœur*. — *The Nation, New York.*

The author has shown a rare discrimination in the treatment of her subjects. And in nothing has this faculty been better displayed than in her selection of authors. This alone is a difficult task, — one in which any writer would be sure to offend, at least by omission. But the table of contents of this book is a gratifying success, and the menu here provided will abundantly satisfy the most of readers. — *The Express, Buffalo.*

This is a very charming book. Mrs. Griswold has a very happy faculty of weaving literary illustrations from the different authors into her descriptions of their domestic lives. She has made a book about the home life of great authors that will be sure to make the home life of many who are not authors somewhat more sweet and glad. — *Christian Register, Boston.*

These glimpses into the home life and heart life of famous authors, English and American, some of whom are still living, will impart fresh interest to their writings, for readers always welcome information about the personal character and domestic habits of writers whose productions engage their attention. — *Home Journal, New York.*

The work is admirably done throughout, and deserves a wide circulation. It will not disappoint a single reader. — *Interior, Chicago.*

Sold by all booksellers, or mailed, on receipt of price, by
A. C. McCLURG & CO., Publishers, CHICAGO.

THE GREAT FRENCH WRITERS.

A SERIES OF STUDIES OF THE LIVES, WORKS, AND INFLUENCE OF THE GREAT WRITERS OF THE PAST, BY GREAT WRITERS OF THE PRESENT, COMPRISING:—

Madame de Sévigné. By GASTON BOISSIER.

George Sand. By E. CARO.

Montesquieu. By ALBERT SOREL.

Victor Cousin. By JULES SIMON.

Turgot. By LÉON SAY.

Thiers. By PAUL DE RÉMUSAT.

Madame de Staël. By ALBERT SOREL.

With other volumes in preparation.

Translated by Prof. MELVILLE B. ANDERSON, Prof. PLAYFAIR ANDERSON, and FANNY HALE GARDINER.

12mo. Price, $1.00 per volume; in half morocco, gilt top, $2.50.

Emphatic commendation must be given to the Chicago house that brings out the translation of the Great French Writers' series. Surely these brilliant books, by setting forth such admirable examples of critical work, must have a potent effect on American criticism. It is the work that the French do so well, and that we do so poorly. — *The Critic, New York.*

No writers of the century have exerted more influence upon English and American thought than the writers of France, whether in fiction, in criticism, or in metaphysics. . . . It was fortunate for Americans especially, that the scheme was conceived of having eminent French writers of this generation prepare monographs upon the great writers of past generations whose books are still the living thought not only of their own country but of the age; and the translations of these monographs and their republications in this country is a literary event of considerable importance. — *Tribune, Chicago.*

When the reader has finished either of these volumes, he must certainly lay it down with the feeling that he has been admitted into the intimate life of the great writer in whose charming company he has been spending a few delightful hours, and that his knowledge of the author's position in literature, and of his influence in the world, is surprisingly enlarged and broadened. — *Nation, New York.*

These French monographs have a power of compression and lightness of touch which may well appear marvellous to American readers not acquainted with the Gallic genius for biographical and critical essay. — *Beacon, Boston.*

Sold by all booksellers, or mailed, on receipt of price, by

A. C. McCLURG & CO., Publishers. CHICAGO.

LIFE OF ABRAHAM LINCOLN.

By THE HON. ISAAC N. ARNOLD.

**With steel portrait, 8vo, cloth, gilt top, 471 pages, price, $1.50;
in half calf or half morocco, $3.50.**

It is decidedly the best and most complete Life of Lincoln that has yet appeared. — *Contemporary Review, London.*

Mr. Arnold succeeded to a singular extent in assuming the broad view and judicious voice of posterity and exhibiting the greatest figure of our time in its true perspective. — *The Tribune, New York.*

It is the only Life of Lincoln thus far published that is likely to live, — the only one that has any serious pretensions to depict him with adequate veracity, completeness, and dignity. — *The Sun, New York.*

The author knew Mr. Lincoln long and intimately, and no one was better fitted for the task of preparing his biography. He has written with tenderness and fidelity, with keen discrimination, and with graphic powers of description and analysis. — *The Interior, Chicago.*

Mr. Arnold's "Life of President Lincoln" is excellent in almost every respect. . . . The author has painted a graphic and life-like portrait of the remarkable man who was called to decide on the destinies of his country at the crisis of its fate. — *The Times, London.*

The book is particularly rich in incidents connected with the early career of Mr. Lincoln; and it is without exception the most satisfactory record of his life that has yet been written. Readers will also find that in its entirety it is a work of absorbing and enduring interest that will enchain the attention more effectually than any novel. — *Magazine of American History, New York.*

It is sure to be considered henceforth as an authority, not only upon the character and career of Lincoln, but upon the history of the period to which it is devoted. — *The Critic, New York.*

The author's portrayal of the character of Mr. Lincoln is distinct and just in every line; his picture of the times in which he lived, and of the mighty struggle between Freedom and Slavery, vivid and complete. His selection of the materials for his work is judicious, and their arrangement admirable. Nothing trivial is admitted, nothing important is omitted. . . . The work is one which on its own merits will doubtless take rank as an American classic. — *Evangelist, New York.*

A book which should be read by all Americans, and should stand on the shelves of every library in the land, however small, in an honored place. — *Unity, Chicago.*

It is a careful and scholarly work, uniformly dignified even in its anecdotes; takes the point of the patriotic statesman and keeps it. . . . Mr. Arnold's volume is typographically irreproachable. — *Literary World, Boston.*

Sold by all booksellers, or mailed, on receipt of price, by

A. C. McCLURG & CO., Publishers, CHICAGO.

THE LIFE OF
JOSHUA R. GIDDINGS.

By THE HON. GEORGE W. JULIAN, author of "Political Recollections." With two Portraits and a complete Index. 8vo, 473 pages, gilt top, $2.50; half morocco, gilt top, $5.00.

Joshua R. Giddings was one of those giants in formulating opinion that has made the country the foremost upon the earth. . . . The book is one for all young Americans to read, for it will teach them what a boy, no matter how poor, who is determined to do right, can accomplish in a country like ours. — *Evening Telegram, New York.*

The history of the abolition movement is also a history of Giddings, and the two are well told in this fine volume written by his son-in-law. A life so full of whole-souled activity could not have been better described in a volume of this size. It covers all the events of his rugged career, his speeches in and out of Congress, and his various writings on the subject nearest to his heart. . . . The biography is a noble one of a noble man. He lived to see the war of the rebellion almost concluded and the abolition of slavery accomplished. As an important part of our national history and a piece of literary work, we regard this biography as the best book of the kind that has appeared for several years. — *The Evening Bulletin, Philadelphia.*

It is an important contribution to the history of the early days of the anti-slavery party. — *Times, New York.*

Mr. Giddings was a plain, sensible, vigorous representative of the great body of the Northern people. He lacked some of the more superficial graces, but was rich in the essentials of manhood and was no man's inferior in the sagacity and fearlessness necessary to an anti-slavery leader in Congress during the years of his service there. There are many claims to the supreme place among the champions of freedom, and possibly it never can be determined who, if any one, really occupied it. But it cannot be denied that Giddings rendered a service unsurpassed in important particulars by that of any one else. — *Congregationalist, Boston.*

The book is a revelation of rare personal worth, and gives the keynote to the public life and services of a truly great man. — *Public Ledger, Philadelphia.*

Mr. Julian has done his work admirably, and has produced from ample materials and careful study a volume which will preserve the memory of one of the noblest of American patriots, whose name and service will remain a perpetual example and inspiration to his countrymen. — *Hon. Edward L. Pierce, in Boston Transcript.*

Sold by all booksellers, or mailed, on receipt of price, by

A. C. McCLURG & CO., Publishers, CHICAGO.

SAVONAROLA,

His Life and Times.

By WILLIAM CLARK, M.A., LL.D. 12mo, gilt top, 358 pages, $1.50; half calf or half morocco, $3.50.

PROFESSOR CLARK writes in popular style, thoroughly explains the intricate political system of Florence in its transition state, and succeeds in giving a well-rounded history of a man whose character will always be one of the most interesting in history to study.

The whole story is compactly and simply told in this volume, and in such a fascinating and charming way as to delight the reader. As a contribution to a proper estimate of a life that presents so many difficulties to the historian, this study of Professor Clark's is especially valuable. — *Living Church, Chicago.*

This is one of the best pieces of biographical work that have fallen under our eye during the present year. The author exhibits a thorough acquaintance with the history of the age in which the great Italian reformer's life was spent. All the information contained in the pages of the most trustworthy authorities has been critically examined, sifted, and condensed into this work. It is a pleasure to commend work which has been so excellently done. . . . The book is written in terse, forceful, and perfectly lucid English; the style of the author is strikingly vivid; and the reader obtains from the volume a very satisfactory conception of Savonarola's aims, deeds, and influence. — *Public Opinion, Washington.*

The book is a very careful study, kept candid and fair as far as it is possible for an enthusiastic admirer to be so. It is frank and full also in reference to authorities. — *Times, Chicago.*

The volume covers just about as much ground as the general reader is likely to want, and is the best popular book yet produced concerning one of the most interesting figures of the last half of the fifteenth century. — *Epoch, New York.*

This is probably the best popular life of Savonarola in the English language, or, for the matter of that, in any language. — *Examiner, New York.*

It is the work of a masterly hand, and we must add, of a master mind. . . . Professor Clark has achieved in this modest book a great work. It is the product of learning and of fastidious taste; of penetrative judgment and patient research; of careful sifting and of wisely compacted selections. *Churchman, New York.*

Professor Clark has written with the carefulness of a scholar and the fervor of a novelist or poet. — *Congregationalist, Boston.*

Sold by all booksellers, or mailed, on receipt of price, by

A. C. McCLURG & CO., Publishers, CHICAGO.

THE AZTECS,

THEIR HISTORY, MANNERS, AND CUSTOMS. From the French of LUCIEN BIART. Authorized translation by J. L. GARNER. Illustrated, 8vo, 340 pages. Price, $2.00; half calf, $4.25; half morocco, $4.50.

The author has travelled through the country of whose former glories his book is a recital, and his studies and discoveries leaven the book throughout. The volume is absorbingly interesting, and is as attractive in style as it is in material. — *Saturday Evening Gazette, Boston.*

Nowhere has this subject been more fully and intelligently treated than in this volume, now placed within reach of American readers. The mythology of the Aztecs receives special attention, and all that is known of their lives, their hopes, their fears, and aspirations finds record here. — *The Tribune, Chicago.*

The man who can rise from the study of Lucien Biart's invaluable work, "The Aztecs," without feelings of amazement and admiration for the history and the government, and for the arts cultivated by these Romans of the New World, is not to be envied. — *The Advance, Chicago.*

The twilight origin of the present race is graphically presented; those strange people whose traces have almost vanished from off the face of the earth again live before us. Their taxes and tributes, their marriage ceremonies, their burial customs, laws, medicines, food, poetry, and dances are described. . . . The book is a very interesting one, and is brought out with copious illustrations. — *The Traveller, Boston.*

We can cordially recommend this book to those desirous of obtaining a clear and correct outline of the history of the original settlement of the valley of Anahuac, and of the successive tribes that inhabited it until the Aztecs established themselves here. — *Sun, New York.*

M. Biart is the most competent authority living on the subject of the Aztecs. He spent many years in Mexico, studied his subject carefully through all means of information, and wrote his book from the view-point of a scientist. His style is very attractive, and it has been very successfully translated. The general reader, as well as all scholars, will be much taken with the work. — *Chronicle Telegraph, Pittsburg.*

M. Biart draws much more freely from the Spanish chronicles than Prescott did in the introductory chapters of his Mexico, and the additional knowledge which he obtains from works published since Prescott's time is often highly important. A number of illustrations add largely to the interest of his treatise. — *Tribune, New York.*

The young Americans who are flocking to modern Mexico should study this remarkable and extremely interesting history of ancient Mexico. They will learn many details of an antique civilization there that was perhaps as high as that of some contemporaneous nations of the Old World. *Bulletin, Philadelphia.*

Sold by all booksellers, or mailed, on receipt of price, by

A. C. McCLURG & CO., Publishers, CHICAGO.

LAUREL-CROWNED VERSE.

EDITED BY FRANCIS F. BROWNE.

The Lady of the Lake. By SIR WALTER SCOTT.
Childe Harold's Pilgrimage. A Romaunt. By LORD BYRON.
Lalla Rookh. An Oriental Romance. By THOMAS MOORE.
Idylls of the King. By ALFRED LORD TENNYSON.
Paradise Lost. By JOHN MILTON.
The Illiad of Homer. Translated by ALEXANDER POPE. 2 vols.

All the volumes of this series are from a specially prepared and corrected text, based upon a careful collation of all the more authentic editions.

The special merit of these editions, aside from the graceful form of the books, lies in the editor's reserve. Whenever the author has provided a preface or notes, this apparatus is given, and thus some interesting matter is revived; but the editor himself refrains from loading the books with his own writing. — *The Atlantic Monthly.*

A series noted for their integral worth and typographical beauties. — *Public Ledger, Philadelphia.*

A contribution to current literature of quite unique value and interest. They are furnished with a tasteful outfit, with just the amount of matter one likes to find in books of this class, and are in all ways very attractive. *Standard, Chicago.*

The requirements of good reprints of standard literature, such as may be offered at a low price but are yet worthy of their subject matter, are, good paper, clear type, scholarly editing, careful proof-reading, and neat binding. To these may be added freedom from illustrations, which necessarily add to the cost, and are too often a hindrance rather than a help to the enjoyment of the text, — an impertinent intrusion. All those requirements these reprints by McClurg & Co. seem to satisfy. — *Home Journal, New York.*

These volumes are models of good taste in covers, typography, dimensions, and presswork. . . . They present the most perfect texts of these works in existence, even Tennyson being an improvement upon the best standard edition. — *Journal, Chicago.*

For this series the publishers are entitled to the gratitude of lovers of classical English. — *School Journal, New York.*

Those who wish either or all of these volumes for their own libraries or gifts to others, will be charmed by them; and possession of them will be more precious because of the attractive dress in which they are presented. *Times, Boston.*

Each volume is finely printed and bound. 16mo, cloth, gilt tops. Price per volume, $1.00; in half calf or half morocco, per vol., $2.75.

Sold by all booksellers, or mailed, on receipt of price, by

A. C. McCLURG & CO., Publishers, CHICAGO.

LAUREL-CROWNED LETTERS.

The Best Letters of Lord Chesterfield. Edited, with an Introduction, by EDWARD GILPIN JOHNSON.

The Best Letters of Lady Mary Wortley Montagu. Edited, with an Introduction, by OCTAVE THANET.

The Best Letters of Horace Walpole. Edited, with an Introduction, by ANNA B. MCMAHAN.

The Best Letters of Madame de Sévigné. Edited, with an Introduction, by EDWARD PLAYFAIR ANDERSON.

The Best Letters of Charles Lamb. Edited, with an Introduction, by EDWARD GILPIN JOHNSON.

The Best Letters of Percy Bysshe Shelley. Edited, with an Introduction, by SHIRLEY C. HUGHSON.

The Best Letters of William Cowper. Edited, with an Introduction, by ANNA B. MCMAHAN.

Handsomely printed on fine laid paper. 16mo, cloth, with gilt tops. Price per volume, $1.00; in half calf or half morocco, $2.75.

Amid the great flood of ephemeral literature that pours from the press, it is well to be recalled by such publications as the "Laurel-Crowned Letters" to books that have won an abiding place in the classical literature of the world. — *The Independent, New York.*

We cannot commend too highly the good taste and judgment displayed by publishers and editors alike in the preparation of these charming volumes. They are in every respect creditable to those who share the responsibility for their existence. — *Journal, Chicago.*

The "Laurel-Crowned Series" recommends itself to all lovers of good literature. The selection is beyond criticism, and puts before the reader the very best literature in most attractive and convenient form. The size of the volumes, the good paper, the clear type and the neat binding are certainly worthy of all praise. — *Public Opinion, Washington.*

A contribution to current literature of quite unique value and interest. They are furnished with a tasteful outfit, with just the amount of matter one likes to find in books of this class, and are in all ways very attractive. — *Standard, Chicago.*

It was an admirable idea to issue in such beautiful and handy form a selection full enough to give an adequate idea of the writers and their times, yet small enough to require not more than a due proportion of time for their reading. — *Evangelist, New York.*

These "Laurel-Crowned" volumes are little gems in their way, and just the books to pick up at odd times and at intervals of waiting. — *Herald, Chicago.*

Sold by all booksellers, or mailed, on receipt of price, by

A. C. McCLURG & CO., Publishers, CHICAGO.

LAUREL-CROWNED TALES.

Abdallah; or, The Four-Leaved Shamrock. By EDOUARD LABOULAYE. Translated by MARY L. BOOTH.

Rasselas, Prince of Abyssinia. By SAMUEL JOHNSON.

Raphael; or, Pages of the Book of Life at Twenty. From the French of ALPHONSE DE LAMARTINE.

The Vicar of Wakefield. By OLIVER GOLDSMITH.

The Epicurean. By THOMAS MOORE.

Picciola. By X. B. SAINTINE.

Other volumes in preparation.

Handsomely printed from new plates, on fine laid paper. 16mo, cloth, with gilt tops, price per volume, $1.00; in half calf or half morocco, $2.75.

IN planning this series, the publishers have aimed at a form which should combine an unpretentious elegance suited to the fastidious book-lover with an inexpensiveness that must appeal to the most moderate buyer.

It is the intent to admit to the series only such tales as have for years or for generations commended themselves not only to the fastidious and the critical, but also to the great multitude of the refined reading public, — tales, in short, which combine purity and classical beauty of style with perennial popularity.

These "Laurel-Crowned" volumes are little gems in their way, and just the books to pick up at odd times and at intervals of waiting. — *Herald, Chicago.*

The publishers have shown excellent discrimination in their choice of material for their projected library of choice fiction, and they have certainly given these initial volumes a form that bespeaks the warmest praise. They are the books that the student of literature will not be ashamed to have upon his shelves, and at the same time they are not too fine for general use in the family library, for which they are eminently fitted. — *The Beacon, Boston.*

No better editions for the price have ever appeared in this country. — *The Critic, New York.*

We have alluded repeatedly to the good taste with which this series is issued. — *Congregationalist, Boston.*

The excellent judgment exhibited in the selection and the unusually pleasing form in which they appear are such as would make one subscribe for the entire series in advance, however long it might be. — *Advance, Chicago.*

Sold by all booksellers, or mailed, on receipt of price, by

A. C. McCLURG & CO., Publishers, CHICAGO.

TALES FROM FOREIGN LANDS.

··· COMPRISING ···

Memories: A Story of German Love. By MAX MÜLLER.

Graziella: A Story of Italian Love. By ALPHONSE DE LAMARTINE.

Marie: A Story of Russian Love. By ALEXANDER PUSHKIN.

Madeleine: A Story of French Love. By JULES SANDEAU.

Marianela: A Story of Spanish Love. By B. PEREZ GALDOS.

Cousin Phillis: A Story of English Love. By MRS. GASKELL.

In cloth, gilt top, per volume $1.00
The same, in neat box, per set 6.00
In half calf or half morocco, gilt top, per set 13.50
In half calf or half morocco, gilt edges, per set 15.00
In flexible calf or flexible russia, gilt edges, per set 18.00

THE series of six volumes forms, perhaps, the choicest addition to the literature of the English language that has been made in recent years.

Of "MEMORIES," the London *Academy* says: — "It is a prose poem. . . . Its beauty and pathos show us a fresh phase of a many-sided mind to which we already owe large debts of gratitude."

Of "GRAZIELLA," the *Boston Post* says: — "It is full of beautiful sentiment, unique and graceful in style, of course, as were all the writings of this distinguished French author."

Of "MARIE," the New York *Independent* says: — "The whole spirit and atmosphere of the story is fresh and bracing; and we promise the readers of the book a new treat."

Of "MADELEINE," the Philadelphia *Times* says: — "It is a theme of exceeding purity and beauty, treated by an artist whose style is as finished and delicate as it is firm, and whose French is a model of simplicity. It is not surprising that 'Madeleine' has become a classic, ranking with 'The Attic Philosopher,' and only a little below 'Paul and Virginia.'"

Of "MARIANELA," an appreciative critic says: — "This famous series of Tales from Foreign Lands receives a rich acquisition in this exquisitely beautiful and pathetic story by the great Spanish writer."

Of "COUSIN PHILLIS" the *British Quarterly* says: — "It is hardly possible to read a page of Mrs. Gaskell's writings without getting some good from it. Her style is clear and forcible, the tone pure, the matter wholesome."

Sold by all booksellers, or mailed, on receipt of price, by

A. C. McCLURG & CO., Publishers, CHICAGO.

UPTON'S HANDBOOKS ON MUSIC.

Comprising The Standard Operas, The Standard Oratorios, The Standard Cantatas, The Standard Symphonies.

By GEORGE P. UPTON.

12mo, flexible cloth, extra, per volume, **$1.50**; **extra gilt**, gilt edges, $2.00.

THE SAME IN NEAT BOX, PER SET:

Cloth	$6.00	Half morocco, gilt tops	$14.00
Extra gilt	8.00	Half morocco, gilt edges	15.00
Half calf, gilt tops	13.00	Tree calf, gilt edges	22.00

Of "THE STANDARD OPERAS," R. H. Stoddard, in *Evening Mail and Express* (New York) says: — "Among the multitude of handbooks described by easy-going writers of book-notices as supplying a long felt want, we know of none which so completely carries out the intention of the writer as 'The Standard Operas,' by Mr. George P. Upton, whose object is to present to his readers a comprehensive sketch of each of the operas contained in the modern repertory. . . . There are thousands of music-loving people who will be glad to have the kind of knowledge which Mr. Upton has collected for their benefit, and has cast in a clear and compact form."

Of "THE STANDARD ORATORIOS," the *Observer* (New York) says: — "Nothing in musical history is so interesting to the general reader as the story of the great oratorios, — the scenes and incidents which gave them rise, how they were composed, and how first performed. These things are told in Mr. Upton's volume with a grace and charm comporting with the character of the subject."

Of "THE STANDARD CANTATAS," the *Boston Post* says: — "Mr. Upton has done a genuine service to the cause of music and to all music-lovers in the preparation of this work, and that service is none the less important in that while wholly unassuming and untechnical, it is comprehensive, scholarly, and thorough."

Of "THE STANDARD SYMPHONIES," the *Mail and Express* (New York) says: — "The information conveyed is of great value, not only to the musical student, but also to music lovers who wish to add to the capabilities of their enjoyment. Mr. Upton has done a real service to this rapidly increasing class of persons, and the merit of his useful volumes has only to be properly known to be thoroughly appreciated. . . . A remarkable amount of information is given in a limited space."

Sold by all booksellers, or mailed, on receipt of price, by

A. C. McCLURG & CO., Publishers, CHICAGO.

BIOGRAPHIES OF MUSICIANS.

LIFE OF LISZT. With portrait.

LIFE OF HAYDN. With portrait.

LIFE OF MOZART. With portrait.

LIFE OF WAGNER. With portrait.

LIFE OF BEETHOVEN. With portrait.

From the German of Dr. Louis Nohl.

In cloth, per volume	$1.00
The same, in neat box, per set	5.00
In half calf, per set,	12.50
In half morocco, per set	13.50

A series of biographies which ought to be on the shelves of all intelligent musical amateurs. Being written in a most readable style, they enjoy much popularity, and in this manner do much good for music in America. — The Musical World.

Of the "LIFE OF LISZT," the *Congregationalist* (Boston) says: "Independently of its interest from a musical point of view, it is fascinating as a romance from the peculiarly interesting character of the subject. The life of the great 'Magician of the Hungarian Land,' as he was called, is itself a beautiful story, which Dr. Nohl delineates, not simply as a biographer, but as an enthusiastic friend."

Of the "LIFE OF HAYDN," the *Gazette* (Boston) says: "No fuller history of Haydn's career, the society in which he moved, and of his personal life can be found than is given in this work."

Of the "LIFE OF MOZART," the *Standard* says: "Mozart supplies a fascinating subject for biographical treatment. He lives in these pages somewhat as the world saw him, from his marvellous boyhood till his untimely death."

Of the "LIFE OF WAGNER," the *American* (Baltimore) says: "It gives in vigorous outlines those events of the life of the tone poet which exercised the greatest influences upon his artistic career, — his youth, his early studies, his first works, his sufferings, disappointments, his victories. . . . It is a story of a strange life devoted to lofty aims."

Of the "LIFE OF BEETHOVEN," the *National Journal of Education* says: "Beethoven was great and noble as a man, and his artistic creations were in harmony with his great nature. The story of his life, outlined in this volume, is of the deepest interest."

Sold by all booksellers, or mailed, on receipt of price, by

A. C. McCLURG & CO., Publishers, CHICAGO.

FACT, FANCY, AND FABLE.

A NEW HANDBOOK FOR READY REFERENCE ON SUBJECTS COMMONLY OMITTED FROM CYCLOPÆDIAS. COMPILED BY HENRY FREDERIC REDDALL. Large 8vo, 536 pages. Half leather, $2.50.

The motto, "Trifles make the sum of human things," could have no better illustration than this noble collection furnishes. It comprises personal sobriquets, familiar phrases, popular appellations, geographical nicknames, literary pseudonyms, mythological characters, red-letter days, political slang, contractions and abbreviations, technical terms, foreign words and phrases, Americanisms, etc. The work is compiled after a distinct plan, and with keen discrimination in regard to what is admitted and what excluded. — *Journal of Education, Boston.*

We have carefully tested the book, and find it to be one likely to be very useful to almost any reader, and even to the student in some cases. — *Examiner, New York.*

It is original in conception and thorough in execution. It brings together alphabetically a surprising number of titles from near and remote sources, that are very necessary in reference when they are not indispensable to the general reader. . . . It supplements and enlarges the usefulness of every dictionary and all the handbooks the dictionary has suggested. — *Globe, Boston.*

It must take its place for the time being as the best work of its kind in existence, particularly as regards American topics. — *Sun, New York.*

There is much matter in the volume that has never before been collated. . . . Writers and readers alike will find this work serviceable and trustworthy. — *Press, Philadelphia.*

The book is one of the best compilations of its kind. — *Critic, New York.*

The volume, a large one, is a collection of out-of-the-way odds and ends, relating to subjects that are constantly spoken of, but of which very many people do not understand the meaning. In gathering these floating items and giving them a permanent form, the author has performed a genuine service, and his book is one that can be read with profit and amusement at any odd moment, and is of permanent value as a handbook of reference for many things that cannot be found readily elsewhere. — *Saturday Evening Gazette, Boston.*

The book is one which, though designed for reference, may be picked up at an odd half hour as a source of entertainment. — *Home Journal, New York.*

Sold by all booksellers, or mailed, on receipt of price, by

A. C. McCLURG & CO., Publishers, CHICAGO.

www.ingramcontent.com/pod-product-compliance
Lightning Source LLC
Chambersburg PA
CBHW021153230426
43667CB00006B/384